Workshop on Computational Approaches to Semitic Languages 2007

Common Issues and Resources

Held in conjunction with ACL 2007

Prague, Czech Republic
28 June 2007

ISBN: 978-1-61738-524-7

Printed from e-media with permission by:

Curran Associates, Inc.
57 Morehouse Lane
Red Hook, NY 12571
www.proceedings.com

Some format issues inherent in the e-media version may also appear in this print version.

Printed by Curran Associates, Inc. (2010)

Association for Computational Linguistics
209 N. Eighth Street
Stroudsburg, Pennsylvania 18360

Phone: 1-570-476-8006
Fax: 1-570-476-0860

acl@aclweb.org

Organizers

Chairs:

Violetta Cavalli-Sforza (Carnegie Mellon University, USA)
Imed Zitouni (IBM Research, USA)

Program Committee:

Sherif Mahdy Abdou (Cairo University, Egypt)
Yaser Al-Onaizan (IBM, USA)
Ann Bies (LDC/University of Pennsylvania, USA)
Malek Boualem (France Telecom, France)
Tim Buckwalter (LDC/University of Pennsylvania, USA)
Achraf Chalabi (Sakhr Software Co., Egypt)
Anne DeRoeck (Open University, UK)
Mona Diab (Columbia University, USA)
Joseph Dichy (University of Lyon 2, France)
Abdelhamid ElJihad (Institut d'Etudes et Recherches sur l'Arabisation, Morocco)
Martha W. Evens (Illinois Institute of Technology, USA)
Ali Farghaly (Oracle, USA)
Alexander Fraser (USC/ISI, USA)
Andrew Freeman (Washington University, USA)
Nizar Habash (Columbia University, USA)
Alon Itai (Technion/Israel Institute of Technology, Israel)
Steven Krauwer (Utrecht University, Netherlands)
Alon Lavie (Carnegie Mellon University, USA)
Mohamed F. Noamany (Carnegie Mellon University, USA)
Uzzi Ornan (Technion, Israel)
Slim Ouni (LORIA/University of Nancy 2, France)
Mike Rosner (University of Malta, Malta)
Khalil Sima'an (University of Amsterdam, Netherlands)
Abdelhadi Soudi (Ecole Nationale de l'Industrie Minerale, Morocco)
Shuly Wintner (University of Haifa, Israel)
Mustafa Yaseen (Amman University, Jordan)
Abdellah Yousfi (Institut d'Etudes et Recherches sur l'Arabisation, Morocco)

Invited Speaker:

Jan Hajic (Charles University, Czech Republic)

Table of Contents

Conference Program

Thursday, June 28, 2007

09:00–09:05 Welcome and Introduction

09:05–09:55 Invited Talk – From print to meaning: the case of Arabic. Jan Hajic, Charles University, Czech Republic

Session 1:

10:45–11:15 Coffee Break

Session 2:

Friday, June 29, 2007

Session 1:

Session 2:

ElixirFM — Implementation of Functional Arabic Morphology

Otakar Smrž
Institute of Formal and Applied Linguistics
Faculty of Mathematics and Physics
Charles University in Prague
otakar.smrz@mff.cuni.cz

Abstract

Functional Arabic Morphology is a formulation of the Arabic inflectional system seeking the working interface between morphology and syntax. ElixirFM is its high-level implementation that reuses and extends the Functional Morphology library for Haskell. Inflection and derivation are modeled in terms of paradigms, grammatical categories, lexemes and word classes. The computation of analysis or generation is conceptually distinguished from the general-purpose linguistic model. The lexicon of ElixirFM is designed with respect to abstraction, yet is no more complicated than printed dictionaries. It is derived from the open-source Buckwalter lexicon and is enhanced with information sourcing from the syntactic annotations of the Prague Arabic Dependency Treebank.

1 Overview

One can observe several different streams both in the computational and the purely linguistic modeling of morphology. Some are motivated by the need to analyze word forms as to their compositional structure, others consider word inflection as being driven by the underlying system of the language and the formal requirements of its grammar.

In Section 2, before we focus on the principles of ElixirFM, we briefly follow the characterization of morphological theories presented by Stump (2001) and extend the classification to the most prominent computational models of Arabic morphology (Beesley, 2001; Buckwalter, 2002; Habash et al., 2005; El Dada and Ranta, 2006).

In Section 3, we survey some of the categories of the syntax–morphology interface in Modern Written Arabic, as described by the Functional Arabic Morphology. In passing, we will introduce the basic concepts of programming in Haskell, a modern purely functional language that is an excellent choice for declarative generative modeling of morphologies, as Forsberg and Ranta (2004) have shown.

Section 4 will be devoted to describing the lexicon of ElixirFM. We will develop a so-called domain-specific language embedded in Haskell with which we will achieve lexical definitions that are simultaneously a source code that can be checked for consistency, a data structure ready for rather independent processing, and still an easy-to-read-and-edit document resembling the printed dictionaries.

In Section 5, we will illustrate how rules of inflection and derivation interact with the parameters of the grammar and the lexical information. We will demonstrate, also with reference to the Functional Morphology library (Forsberg and Ranta, 2004), the reusability of the system in many applications, including computational analysis and generation in various modes, exploring and exporting of the lexicon, printing of the inflectional paradigms, etc.

2 Morphological Models

According to Stump (2001), morphological theories can be classified along two scales. The first one deals with the core or the process of inflection:

lexical theories associate word's morphosyntactic properties with *affixes*

inferential theories consider inflection as a result of operations on *lexemes*; morphosyntactic prop-

Proceedings of the 5th Workshop on Important Unresolved Matters, pages 1–8,
Prague, Czech Republic, June 2007.

erties are expressed by the *rules* that relate the form in a given paradigm to the lexeme

The second opposition concerns the question of inferability of meaning, and theories divide into:

incremental words *acquire* morphosyntactic properties only in connection with acquiring the inflectional exponents of those properties

realizational association of a set of properties with a word *licenses* the introduction of the exponents into the word's morphology

Evidence favoring inferential–realizational theories over the other three approaches is presented by Stump (2001) as well as Baerman et al. (2006) or Spencer (2004). In trying to classify the implementations of Arabic morphological models, let us reconsider this cross-linguistic observation:

> The morphosyntactic properties associated with an inflected word's individual inflectional markings may underdetermine the properties associated with the word as a whole. (Stump, 2001, p. 7)

How do the current morphological analyzers interpret, for instance, the number and gender of the Arabic broken masculine plurals *ǧudud* جُدُد *new ones* or *quḍāh* قُضَاة *judges*, or the case of *mustawan* مُسْتَوًى *a level*? Do they identify the values of these features that the syntax actually operates with, or is the resolution hindered by some too generic assumptions about the relation between meaning and form?

Many of the computational models of Arabic morphology, including in particular (Beesley, 2001), (Ramsay and Mansur, 2001) or (Buckwalter, 2002), are *lexical* in nature. As they are not designed in connection with any syntax–morphology interface, their interpretations are destined to be *incremental*.

Some signs of a *lexical–realizational* system can be found in (Habash, 2004). The author mentions and fixes the problem of underdetermination of inherent number with broken plurals, when developing a generative counterpart to (Buckwalter, 2002).

The computational models in (Soudi et al., 2001) and (Habash et al., 2005) attempt the *inferential–realizational* direction. Unfortunately, they implement only sections of the Arabic morphological system. The Arabic resource grammar in the Grammatical Framework (El Dada and Ranta, 2006) is perhaps the most complete inferential–realizational implementation to date. Its style is compatible with the linguistic description in e.g. (Fischer, 2001) or (Badawi et al., 2004), but the lexicon is now very limited and some other extensions for data-oriented computational applications are still needed.

ElixirFM is inspired by the methodology in (Forsberg and Ranta, 2004) and by functional programming, just like the Arabic GF is (El Dada and Ranta, 2006). Nonetheless, ElixirFM reuses the Buckwalter lexicon (2002) and the annotations in the Prague Arabic Dependency Treebank (Hajič et al., 2004), and implements yet more refined linguistic model.

3 Morphosyntactic Categories

Functional Arabic Morphology and ElixirFM re-establish the system of *inflectional* and *inherent* morphosyntactic properties (alternatively named grammatical categories or features) and distinguish precisely the senses of their use in the grammar.

In Haskell, all these categories can be represented as distinct data types that consist of uniquely identified values. We can for instance declare that the category of case in Arabic discerns three values, that we also distinguish three values for number or person, or two values of the given names for verbal voice:

```
data Case = Nominative | Genitive |
            Accusative
data Number = Singular | Dual | Plural
data Person = First | Second | Third
data Voice = Active | Passive
```

All these declarations introduce new enumerated types, and we can use some easily-defined methods of Haskell to work with them. If we load this (slightly extended) program into the interpreter,[1] we can e.g. ask what category the value `Genitive` belongs to (seen as the `::` type signature), or have it evaluate the list of the values that `Person` allows:

```
? :type Genitive    → Genitive :: Case
? enum :: [Person]  → [First,Second,Third]
```

Lists in Haskell are data types that can be parametrized by the type that they contain. So, the value `[Active, Active, Passive]` is a list of three elements of type `Voice`, and we can write this if necessary as the signature `:: [Voice]`. Lists can also

[1] http://www.haskell.org/

be empty or have just one single element. We denote lists containing some type `a` as being of type `[a]`.

Haskell provides a number of useful types already, such as the enumerated boolean type or the parametric type for working with optional values:

```
data Bool = True | False
data Maybe a = Just a | Nothing
```

Similarly, we can define a type that couples other values together. In the general form, we can write

```
data Couple a b = a :-: b
```

which introduces the value `:-:` as a container for some value of type `a` and another of type `b`.[2]

Let us return to the grammatical categories. Inflection of nominals is subject to several formal requirements, which different morphological models decompose differently into features and values that are not always complete with respect to the inflectional system, nor mutually orthogonal. We will explain what we mean by revisiting the notions of state and definiteness in contemporary written Arabic.

To minimize the confusion of terms, we will depart from the formulation presented in (El Dada and Ranta, 2006). In there, there is only one relevant category, which we can reimplement as `State'`:

```
data State' = Def | Indef | Const
```

Variation of the values of `State'` would enable generating the forms *al-kitābu* الكِتَابُ def., *kitābun* كِتَابٌ indef., and *kitābu* كِتَابُ const. for the nominative singular of *book*. This seems fine until we explore more inflectional classes. The very variation for the nominative plural masculine of the adjective *high* gets *ar-rafīʿūna* الرَّفِيعُونَ def., *rafīʿūna* رَفِيعُونَ indef., and *rafīʿū* رَفِيعُو const. But what value does the form *ar-rafīʿū* الرَّفِيعُو, found in improper annexations such as in *al-masʾūlūna 'r-rafīʿū 'l-mustawā* المَسؤُولُونَ الرَّفِيعُو المُستَوَى *the-officials the-highs-of the-level*, receive?

It is interesting to consult for instance (Fischer, 2001), where state has exactly the values of `State'`, but where the definite state `Def` covers even forms without the prefixed *al-* ال article, since also some separate words like *lā* لَا *no* or *yā* يَا *oh* can have the effects on inflection that the definite article has. To distinguish all the forms, we might think of keeping state in the sense of Fischer, and adding a boolean feature for the presence of the definite article... However, we would get one unacceptable combination of the values claiming the presence of the definite article and yet the indefinite state, i.e. possibly the indefinite article or the diptotic declension.

Functional Arabic Morphology refactors the six different kinds of forms (if we consider all inflectional situations) depending on two parameters. The first controls prefixation of the (virtual) definite article, the other reduces some suffixes if the word is a head of an annexation. In ElixirFM, we define these parameters as type synonyms to what we recall:

```
type Definite = Maybe Bool
type Annexing = Bool
```

The `Definite` values include **`Just True`** for forms with the definite article, **`Just False`** for forms in some compounds or after *lā* لَا or *yā* يَا (absolute negatives or vocatives), and **`Nothing`** for forms that reject the definite article for other reasons.

Functional Arabic Morphology considers state as a result of coupling the two independent parameters:

```
type State = Couple Definite Annexing
```

Thus, the indefinite state `Indef` describes a word void of the definite article(s) and not heading an annexation, i.e. **`Nothing`** `:-:` **`False`**. Conversely, *ar-rafīʿū* الرَّفِيعُو is in the state **`Just True`** `:-:` **`True`**. The classical construct state is **`Nothing`** `:-:` **`True`**. The definite state is **`Just`** `_` `:-:` **`False`**, where _ is **`True`** for El Dada and Ranta and **`False`** for Fischer. We may discover that now all the values of `State` are meaningful.[3]

Type declarations are also useful for defining in what categories a given part of speech inflects. For verbs, this is a bit more involved, and we leave it for Figure 2. For nouns, we set this algebraic data type:

```
data ParaNoun = NounS Number Case State
```

In the interpreter, we can now generate all 54 combinations of inflectional parameters for nouns:

```
? [ NounS n c s | n <- enum, c <- enum,
                  s <- values ]
```

The function `values` is analogous to `enum`, and both need to know their type before they can evaluate.

[2]Infix operators can also be written as prefix functions if enclosed in `()`. Functions can be written as operators if enclosed in ` `` `. We will exploit this when defining the lexicon's notation.

[3]With **`Just False`** `:-:` **`True`**, we can annotate e.g. the 'incorrectly' underdetermined *rafīʿū* رَفِيعُو in *hum-u 'l-masʾūlū-na rafīʿū 'l-mustawā* هم المسؤولون رَفِيعُو المستوى *they-are the-officials highs-of the-level*, i.e. *they are the high-level officials*.

The 'magic' is that the bound variables `n`, `c`, and `s` have their type determined by the `Nouns` constructor, so we need not type anything explicitly. We used the list comprehension syntax to cycle over the lists that `enum` and `values` produce, cf. (Hudak, 2000).

4 ElixirFM Lexicon

Unstructured text is just a list of characters, or string:

```
type String = [Char]
```

Yet words do have structure, particularly in Arabic. We will work with strings as the superficial word forms, but the internal representations will be more abstract (and computationally more efficient, too).

The definition of *lexemes* can include the derivational *root and pattern* information if appropriate, cf. (Habash et al., 2005), and our model will encourage this. The surface word *kitāb* كِتَاب *book* can decompose to the triconsonantal root *k t b* كتب and the morphophonemic pattern `FiCAL` of type `PatternT`:

```
data PatternT = FaCaL | FAL | FaCY |
                FiCAL | FuCCAL | {- ... -}
                MustaFCaL | MustaFaCL
    deriving (Eq, Enum, Show)
```

The **deriving** clause associates `PatternT` with methods for testing equality, enumerating all the values, and turning the names of the values into strings:

```
? show FiCAL → "FiCAL"
```

We choose to build on morphophonemic patterns rather than CV patterns and vocalisms. Words like *istaǧāb* إِستَجَاب *to respond* and *istaǧwab* إِستَجوَب *to interrogate* have the same underlying VstVCCVC pattern, so information on CV patterns alone would not be enough to reconstruct the surface forms. Morphophonemic patterns, in this case `IstaFAL` and `IstaFCaL`, can easily be mapped to the hypothetical CV patterns and vocalisms, or linked with each other according to their relationship. Morphophonemic patterns deliver more information in a more compact way. Of course, ElixirFM provides functions for properly interlocking the patterns with the roots:

```
? merge "k t b"  FiCAL    → "kitAb"
? merge "^g w b" IstaFAL  → "ista^gAb"
? merge "^g w b" IstaFCaL → "ista^gwab"
? merge "s ' l"  MaFCUL   → "mas'Ul"
? merge "z h r"  IFtaCaL  → "izdahar"
```

The *izdahar* إِزدَهَر *to flourish* case exemplifies that exceptionless assimilations need not be encoded in the patterns, but can instead be hidden in rules.

The whole generative model adopts the multi-purpose notation of ArabTEX (Lagally, 2004) as a meta-encoding of both the orthography and phonology. Therefore, instantiation of the `"'"` *hamza* carriers or other merely orthographic conventions do not obscure the morphological model. With Encode Arabic[4] interpreting the notation, ElixirFM can at the surface level process the original Arabic script (non-)vocalized to any degree or work with some kind of transliteration or even transcription thereof.

Morphophonemic patterns represent the stems of words. The various kinds of abstract prefixes and suffixes can be expressed either as atomic values, or as literal strings wrapped into extra constructors:

```
data Prefix = Al | LA | Prefix String

data Suffix = Iy | AT | At | An | Ayn |
              Un | In | Suffix String

al = Al; lA = LA    -- function synonyms

aT = AT; ayn = Ayn; aN = Suffix "aN"
```

Affixes and patterns are arranged together via the `Morphs a` data type, where `a` is a triliteral pattern `PatternT` or a quadriliteral `PatternQ` or a non-templatic word stem `Identity` of type `PatternL`:

```
data PatternL = Identity
data PatternQ = KaRDaS | KaRADiS {- ... -}

data Morphs a = Morphs a [Prefix] [Suffix]
```

The word *lā-silkīy* لَاسِلكِي *wireless* can thus be decomposed as the root *s l k* سلك and the value `Morphs FiCL [LA] [Iy]`. Shunning such concrete representations, we define new operators `>|` and `|<` that denote prefixes, resp. suffixes, inside `Morphs a`:

```
? lA >| FiCL |< Iy → Morphs FiCL [LA][Iy]
```

Implementing `>|` and `|<` to be applicable in the intuitive way required Haskell's multi-parameter type classes with functional dependencies (Jones, 2000):

```
class Morphing a b | a -> b where
    morph :: a -> Morphs b

instance Morphing (Morphs a) a where
    morph = id

instance Morphing PatternT PatternT where
    morph x = Morphs x [] []
```

The **instance** declarations ensure how the `morph` method would turn values of type `a` into `Morphs b`.

[4] http://sf.net/projects/encode-arabic/

```
|> "k t b" <| [

    FaCaL          `verb`   [ "write", "be destined" ]         `imperf`  FCuL,

    FiCAL          `noun`   [ "book" ]                         `plural`  FuCuL,

    FiCAL |< aT    `noun`   [ "writing" ],

    FiCAL |< aT    `noun`   [ "essay", "piece of writing" ]    `plural`  FiCAL |< At,

    FACiL          `noun`   [ "writer", "author", "clerk" ]    `plural`  FaCaL |< aT
                                                               `plural`  FuCCAL,

    FuCCAL         `noun`   [ "kuttab", "Quran school" ]       `plural`  FaCACIL,

    MaFCaL         `noun`   [ "office", "department" ]         `plural`  MaFACiL,

    MaFCaL |< Iy   `adj`    [ "office" ],

    MaFCaL |< aT   `noun`   [ "library", "bookstore" ]         `plural`  MaFACiL     ]
```

Figure 1: Entries of the ElixirFM lexicon nested under the root *k t b* كتب using morphophonemic templates.

Supposing that `morph` is available for the two types, `(|<)` is a function on `y :: a` and `x :: Suffix` giving a value of type `Morphs b`. The intermediate result of `morph y` is decomposed, and `x` is prepended to the stack `s` of the already present suffixes.

```
(|<) :: Morphing a b =>
        a -> Suffix -> Morphs b

y |< x = Morphs t p (x : s)
    where Morphs t p s = morph y
```

With the introduction of patterns, their synonymous functions and the `>|` and `|<` operators, we have started the development of what can be viewed as a domain-specific language embedded in the general-purpose programming language. Encouraged by the flexibility of many other domain-specific languages in Haskell, esp. those used in functional parsing (Ljunglöf, 2002) or pretty-printing (Wadler, 2003), we may design the lexicon to look like e.g.

```
module Elixir.Data.Lexicon
import Elixir.Lexicon

lexicon = listing  {- lexicon's header -}

  |> {- root one -} <| [ {- Entry a -} ]

  |> {- root two -} <| [ {- Entry b -} ]

  -- other roots or word stems and entries
```

and yet be a verifiable source code defining a data structure that is directly interpretable. The meaning of the combinators `|>` and `<|` could be supplied via an external module `Elixir.Lexicon`, so is very easy to customize. The effect of these combinators might be similar to the `:` and `:-:` constructors that we met previously, but perhaps other data structures might be built from the code instead of lists and pairs.

Individual entries can be defined with functions in a convenient notational form using ``. Infix operators can have different precedence and associativity, which further increases the options for designing a lightweight, yet expressive, embedded language.

In Figure 1, each entry reduces to a record of type `Entry PatternT` reflecting internally the lexeme's inherent properties. Consider one such reduction below. Functions like `plural` or `gender` or `humanness` could further modify the `Noun`'s default information:

```
? FiCAL |< aT `noun` [ "writing" ] →

  noun (FiCAL |< aT) [ "writing" ] →

  Entry (Noun [] Nothing Nothing)
        (morph (FiCAL |< aT))
        [ "writing" ]                →

  Entry (Noun [] Nothing Nothing)
        (Morphs FiCAL [] [AT])
        [ "writing" ]
```

The lexicon of ElixirFM is derived from the open-source Buckwalter lexicon (Buckwalter, 2002).[5] We devised an algorithm in Perl using the morpho-

[5]Habash (2004) comments on the lexicon's internal format.

```
data Mood = Indicative | Subjunctive | Jussive | Energetic  deriving (Eq, Enum)
data Gender = Masculine | Feminine                          deriving (Eq, Enum)

data ParaVerb = VerbP      Voice Person Gender Number
              | VerbI Mood Voice Person Gender Number
              | VerbC                   Gender Number        deriving Eq


paraVerbC :: Morphing a b => Gender -> Number -> [Char] -> a -> Morphs b
paraVerbC g n i = case n of

            Singular    -> case g of    Masculine -> prefix i . suffix ""
                                        Feminine  -> prefix i . suffix "I"

            Plural      -> case g of    Masculine -> prefix i . suffix "UW"
                                        Feminine  -> prefix i . suffix "na"

            _           ->                           prefix i . suffix "A"
```

Figure 2: Excerpt from the implementation of verbal inflectional features and paradigms in ElixirFM.

phonemic patterns of ElixirFM that finds the roots and templates of the lexical items, as they are available only partially in the original, and produces the lexicon in formats for Perl and for Haskell.

Information in the ElixirFM lexicon can get even more refined, by lexicographers or by programmers. Verbs could be declared via indicating their derivational verbal form (that would, still, reduce to some `Morphs a` value), and deverbal nouns and participles could be defined generically for the extended forms. The identification of patterns as to their derivational form is implemented easily with the `isForm` method:

```
data Form = I | II | III | IV {- .. -} XV

? isForm VIII IFtaCaL              → True
? isForm II   TaKaRDuS             → True
? filter (`isForm` MuFCI) [I ..]   → [IV]
```

Nominal parts of speech need to be enhanced with information on the inherent number, gender and humanness, if proper modeling of linguistic agreement in Arabic is desired.[6] Experiments with the Prague Arabic Dependency Treebank (Hajič et al., 2004) show that this information can be learned from annotations of syntactic relations (Smrž, 2007).

5 Morphological Rules

Inferential–realizational morphology is modeled in terms of paradigms, grammatical categories, lexemes and word classes. ElixirFM implements the comprehensive rules that draw the information from the lexicon and generate the word forms given the appropriate morphosyntactic parameters. The whole is invoked through a convenient `inflect` method.

The lexicon and the parameters determine the choice of paradigms. The template selection mechanism differs for nominals (providing plurals) and for verbs (providing all needed stem alternations in the extent of the entry specifications of e.g. Hans Wehr's dictionary), yet it is quite clear-cut (Smrž, 2007).

In Figure 2, the algebraic data type `ParaVerb` restricts the space in which verbs are inflected by defining three Cartesian products of the elementary categories: a verb can have `VerbP` perfect forms inflected in voice, person, gender, number, `VerbI` imperfect forms inflected also in mood, and `VerbC` imperatives inflected in gender and number only.[7]

The paradigm for inflecting imperatives, the one and only such paradigm in ElixirFM, is implemented as `paraVerbC`. It is a function parametrized by some particular value of gender `g` and number `n`. It further takes the initial imperative prefix `i` and the verbal stem (both inferred from the morphophonemic patterns in the lexical entry) to yield the inflected imperative form. Note the polymorphic type of the function, which depends on the following:

```
prefix, suffix :: Morphing a b =>
                     [Char] -> a -> Morphs b

prefix x y = Prefix x >| y
suffix x y = y |< Suffix x
```

[6]Cf. e.g. (El Dada and Ranta, 2006; Kremers, 2003).

[7]Cf. (Forsberg and Ranta, 2004; El Dada and Ranta, 2006).

If one wished to reuse the paradigm and apply it on strings only, it would be sufficient to equate these functions with standard list operations, without any need to reimplement the paradigm itself.

The definition of `paraVerbC` is simple and concise due to the chance to compose with `.` the partially applied `prefix` and `suffix` functions and to virtually omit the next argument. This advanced formulation may seem not as minimal as when specifying the literal endings or prefixes, but we present it here to illustrate the options that there are. An abstract paradigm can be used on more abstract types than just strings.[8] Inflected forms need not be merged with roots yet, and can retain the internal structure:

```
? paraVerbC Feminine Plural "u" FCuL →
  Prefix "u" >| FCuL |< Suffix "na"

? merge "k t b" ({- previous value -}) →
```

`"uktubna"` *uktubna* أُكْتُبْنَ fem. pl. *write!*

```
? [ merge "q r '" (paraVerbC g n "i"
    FCaL) | g <- values, n <- values ] →
```

masc.: `"iqra'"` *iqraʾ* إِقْرَأْ sg. `"iqra'A"` *iqraʾā* إِقْرَآ *du.* `"iqra'UA"` *iqraʾū* إِقْرَؤُوا pl.

fem.: `"iqra'I"` *iqraʾī* إِقْرَئِي sg. `"iqra'A"` *iqraʾā* إِقْرَآ *du.* `"iqra'na"` *iqraʾna* إِقْرَأْنَ pl. *read!*

The highlight of the Arabic morphology is that the 'irregular' inflection actually rests in strictly observing some additional rules, the nature of which is phonological. Therefore, surprisingly, ElixirFM does not even distinguish between verbal and nominal word formation when enforcing these rules. This reduces the number of paradigms to the prototypical 3 verbal and 5 nominal! Yet, the model is efficient.

Given that the morphophonemic patterns already do reflect the phonological restrictions, the only places of further phonological interaction are the prefix boundaries and the junction of the last letter of the pattern with the very adjoining suffix. The rules are implemented with `->-` and `-<-`, respectively, and are invoked from within the `merge` function:

```
merge :: (Morphing a b, Template b) =>
         [Char] -> a -> [Char]

(->-) :: Prefix -> [Char] -> [Char]
(-<-) :: Char -> Suffix -> [Char]
```

[8]Cf. some morphology-theoretic views in Spencer (2004).

```
'I' -<- x = case x of

    AT      -> "iyaT"  ;   Un      -> "Una"
    Iy      -> "Iy"    ;   In      -> "Ina"

    Suffix ""      -> "i"

    Suffix "Una"   -> "Una"
    Suffix "U"     -> "U"
    Suffix "UW"    -> "UW"

    Suffix "Ina"   -> "Ina"
    Suffix "I"     -> "I"

    Suffix x | x `elem` ["i",  "u"]  -> "I"
             | x `elem` ["iN", "uN"] -> "iN"

          | "n" `isPrefixOf` x ||
            "t" `isPrefixOf` x      -> "I" ++ x

    _        -> "iy" ++ show x
```

`(-<-)` is likewise defined when matching on `'Y'`, `'A'`, `'U'`, and when not matching. `(->-)` implements definite article assimilation and occasional prefix interaction with weak verbs.

Nominal inflection is also driven by the information from the lexicon and by phonology. The reader might be noticing that the morphophonemic patterns and the `Morphs a` templates are actually extremely informative. We can use them as determining the inflectional class and the paradigm function, and thus we can almost avoid other unintuitive or excessive indicators of the kind of weak morphology, diptotic inflection, and the like.

6 Applications and Conclusion

The ElixirFM linguistic model and the data of the lexicon can be integrated into larger applications or used as standalone libraries and resources.

There is another, language-independent part of the system that implements the compilation of the inflected word forms and their associated morphosyntactic categories into morphological analyzers and generators. This part is adapted from (Forsberg and Ranta, 2004). The method used for analysis is deterministic parsing with tries (Ljunglöf, 2002).

ElixirFM also provides functions for exporting and pretty-printing the linguistic model into XML, LaTeX, Perl, SQL, and other custom formats.

We have presented ElixirFM as a high-level functional implementation of Functional Arabic Morphology. Next to some theoretical points, we proposed a model that represents the linguistic data in an abstract and extensible notation that encodes both *orthography* and *phonology*, and whose interpretation is customizable. We developed a domain-specific language in which the lexicon is stored and which allows easy manual editing as well as automatic verification of consistency. We believe that the modeling of both the *written* language and the *spoken* dialects can share the presented methodology.

ElixirFM and its lexicons are open-source software licensed under GNU GPL and available on `http://sf.net/projects/elixir-fm/`.

This work has been supported by the Ministry of Education of the Czech Republic (MSM00216208-38), by the Grant Agency of Charles University in Prague (UK 373/2005), and by the Grant Agency of the Czech Academy of Sciences (1ET101120413).

References

Elsaid Badawi, Mike G. Carter, and Adrian Gully. 2004. *Modern Written Arabic: A Comprehensive Grammar*. Routledge.

Matthew Baerman, Dunstan Brown, and Greville G. Corbett. 2006. *The Syntax-Morphology Interface. A Study of Syncretism*. Cambridge Studies in Linguistics. Cambridge University Press.

Kenneth R. Beesley. 2001. Finite-State Morphological Analysis and Generation of Arabic at Xerox Research: Status and Plans in 2001. In *EACL 2001 Workshop Proceedings on Arabic Language Processing: Status and Prospects*, pages 1–8, Toulouse, France.

Tim Buckwalter. 2002. Buckwalter Arabic Morphological Analyzer Version 1.0. LDC catalog number LDC2002L49, ISBN 1-58563-257-0.

Ali El Dada and Aarne Ranta. 2006. Open Source Arabic Grammars in Grammatical Framework. In *Proceedings of the Arabic Language Processing Conference (JETALA)*, Rabat, Morocco, June 2006. IERA.

Wolfdietrich Fischer. 2001. *A Grammar of Classical Arabic*. Yale Language Series. Yale University Press, third revised edition. Translated by Jonathan Rodgers.

Markus Forsberg and Aarne Ranta. 2004. Functional Morphology. In *Proceedings of the Ninth ACM SIGPLAN International Conference on Functional Programming, ICFP 2004*, pages 213–223. ACM Press.

Nizar Habash, Owen Rambow, and George Kiraz. 2005. Morphological Analysis and Generation for Arabic Dialects. In *Proceedings of the ACL Workshop on Computational Approaches to Semitic Languages*, pages 17–24, Ann Arbor, Michigan. Association for Computational Linguistics.

Nizar Habash. 2004. Large Scale Lexeme Based Arabic Morphological Generation. In *JEP-TALN 2004, Session Traitement Automatique de l'Arabe*, Fes, Morocco, April 2004.

Jan Hajič, Otakar Smrž, Petr Zemánek, Jan Šnaidauf, and Emanuel Beška. 2004. Prague Arabic Dependency Treebank: Development in Data and Tools. In *NEMLAR International Conference on Arabic Language Resources and Tools*, pages 110–117. ELDA.

Paul Hudak. 2000. *The Haskell School of Expression: Learning Functional Programming through Multimedia*. Cambridge University Press.

Mark P. Jones. 2000. Type Classes with Functional Dependencies. In *ESOP '00: Proceedings of the 9th European Symposium on Programming Languages and Systems*, pages 230–244, London, UK. Springer.

Joost Kremers. 2003. *The Arabic Noun Phrase. A Minimalist Approach*. Ph.D. thesis, University of Nijmegen. LOT Dissertation Series 79.

Klaus Lagally. 2004. ArabTEX: Typesetting Arabic and Hebrew, User Manual Version 4.00. Technical Report 2004/03, Fakultät Informatik, Universität Stuttgart.

Peter Ljunglöf. 2002. *Pure Functional Parsing. An Advanced Tutorial*. Licenciate thesis, Göteborg University & Chalmers University of Technology.

Allan Ramsay and Hanady Mansur. 2001. Arabic morphology: a categorial approach. In *EACL 2001 Workshop Proceedings on Arabic Language Processing: Status and Prospects*, pages 17–22, Toulouse, France.

Otakar Smrž. 2007. *Functional Arabic Morphology. Formal System and Implementation*. Ph.D. thesis, Charles University in Prague.

Abdelhadi Soudi, Violetta Cavalli-Sforza, and Abderrahim Jamari. 2001. A Computational Lexeme-Based Treatment of Arabic Morphology. In *EACL 2001 Workshop Proceedings on Arabic Language Processing: Status and Prospects*, pages 155–162, Toulouse.

Andrew Spencer. 2004. Generalized Paradigm Function Morphology. `http://privatewww.essex.ac.uk/~spena/papers/GPFM.pdf`, October 6.

Gregory T. Stump. 2001. *Inflectional Morphology. A Theory of Paradigm Structure*. Cambridge Studies in Linguistics. Cambridge University Press.

Philip Wadler. 2003. A Prettier Printer. In Jeremy Gibbons and Oege de Moor, editors, *The Fun of Programming*, Cornerstones of Computing, pages 223–243. Palgrave Macmillan, March 2003.

Implementation of the Arabic Numerals and their Syntax in GF

Ali Dada
SAP Research CEC
Blumenbergplatz 9
9000 St. Gallen, Switzerland
`ali.dada@sap.com`

Abstract

The numeral system of Arabic is rich in its morphosyntactic variety yet suffers from the lack of a good computational resource that describes it in a reusable way. This implies that applications that require the use of rules of the Arabic numeral system have to either reimplement them each time, which implies wasted resources, or use simplified, imprecise rules that result in low quality applications. A solution has been devised with Grammatical Framework (GF) to use language constructs and grammars as libraries that can be written once and reused in various applications. In this paper, we describe our implementation of the Arabic numeral system, as an example of a bigger implementation of a grammar library for Arabic. We show that users can reuse our system by accessing a simple language-independent API rule.

1 Introduction

1.1 Problem

Language technology and software localization consume a significant share of many companies' time and work. Translating an operating system or an application to different languages involves, in the traditional approach, translating out-of-context strings into different languages. This requires a language expert for each new language, and will still involve language-related problems because of the difficulty in translating out-of-context strings and taking care of morphological and syntactic variations at the same time. We illustrate this with an example. A mail reader application wants to display messages like

```
You have 1 new message
You have 2 new messages
You have 3 new messages
You have 100 new messages
```

If these are to be translated into Arabic, special morphological and syntactic considerations should be made, which include inflecting "message" in number:

`1 message`	رِسَالَةٌ	*risālatun*
`2 messages`	رِسَالَتَانِ	*risālatāni*
`(3-10) messages`	رَسَائِلَ	*rasāʾila*
`(11-99) messages`	رِسَالَةً	*risālatan*
`x100 messages`	رِسَالَةٍ	*risālatin*

So the word "messages" is translated into different words in Arabic, depending on the numeral counting it. Counted nouns are an extreme example of how varied case inflection can be: The case of the singular and the dual is determined by their syntactic function (nominative in the example above). This is not the case for plurals, which assume the genitive case from three to ten (رَسَائِل is diptote, thus the فتحة marker), then accusative (singular) from eleven to nighty-nine, and genitive again for plurals that are multiples of hundred. This is not to mention noun-adjective agreement which should be taken care of when translating "new messages" into Arabic.

The aforementioned details should not be the responsibility of the application programmer, and hav-

Proceedings of the 5th Workshop on Important Unresolved Matters, pages 9–16,
Prague, Czech Republic, June 2007. ©2007 Association for Computational Linguistics

ing translators do this work over and over again for each application can be costly and lead to repeated work and/or poor results.

1.2 Solution and Contributions

We reviewed in other works (Dada and Ranta, 2007) an approach that addresses problems in language technology similar but not limited to the above. We applied this approach to Arabic, thus developing a resource grammar for Arabic in which we implement rules that cover the orthography, morphology, and syntax. In short, this approach is based on developing libraries of natural language constructs and rules, which can be used by an application programmer who is not knowledgeable in a specific language. The core programming language is Grammatical Framework (GF) (Ranta, 2004). The language library, called a resource grammar (Khegai and Ranta, 2004) and comprising the linguistic rules, can be reused in applications through an *Application Programming Interface* (API) by programmers that are unaware of the details of the specific natural language. Such a programmer uses a resource grammar assuming it will take care of morphological and syntactic rules. So far, we have implemented significant parts of the Arabic morphology, syntax, orthographic rules, and provided a sample lexicon of 300 words based on the Swadesh list (Hymes, 1960).

In this paper, we only describe part of the work, namely the numeral system of Arabic and its syntax. In the next section we elaborate on the approach, the programming language that implements it, and on Resource Grammars.

2 GF and the Resource Library

GF is a special-purpose functional programming language for defining grammars of (formal or natural) languages. A common API and resource grammars for various natural languages accompany GF with a purpose similar to that of libraries in general programming languages: implementing pieces of code that can be reused by the application programmer.

GF makes a distinction between abstract and concrete syntaxes. The common API specifies a set of syntactic rules that are language independent (abstract syntax), and the resource grammar implements each rule according to the particular rules of the language (concrete syntax). This latter involves word order, agreement, case inflection, etc. This distinction can abstract over language-dependent features and enables an application programmer to write sentences in a language only by describing their abstract syntax trees or by translating them from another language, preferably in a limited domain. The abstract representation would then act as interlingua.

3 The Numerals

We give here an explanation of our treatment of the Arabic number system, namely the numerals and their counted nouns. Our implementation is based on the work done by Hammarström and Ranta (2004) in defining the cardinal numerals in GF. We will gradually give the governing grammar rules along with their our formal description in GF.

The numbers from one to nineteen in Arabic have two forms, a masculine form and a feminine one, so in general we will take gender to be one of the inflecting attributes of numbers. Which of these two forms to use depends on the counted noun and the counting number:

- The numerals 1 and 2 show gender agreement with the counted noun (their grammatical role is an adjective modifying this noun).
- Numerals 3-10 show gender polarity with the counted noun, so a masculine noun is counted with a number in its feminine form and vice versa, e.g. ثَلَاثة رِجَال (three [+FEM] men [+MASC]) but ثَلَاث نِسَاء (three [+MASC] women [+FEM]).
- Numbers 11 and 12 have two constituents which show gender agreement with each other and with the counted noun, e.g. أَحد عَشَر رجلًا (eleven [+MASC] men [+MASC]).
- Numbers 13-19 show gender polarity between their first constituent and the counted noun.
- Numbers further on, except those ending in 01 and 02, show no gender distinction.

Numerals dictate the number of the counted noun is a way different to what is the case in other languages:

- Numeral One: The noun is in the singular form.

- Numeral Two: The noun is in the dual form.
- Numerals 3-10: The noun is in the plural form, e.g. ثلَاثة رِجَال (three men [+PLUR]).
- Numerals $\geq$ 10: The noun is in singular form again, e.g. ثلاثون رجلًا (thirty men [+SING]).

The numbers inflect also in case, so in the general case the number can have different forms for the three cases: nominative, accusative, and genitive. But again, as with gender, this will depend on the particular range of numerals:

- Numeral 1: full case distinction (it is an adjective)
- Number 2: usually the noun in dual is used alone, and if the number 2 is specified then it is usually only for emphasis. In this case it's an adjective in the dual form, thus it has two cases: nominative and oblique, e.g. ولَدَان اثنَان [+NOM] and ولَدَين اثنَين [+OBL].
- Numerals 3-10 : full case distinction for the numbers; the counted noun is always genitive, e.g. خمسةُ كتبٍ (five [+NOM] books [+GEN]), خمسةً كتبٍ (five [+ACC] books [+GEN]), خمسةِ كتبٍ (five [+GEN] books [+GEN]).
- Numerals 11 and 13-19: only accusative, same as their counted noun, e.g. أربعةَ عشرَ قلمًا (fourteen [+ACC] pens [+ACC]).
- 12: same as 2, but the counted noun is always accusative
- The tens (20, 30, ... 90): nominative and oblique cases, the counted noun is accusative
- multiples of 100 or 1000: the counted noun is genitive.
- composites: the case distinction of the number is the same as each of its constituent parts, and the case of the counted noun is determined by the rule of the last part of the compound construction. For example, 23: the three follows the rule of 3-10, the 20 follows the rule of the tens, and the counted noun is accusative as in the rule of the tens, the last part of the construction twenty three (three and twenty in Arabic).

The rules above only treat the indefinite state of the numerals, since the numerals in the definite state will be an adjective modifying the noun. The case of such a noun will not then follow the rules above but will assume the case dictated by its syntactic role in the sentence. We do however give below the type of the numerals inflection table including all the attributes that a number can inflect in: gender, state, and case.

```
lincat Numeral = {
  s : Gender => State => Case => Str ;
  n : Size
} ;

param Size =
  One | Two | ThreeTen | Teen
| NonTeen | Hundreds | None ;

param
   Gender   = Masc | Fem ;
   State    = Def | Indef | Const ;
   Case     = Nom | Acc | Gen ;
```

The `lincat` (`lin`earize `cat`egory) statement defines the type of a numeral in Arabic. It states that in GF, an Arabic numeral is a record that comprises two fields. The first is a string `s` which is in this case an inflection table specifying that a numeral is inflected in gender, state, and case. The => operator is the table operator in GF, so having three inputs to the table means that a `Numeral` is inflected in these three attributes. The three inflectional attributes are defined as `param`eters that take one of predefined values: gender can be masculine or feminine, case can be nominative, accusative, or genitive, and state can be definite with *al*, definite with a genitive construction (إضافة) or indefinite. The second field is `n` of type `Size`, which is also defined as a `param`eter with several possible values. These values specify which range of numbers does the numeral belong to. This is needed to be able to apply the rules above properly at all stages, including the formation of the number and the formation of the noun phrase from the number and the counted noun.

As mentioned earlier, GF differentiates between abstract and concrete syntaxes, and this differentiation also applies for the numeral system. So first an abstract syntax defines how numbers are formed in a language-independent way. The numbers are defined in a way that draws similarities found across languages in the formation of compound numbers. We linearize the rules into Arabic thus making use of this division but making distinctions because of the special rules that govern numerals in Arabic. A typical example of such numbers is the special treatment that numbers ending in 2 have in Arabic due to the notion of the dual.

We give here the rules for the first division of numbers and show how we implement them for Arabic. The API specifies the following categories and rules for numbers less than ten:

```
cat
  Digit ;                                -- 2..9
  Sub10 ;                                -- 1..9

fun
  n2, n3, n4, n5, n6, n7, n8, n9 : Digit ;

  pot01 : Sub10 ;                        -- 1
  pot0 : Digit -> Sub10 ;                -- d * 1
```

So the number 1 is treated separately from the remaining digits. We want to preserve a difference in our Arabic implementation between `n2` and the remaining digits because of the different way the digit 2 combines in compound numbers later on. This is the motivation between the division seen in `Size` between `Two` and `ThreeTen`.

Following is the type of the categories above in Arabic (the concrete syntax):

```
lincat Digit = {
s : DForm => Gender => State => Case => Str;
n : Size
} ;

lincat Sub10 = {
s : DForm => Gender => State => Case => Str;
n : Size
} ;

param DForm = unit | ten ;
```

The inflection table shows what we discussed earlier, that Arabic numbers get in the general case inflected in gender, state, and case. The `DForm` is used to calculate both the digit and its multiple of ten.

We write functions that form the inflection tables of the digits: one function for numeral 2 (`num2`, not shown here) and one function for the rest of the digits, including 1 (`num1_10`, shown below). [1]

```
oper num1_10 : Str -> { s : DForm => Gender
  => State => Case => Str } = \xams ->
let xamsa = xams + "ap" in {
 s= table {
    unit => table {
     Masc => \\s,c => (sing xams) ! s ! c;
     Fem => \\s,c => Al ! s + xamsa
                    + declsg ! s ! c
    };
    ten => \\_,s,c => Al ! s + xams +
                    m_pl ! Indef ! c
  }
};
```

[1]Our grammar files are in unicode, but the example codes shown here are written using the Buckwalter (2003) transliteration with a few changes that suit our needs. We note our use of 'c' to denote the *ʿayn*.

Note the following GF syntax notations: The keyword `oper` defines a GF function. An `oper` judgment includes the name of the defined operation (e.g. `num1_10` in the example above), its type (e.g. `Str -> { s : DForm => Gender => State => Case => Str }`), and an expression defining it (everything after the = operator). As for the syntax of the defining expression, notice the lambda abstraction form `\x -> t` of the function. Inflection tables are either specified by the `table` keyword or using the shorthand `\\... =>` notation. Finally, + is the character concatenation operator and ! is the table selection operator.

The `num1_10` function takes a string which can be any of the stems of the numerals from one to ten excluding two, e.g. *ḫams*. From this stem, and using helping functions from the nominal morphology modules, we build the inflection table of the numeral. For example, for the case where `DForm` is `unit` and the `Gender` is feminine (e.g. *ḫamsah*), the actual numeral string would be the concatenation of a possible definite marker (*al*), the stem, and a suffix determined by the state and the case of the numeral, `s` and `c` respectively. The helping function that determines if the definite marker is needed is the following:

```
Al : State => Str =
  table {
    Def => "Al";
    _   => ""
  };
```

The second helping function defines the suffixes that attach to singular or broken plurals of the first (strong) declension of Arabic nominal words (Retsö, 1984). It calculates, given the state of the word and its case, what its suffix will be. Note that `N`, `F`, and `K` are the nominative, accusative, and genitive nunation diacritics.

```
declsg : State => Case => Str =
  table {
    Indef =>
      table {
        Nom => "N";
        Acc => "F";
```

```
        Gen => "K"
      };
    _ =>
      table {
        Nom => "u";
        Acc => "a";
        Gen => "i"
      }
  };
```

As expected, only words with indefinite state take double diacritics (nunation), where as the rest (*al*-definite or construct-definite words) take simple diacritics. The remaining helping functions will not be all explained here as they follow similar logic.

The `num1_10` and `num2` produce only the inflection tables (the `s` field of the digit record). We simply add the correct `Size` parameter to each digit as follows:

```
oper num3_10 : Str -> { s : DForm => Gender
  => State => Case => Str ; n : Size } =
    \xams ->
    num1_10 xams ** { n = ThreeTen } ;

lin n2 = num2 ** {n = Two };

lin n3 = num3_10   "valAv";
lin n4 = num3_10  ">arbac";
lin n5 = num3_10    "xams";
lin n6 = num3_10    "sit~";
lin n7 = num3_10    "sabc";
lin n8 = num3_10  "vamAnI";
lin n9 = num3_10    "tisc";

lin pot01 = num1_10 "wAHid" ** { n = One } ;

lin pot0 d = d ;
```

The last function in the linearization shown above, `pot0`, is used to promote a `Digit` into a `Sub10` in order to use it later on as any numeral less that ten. This is the way the API specifies different numerals, dividing them into categories based on the decimal system. We give here the rest of the API categories and their linearization in Arabic:

```
cat
  Sub100 ;        -- 1..99
  Sub1000 ;       -- 1..999
  Sub1000000 ;    -- 1..999999

lincat Sub100 = {
 s : Gender => State => Case => Str ;
 n : Size
} ;
```

We will now show only a few implementation examples of the rules that specify the formation of the `Sub100` category. The rest of the rules for this and other categories don't show any different logic and will not be detailed here. The first rule we give is for the special cases of numeral 11:

```
fun
  pot111 : Sub100 ;

lin pot111 = {
 s = \\g,d,_ =>
  case g of {
   Masc => Al ! d + ">aHada" ++ teen ! Masc;
   Fem => Al ! d + "<iHdaY" ++ teen ! Fem
  };
 n = NonTeen
};

oper teen : Gender => Str =
  table {
    Masc => "ca$ara";
    Fem  => "ca$rapa"
  };
```

The implementation shows how the qualitative rules stated at the beginning are described formally. The inflection table doesn't give different forms for the three cases, and the accusative is used whatever the context case is. Both parts of the construction show gender agreement.

The numbers 12-19 have a common rule in the API but we should differentiate in the Arabic linearization between 12 and 13-19 because of the special status of the dual in Arabic and the different rules that these numbers assume in Arabic (see rules above).

```
fun
  pot1to19 : Digit -> Sub100 ;   -- 10 + d

lin pot1to19 dig = {
 s = \\g,d,c =>
  case dig.n of {
   Two => Al ! d + num2.s ! unit ! g
          ! Const ! c ++ teen ! g  ;
   _    => dig.s ! unit ! g ! Const ! Acc
          ++ teen ! (genPolarity ! g)
  };
 n =
  case dig.n of {
   Two => NonTeen;
   _ => Teen
  }
 };

oper
  genPolarity : Gender => Gender =
    table {
      Masc => Fem;
      Fem => Masc
    };
```

The `pot1to19` function takes a `Digit` as argument. In our implementation we take cases for the

Size of the digit. When the Size is Two, i.e. the number will be 12, we apply the rules for number 12 as given in the beginning: gender agreement between the two constituents, the first constituent is inflected in case (it is basically number 2 in the Const state). Otherwise (when the digit size is ThreeTen), we apply the rules of numbers 13 - 19: gender polarity between the two constituents and the first constituent is the digit inflected for the construct state and accusative case. The second constituent for all the numbers 11-19 is always accusative as shown in the teen helping function before.

The rest of the rules for forming numbers will not be detailed here. Instead we will explain how all these numbers will combine with nouns to form noun phrases. The different number ranges as defined by the Size parameter will be now used extensively in applying the proper rules. Following is the rule that takes that takes a Determiner (which can, among others, be a numeral) and a common noun to give a noun phrase.

```
fun
    DetCN   : Det -> CN -> NP ;
```

The rule above has the same type in all languages since it's part of the language-independent API (abstract syntax). The advantage of this is that a user of our system can access the Arabic numerals at this high level of abstraction, without being knowledgeable about the details of our implementation.

When determiners combine with common nouns in the general case, it will make a difference whether or not the determiner was a numeral, and if it were then the range of the numeral will probably determine the case of the noun in the resulting NP. Thus the type of the determiner category should include a Size field which is taken directly from the size of the number if that determiner is a numeral:

```
lincat Det = {
  s : Species => Gender => Case => Str ;
  d : State;
  n : Size
} ;

param Species = NoHum | Hum ;
```

If the determiner is not a numeral, then this will be denoted by n = None.

The first determiner-noun modification we will introduce is the determiner's gender. If we don't consider numerals, then a determiner's gender is directly deduced from that of the noun. But, as we saw in the rules for Arabic counted nouns, if the numeral was in the range 3-10 or 13-19 (Size is ThreeTen or Teen), then the numeral will show gender polarity instead of agreement. The rest of the cases continue to show agreement. This is described in detGender:

```
oper
  detGender : Gender -> Size -> Gender =
    \g,s ->
    case s of {
      ThreeTen | Teen => genPolarity ! g;
      _ => g
    };
```

The arguments are the gender of the noun and the size of the determiner. The correct gender of the determiner is calculated after taking cases of the Size.

Again, if we were not to consider numerals, the number in which we should inflect the common noun (singular, dual, or plural) would be directly determined by the number of the determiner. Now with the consideration of numerals and their special rules that dictate the number of the counted noun, we have to specify a correcting function:

```
oper sizeToNumber : Size -> Number = \s ->
  case s of {
    ThreeTen | None => Pl;
    Two => Dl;
    _ => Sg
  } ;

param Number = Sg | Dl | Pl;
```

This function converts from the Size of the determiner to a number in which the noun should be inflected in. As the rules of Arabic numerals specify, only the 3-10 numeral range dictate a noun in the plural form. Apart from the dual, the remaining numeral ranges take a singular noun.

The last way that a numeral will affect the noun it counts is by specifying its case as we have already seen in the rules. Without considering numerals, the case of the noun would always be determined by its grammatical role in the sentence. Again, this changes with the introduction of numerals. We write now a function that takes the case from the sentence, along with the size and state of the determiner, and modifies the case if required:

```
oper
  nounCase : Case -> Size -> State -> Case =
    \c,size,s ->
```

```
case <size,s> of {
  <Teen,_> => Acc;
  <NonTeen,_> => Acc;
  <ThreeTen,_> => Gen;
  <Hundreds,_> => Gen;
  <_,Const> => Gen;
  _        => c
};
```

Numbers from 11 to 99 dictate the accusative case on the nouns they count, numbers from 3 to 10 and multiples of hundred dictate the genitive case of the nouns they count, and the remaining numbers (1 and 2) don't change the case determined by the context. The remaining case of `State = Const` takes care of the *iḍāfah* genitive constructions.

Thus, after applying all the "correction" functions above, we get the following implementation of the noun determination rule:

```
lin DetCN det cn =
let number = sizeToNumber det.n in {
 s = \\c =>
  det.s ! cn.h ! (detGender cn.g det.n) ! c
  ++ cn.s ! number ! (nounState det.d number)
                 ! (nounCase c det.n det.d);
 a = agrP3 cn.h cn.g number
};

oper agrP3 : Species -> Gender -> Number
                -> PerGenNum=
  \h,g,n ->
    case <h,n> of {
      <NoHum,Pl> => Per3 Fem Sg;
      _          => Per3 g n
    };
```

The `agrP3` helping function tests for the case when the species and number are nonhuman and plural. This case is treated in agreement as the feminine singular.

4 Related Work

A large-scale implementation of the Arabic morphological system is the Xerox Arabic Morphological Analyzer and Generator (Beesley and Karttunen, 2000; Beesley, 2001). This system is developed using only the Xerox Finite State Technology tools (Beesley and Karttunen, 2003) from which an Arabic Finite State Lexical Transducer is written. A research version is available for online testing, and an expanded and updated version can be obtained with a commercial license. Another notable computational model of the Arabic morphology is Tim Buckwalter's Arabic Morphological Analyzer (Buckwalter, 2004b,a). Buckwalter's analyzer parses Arabic words and gives all their possible morphological interpretations, each solution having a unique lemma ID, different word constituents, the part-of-speech, and English glosses.

Other works that also use functional languages for the treatment of Arabic include a morphology system by Smrž (in prep.). This work is based on Functional Morphology (Forsberg and Ranta, 2004), a methodology for building morphological systems in the Haskell programming language. Our treatment of Arabic shares similarities with that of Functional Morphology. Both approaches use typed languages, making use of finite algebraic datatypes to define linguistic categories. Both languages are functional, so the approaches use functions to realize linguistic abstractions. A large-scale implementation of this approach, in which a typed functional programming language is used to build a morphology, is Huet's Sanskrit dictionary and morphological system (Huet, 2006) upon which the Zen computational linguistics toolkit is based (Huet, 2005).

Of the available works in Arabic syntax, we mention El-Shishiny (1990) who developed a formal description of Arabic syntax in Definite Clause Grammar. We also make note of the work in Othman et al. (2003), where the authors describe a parser they wrote in Prolog to parse and disambiguate the Arabic sentence. Shaalan (2005) builds on this work to develop a syntax-based grammar checker for Arabic called Arabic GramCheck.

5 Discussion

Our implementation of the Arabic numerals covers all natural numbers in the range 1-999,999. This was accomplished by implementing only a few functions, thanks to the repetitive way in which numerals are composed to form larger numerals. As for performance, Arabic grammars are slower to compile than comparable GF grammars of other languages, partly because of the additional complexity of Arabic and partly because of the general way in which our lexicon is specified. Our implementation stresses more on elegance and generality rather than efficiency, thus more work needs to be done on the latter.

6 Conclusion

We discussed in this paper the details of implementing the Arabic numeral system in GF. We motivated our work by taking an example that shows the value of having the necessary language rules implemented in a reusable fashion. We built up our implementation towards a single language-independent rule that a user can call to access our system. We show how the grammar formalism we use in our implementation parallels the way linguists think.

Acknowledgments

Most of the work was done at Chalmers University of Technology. Thanks to Prof. Aarne Ranta for supervising this work and providing constant help. Also thanks to Björn Bringert, Harald Hammarström, and Otakar Smrž for giving valuable comments.

References

Kenneth Beesley. Finite-State Morphological Analysis and Generation of Arabic at Xerox Research: Status and Plans in 2001. In *Workshop Proceedings on Arabic Language Processing: Status and Prospects*, pages 1–8, Toulouse, 2001. ACL.

Kenneth Beesley and Lauri Karttunen. Finite-state non-concatenative morphotactics. In *Proceedings of the Fifth Workshop of the ACL SIG in Computational Phonology*, pages 1–12, 2000.

Kenneth R. Beesley and Lauri Karttunen. *Finite State Morphology*. CSLI Studies in Computational Linguistics. CSLI Publications, Stanford, California, 2003.

Tim Buckwalter. Arabic transliteration, 2003. `http://www.qamus.org/transliteration.htm`.

Tim Buckwalter. Issues in Arabic Orthography and Morphology Analysis. In *Proceedings of the COLING 2004 Workshop on Computational Approaches to Arabic Script-based Languages*, pages 31–34, 2004a.

Tim Buckwalter. Buckwalter Arabic Morphological Analyzer Version 2.0. LDC catalog number LDC2004L02, ISBN 1-58563-324-0, 2004b.

Ali Dada and Aarne Ranta. Implementing an Open Source Arabic Resource Grammar in GF. In Mustafa Mughazy, editor, *Perspectives on Arabic Linguistics*, volume XX. John Benjamins, 2007.

Hisham El-Shishiny. A formal description of Arabic syntax in definite clause grammar. In *Proceedings of the 13th Conference on Computational Linguistics*, pages 345–347. ACL, 1990.

Markus Forsberg and Aarne Ranta. Functional Morphology. In *Proceedings of the Ninth ACM SIGPLAN International Conference on Functional Programming, ICFP 2004*, pages 213–223. ACM Press, 2004.

Harald Hammarström and Aarne Ranta. Cardinal Numerals Revisited in GF. In *Workshop on Numerals in the World's Languages*, Leipzig, Germany, 2004. Dept. of Linguistics Max Planck Institute for Evolutionary Anthropology.

Gérard Huet. A Functional Toolkit for Morphological and Phonological Processing, Application to a Sanskrit Tagger. *Journal of Functional Programming*, 15:573–614, 2005.

Gérard Huet. Sanskrit Site, 2006. `http://sanskrit.inria.fr/`.

D. H. Hymes. Lexicostatistics so far. *Current Anthropology*, 1:3–44, 1960.

Janna Khegai and Aarne Ranta. Building and Using a Russian Resource Grammar in GF. In *Intelligent Text Processing and Computational Linguistics (CICLing-2004)*, pages 38–41, Korea, 2004.

E. Othman, K. Shaalan, and A. Rafea. A Chart Parser for Analyzing Modern Standard Arabic Sentence. In *Proceedings of the MT Summit IX Workshop on Machine Translation for Semitic Languages*, pages 37–44, 2003.

Aarne Ranta. Grammatical Framework: A Type-theoretical Grammar Formalism. *Journal of Functional Programming*, 14:145–189, 2004.

Jan Retsö. State, Determination and Definiteness in Arabic: A Reconsideration. *Orientalia Suecana*, 33–35:341–346, 1984.

Khaled F. Shaalan. Arabic GramCheck: a grammar checker for Arabic: Research Articles. *Software - Pracice and Experience*, 35(7):643–665, 2005.

Otakar Smrž. *Functional Arabic Morphology. Formal System and Implementation*. PhD thesis, Charles University in Prague, in prep.

Person Name Entity Recognition for Arabic

Khaled Shaalan

Institute of Informatics

The British University in Dubai

P O Box 502216, Dubai, UAE

Khaled.shaalan@buid.ac.ae

Hafsa Raza

Institute of Informatics

The British University in Dubai

P O Box 502216, Dubai, UAE

hafsa.raza@gmail.com

Abstract

Named entity recognition (NER) is nowadays an important task, which is responsible for the identification of proper names in text and their classification as different types of named entity such as people, locations, and organizations. In this paper, we present our attempt at the recognition and extraction of the most important proper name entity, that is, the person name, for the Arabic language. We developed the system, Person Name Entity Recognition for Arabic (PERA), using a rule-based approach. The system consists of a lexicon, in the form of gazetteer name lists, and a grammar, in the form of regular expressions, which are responsible for recognizing person name entities. The PERA system is evaluated using a corpus that is tagged in a semi-automated way. The system performance results achieved were satisfactory and confirm to the targets set forth for the precision, recall, and f-measure.

1 Introduction

The recognition and classification of proper names in text (e.g. persons, locations, and organizations) has recently become considered of major importance in Natural Language Processing (NLP) as it plays a significant role in various types of NLP applications, especially in Information Extraction, Information Retrieval, Machine Translation, Syntactic Parsing/Chunking, Question-Answering, among others. The valuable information in text is usually located around proper names, to collect this information it should be found first (Abuleil, 2004; Chinchor, 1998). In our presentation, we will concentrate on the role of NER in Information Extraction (IE). IE is the NLP task that retrieves relevant information from unstructured texts and produces as a result a structured set of data.

This paper describes work on recognizing and extracting the most important entities, that is, person names for the Arabic language. We have adopted the rule-based approach using linguistic grammar-based techniques to develop PERA. This approach provides flexibility and adaptability features in our system and it can be easily configured to work with different languages, NLP applications, and domains. In order to determine the best rules for recognition of person names, various Arabic text corpora were analyzed. Phrases containing person names were retrieved, the underlying pattern was learned and person indicators such as titles were identified. Apart from this, person names were extracted from the available corpora and other resources to build up a lexicon, in the form of gazetteer name lists, or gazetteer for short. The various Arabic naming conventions and the person indicators identified helped in deriving fine rules that gave high-quality recognition of person names in Arabic text. The recognition was done in two cycles using first the gazetteer and then the grammar rules. The PERA system is evaluated using a reference corpus that is tagged with person names in a semi-automated way. The achieved system performance results were satisfactory and confirm

Proceedings of the 5th Workshop on Important Unresolved Matters, pages 17–24,
Prague, Czech Republic, June 2007.

to the targets set forth for the precision, recall, and f-measure.

The paper is structured as follows. Section 2 presents the related work. Section 3 describes the naming conventions of person names used in Arabic language. Section 4 presents methods of data collection used. Section 5 explains the system architecture and implementation. Section 6 presents the experiment performed to evaluate the system and finally Section 7 concludes the paper, summarizes our achievements, and highlights our plans for future work..

2 Related Work

As in other NLP techniques, there are two main approaches to NER (Toral, 2005). One is based on linguistic knowledge, in particular grammar rules and hence called rule-based, while the other is based on machine learning techniques. The required resources for the knowledge approach are usually gazetteers and rules whereas the learning approach needs an annotated (tagged) corpus. The linguistic knowledge-based model achieve better results in specific domains, as the gazetteers can be adapted very precisely, and it is able to detect complex entities, as the rules can be tailored to meet nearly any requirement. However, if we deal with an unrestricted domain, it is better to choose the machine learning approach, as it would be inefficient to acquire and/or derive rules and gazetteers in this case.

Name identification has been worked on quite intensively for the past few years, and has been incorporated into several products. Many researchers have attacked this problem in a variety of languages but only a few limited researches have focused on NER for Arabic text. This is due to the lack of resources for Arabic NE and the limited amount of progress made in Arabic NLP in general.

Maloney and Niv (1998) developed TAGARAB an Arabic name recognizer that uses a pattern-recognition engine integrated with morphological analysis. The role of the morphological analyzer is to decide where a name ends and the non-name context begins. The decision depends on the part-of-speech of the Arabic word and/or its inflections.

Abuleil (2004) presented a technique to extract proper names from text to build a database of names along with their classification that can be used in question-answering systems. This work was done in three main stages: 1) marking the phrases that might include names, 2) building up graphs to represent the words in these phrases and the relationships between them, and 3) applying rules to generate the names, classify each of them, and saves them in a database.

Larkey et al. (2003) have conducted a study that showed the importance of the proper names component in cross language tasks involving searching, tracking, retrieving, or extracting information. In particular, they have concluded that a combination of static proper name (English-Arabic) translation plus transliteration provides a successful solution.

Pouliquen et al. (2005) developed a tool for multilingual person name recognition that focuses on the "Who" part of the analysis of large news text. As multilingual NER is concerned, the transliteration of the NE has included alternative spelling variants where the origin language of the name is usually not known. Several variants could also be found in the same language.

Samy et al. (2005) has used parallel corpora in Spanish, and Arabic and an NE tagger in Spanish to tag the names in the Arabic corpus. For each sentence pair aligned together, they use a simple mapping scheme to transliterate all the words in the Arabic sentence and return those matching with NEs in the Spanish sentence as the NEs in Arabic. While they report high precision and recall, it should be noted that their approach is applicable only when a parallel corpus is available.

Zitouni et al. (2005) has adopted a statistical approach for the entity detection and recognition (EDR). In this work, a *mention* can be either named (e.g. John Mayor), nominal (the president) or pronominal (she, it). An entity is the aggregate of all the mentions (of any level) which refer to one conceptual entity. This extended definition of the entity has proved the suitability of the approach.

3 Components of an Arabic Full Name

Arabic has well-defined naming practices. The Arabic name elements may be divided into five main categories, Ibn Auda (2003):

1. An ***ism*** (pronounced IZM, as the final syllable in the word *dogmatism*), a personal, proper name given shortly after birth, i.e. the given name. Examples of such names are *Muham-*

mad [Mohammed], *Musa* [Moses], *Ibrahim* [Abraham].

2. A ***kunya*** (pronounced COON-yah), an honorific name or surname, as the father or mother of someone; e.g., *abu Da'ud* [the father of David], *umm Salim* [the mother of Salim]. It is meant as a prefix of respect or reverence. Married persons (especially married ladies) are, as a general rule, simply called by their *kunya* (*abu* or *umm* + the name of their first-born child). When using a person's full name, the *kunya* precedes the personal (given) name: *Abu Yusuf Hasan* [the father of Joseph, Hasan], *Umm Ja'far Aminah* [the mother of Ja'far, Aminah].
3. By a ***nasab*** (pronounced NAH-sahb), a pedigree, as the son or daughter of someone; *e.g.*, *ibn 'Umar* [the son of Omar], *bint 'Abbas* [the daughter of Abbas]. The *nasab* follows the *ism* in usage: *Hasan ibn Faraj* [Hasan the son of Faraj], *Sumayya bint Khubbat* [Sumayya the daughter of Khubbat]. Many historical personages are more familiar to us by their *nasab* than by their *ism*: e.g., the historian *ibn Khaldun*, the traveler *ibn Battuta*, and the philosopher *ibn Sina* [Avicenna].
   *Nasab*s may be extended for several generations, as may be noted in the example below containing two generations nasab:
   Abu al-Qasim Mansur **ibn** al-Zabriqan **ibn** Salamah al-Namari
4. A ***laqab*** (pronounced LAH-kahb), a combination of words into a byname or epithet, usually religious, relating to nature, a descriptive, or of some admirable quality the person had (or would like to have); e.g., *al-Rashid* [the Rightly-guided], *al-Fadl* [the Prominent]. *Laqab*s follow the *ism*: *Harun al-Rashid* [Aaron the Rightly-guided].
5. A ***nisba*** (pronounced NISS-bah), a name derived from a person's: trade or profession, place of residence or birth, religious affiliation, among others; e.g. *al-Hallaj* [the dresser of cotton], *Al Msri* [The Egyptian], *Islami* [Islamic]. Nisbas follow the ism or, if the name contains a nasab (of however many generations), generally follow the nasab.

4 Data Collection

The development of the system PERA depends on collecting dictionaries of proper nouns and their related indicators. Techniques used for acquiring such data to build the dictionaries include:

1. *Automatic collection of person names from annotated corpus.* The person entities in the ACE[1] and Treebank corpus[2] were recognized and extracted using regular expression patterns coded within Python scripts. Python is a strong string processing language and widely used in developing NLP applications and tools.
2. *Identification of person indicators.* Apart from extracting the person names, these corpora were used also to extract noun phrases containing the person names. The surrounding sequence of words around person names was analyzed to identify indicators of person names. A dictionary of these indicators was formed which represented contextual cues of person names.
3. *Name Database provided by government organization.* The person name dictionary was also build from names collected from some organizations including Immigration Departments, Educational bodies, and Brokerage companies.
4. *Internet Resources.* Names were retrieved further from various websites[3] containing lists of Arabic names. Some of these names are Romanized (written using the Latin alphabet) and had to be transliterated from English to Arabic. This was done using the online translation software 'Tarjim' provided by Sakhr Software Company. Notice that the variations in Romanized Arabic due to the lack of one to one correspondence between Arabic letters and Roman letters have also been reflected in the transliteration, in reverse, from Romanized Arabic to Arabic Script.

The raw data received had to be further processed to make it suitable for building gazetteers to

---

[1] ACE reference: http://projects.ldc.upenn.edu/ace/

[2] Treebank Corpus reference: http://www.ircs.upenn.edu/arabic/
Both software are available to BUiD under license agreement.

[3] Web sites include: http://en.wikipedia.org/wiki/List_of_Arabic_names , http://www.islam4you.info/contents/names/fa.php, and http://www.mybabynamessite.com/list.php?letter=a

be incorporated within the system. Some of the automated preprocessing performed on these data includes:

- Removing extra whitespaces between first and last names, or beginning and end of names for the efficient processing of the main gazetteer (dictionary) of complete person names.
- Creating separate dictionaries (i.e. first, last and middle names) without redundancy because the full names had to be parsed. The extraction of each of these individual components from full person names was based on Python code and common sense.

4.1 Typographic Variants

In order to be able to recognize variant Arabic name entities, we added extra expressions in rules and lexicon entries which lead to recognizing named entities and their typographic variants. Examples of typographic variants include:

- The drop of hamza initially, medially, and finally (e.g. احسان vs إحسان - [*Ehessan*])
- Two dots inserted on aleph maqsura, and two dots removed from yaa (e.g. موسي vs موسى-[*Mousa*])
- Dropping the madda from the aleph (e.g. ال خليفة vs آل خليفة - [*Al Khalifa*])
- Hamza insertion below vs. above aleph (e.g. أسراء vs إسراء-[*Essraa*])
- Two dots inserted on final haa, and two dots removed from taa marbouta (e.g. فاطمه vs فاطمة-[*Fatma*])
- Diacritics: partial, full, or none. In the current version we remove diacritics.
- Typing hamza followed by aleph maqsura separately vs. together (e.g. هانىء vs هانئ-[*Hani*]).

4.2 Dictionaries

The following dictionaries (gazetteers) are derived using the aforementioned data collection techniques. A total of 472617 entries were collected.

- A dictionary of full person names (263598 entries)
- A dictionary of first names (78956 entries)
- A dictionary of middle names (67595 entries)
- A dictionary of last names (33517 entries)
- A dictionary of job titles (19245 entries)
- A dictionary of honorifics used before names (173 entries)
- A dictionary of country names including variations in spellings (923 entries)
- A dictionary of nick names and laqabs (8169 entries)
- A dictionary of person titles (20 entries)
- a dictionary of words and phrases that act as person indicators such as 'المشرف الرياضي' (The sports supervisor) (421 entries)

5 System Architecture and Implementation

Figure 1 shows the architecture of the PERA system. Our system has two major components: the *gazetteers* and the *Grammar*. A *filtration mechanism* is employed that enables revision capabilities in the system.

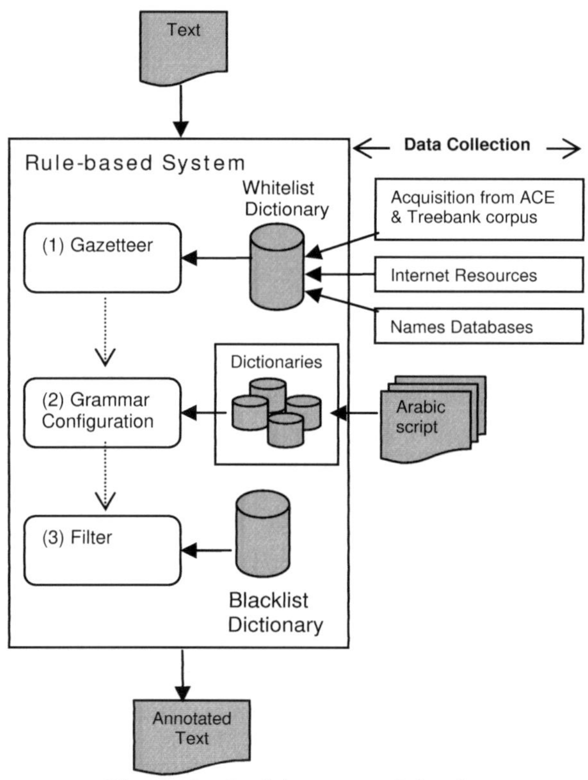

Figure 1: Architecture of the System

5.1 Gazetteers

The main gazetteer (dictionary) of complete person names plays the role of a fixed static dictionary of full person names. It recognizes person name entities by being applied as a *Whitelist* mechanism that accepts matches which are reported as a result of an intersection between the dictionary and the input text. A Whitelist is a list of strings that must be recognized independent of the rules. It contains entries in the following format:

عبدالرحمن قاسم الشيراوى|Abdulrahman Qasim Mohammed Alshirawi

Since the system being developed can be incorporated in various applications independent of language constraints, the English transliterations of the Arabic names are included in the dictionary as meta data.

5.2 Grammar

The grammar performs recognition and extraction of person entities from the input text based on combinations of regular expression patterns. This rule definition is particularly challenging for the Arabic language due to reasons such as:

- Arabic writing systems do not exhibit differences in orthographic case, such as initial capitalized letters to indicate the presence of a proper name. This lack of specific internal structure in the Arabic language poses great challenge for recognizing person entities.
- Arabic is a highly inflected language which entails a requirement of understanding of its morphological nature. The inflected Arabic word maybe composed of prefixes such as prepositions and suffixes such as pronouns. These affixes need to be addressed to ensure recognition of person names alone.

Due to the above complexities in the Arabic language a deep contextual analysis of various Arabic scripts was performed using Python scripts to build grammar rules based on keywords or trigger words forming a window around a person name.

An Example Rule:

The following rule recognizes a person name composed of a first name followed by optional middle and last names based on a preceding person indicator pattern.

```
((honorfic+ws(location(ي|ية)+ws)?)
+firsts_v((ws+middle_vv)|
(ws+lasts_v))?ws+(number)?)
```

Description:

- The names should be verified against their respective dictionaries (i.e. first, middle, and last names).
- The indicator pattern is composed of an honorific such as "الملك" [The king] followed by an optional *Nisba* derived from a location name such as "الأردني" [Jordanian]. These act as trigger words to recognize the person name and should be verified against their respective dictionaries of honorific and locations.
- The rule also matches an optional ordinal number appearing at the end of some names such as "الثاني" [II].
- The Arabic suffix letters "ية" and "ي" used in the above pattern parses the inflections attached to *Nisba* derived from locations that are commonly found in Arabic text.

Implementation:

```
(($honorific$ws*($location
(\x{064A}|\x{0629})*$ws*)?)+
$firsts_v(($ws*$middle_vv)|
($ws*$lasts_v))?$ws*($number)?)
```

Writing conventions:

- `$`: reference to a slave schema.
- `Firsts_v`: dictionary of first names.
- `Middle_vv`: dictionary of middle names.
- `Lasts_v`: dictionary of last names.
- `Ws`: whitespace.
- `Honorific`: dictionary of honorifics appearing before names.
- `Location`: dictionary of locations.
- `Number`: Arabic ordinal numbers.

Example:

The following name would be recognized by the above rule:

الملك الأردني عبد الله الثاني

[The Jordanian king Abdullah II]

Apart from contextual cues, the typical Arabic naming elements were used to formulate rules such as nasab, kunya, etc. Thereby the rules resulted in a good control over critical instances by recognizing complex entities.

5.3 Filter

A *filtration* mechanism is used in the form of a *Blacklist* (rejecter) within the grammar configuration to filter matches that appear after person titles but are invalid person names. In the following example:

'وزير الخارجية العراقي الامين العام' [The Iraqi Foreign Minister the Secretary-General]

The sequence of words 'وزير الخارجية العراقي' [The Iraqi Foreign Minister] acts as a person indicator and the word immediately following it is usually a valid person name. However, in this example, the words following the person indicator that is, ' الامين العام' (the Secretary-General) is not a valid person name. Hence the role of the blacklist comes into play by rejecting the incorrect matches recognized by certain rules.

5.4 The Implementation Platform

The PERA system was implemented through incorporation into the FAST ESP framework, (FAST,_). FAST ESP is an integrated software application that provides searching and filtering services. It is a distributed system that enables information retrieval from any type of information, combining real-time searching, advanced linguistics, and a variety of content access options into a modular, scalable product suite.

The document processing stage within FAST ESP system provides support for Entity Extraction. PERA is implemented through the customizable document processing *pipelines* within FAST ESP, which consists of multiple document processing *stages*. A new search pipeline was created and stages containing the grammar configuration and gazetteers were added to this pipeline. Figure 2 indicates the functionality of the PERA system incorporated in the pipeline within FAST ESP for recognizing and tagging person entity in text.

6 The Experiment

In evaluating the PERA system we follow the standard practice in the IE field of comparing system output against a reference corpus and measuring the performance of the Arabic person named entity.

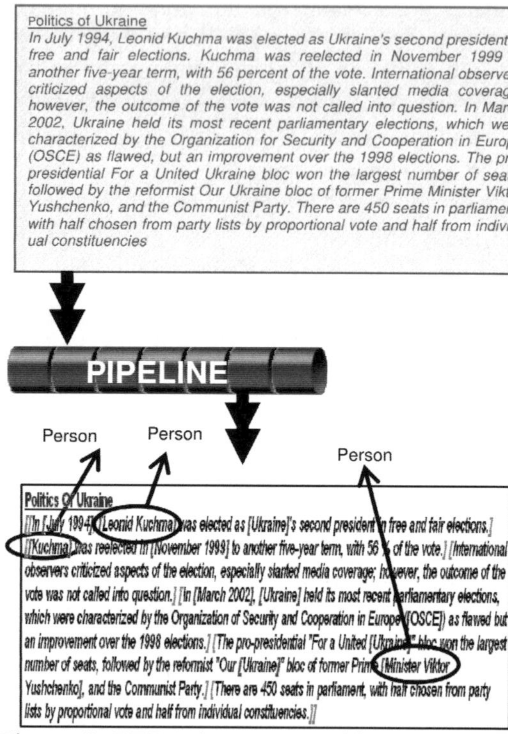

Figure 2: PERA incorporated into FAST ESP pipeline to produce Tagged text

6.1 Reference Corpus

The text within the ACE and Treebank corpus was used for creating the entity tagged reference corpus for evaluating PERA. The text was chosen randomly from files with 'sgm' extension (containing the Arabic script) within ACE & Treebank corpus. The tagging was automatically performed with a Python script and further a post manual check was performed to correct any invalid tags or identify the missing ones. The end product was an annotated text corpus in the *xml* format with the *UTF-8* encoding. This was divided into a 46 test sets and each evaluated individually with hurricane. The total size of the reference corpus build is around 4MB. The size and content of the corpus is such that it contains a representative amount of occurrences of the person entity.

6.2 Evaluation Method

We have adopted the evaluation measures that are standard in the IE community (De Sitter et al., 2004), to evaluate and compare the results (precision, recall and F-measures):

$$\textbf{Precision} = \frac{\text{correct entities recognized}}{\text{total entities recognized}}$$

$$\textbf{Recall} = \frac{\texttt{correct entities recognized}}{\texttt{total correct entities}}$$

$$\textbf{F-measure} = \frac{\texttt{2 x recall x precision}}{\texttt{recall + precision}}$$

Precision indicates how many of the extracted entities are correct. *Recall* indicates how many of the entities that should have been found, are effectively extracted. Usually there is a trade off of recall against precision. Therefore, often an average accuracy is reported in the form of the *F-measure*, a harmonic mean which weights recall and precision equally. It was introduced to provide a single figure to compare different systems' performances. The PERA system implemented within the FAST ESP pipeline was evaluated using an Information Extraction testing tool called 'hurricane' that applies these standard measures.

6.3 Results

Figure 3 is a snapshot of the evaluation performed by hurricane in terms of the above mentioned measure.

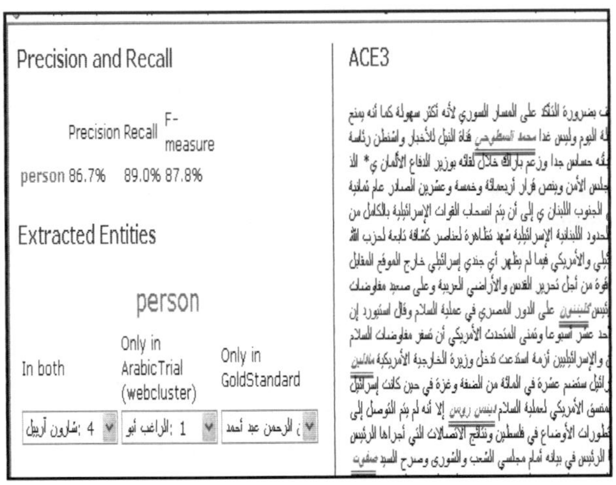

Figure 3: An Extraction from Hurricane Evaluation

The extraction quality of the pipeline created for the person name extractor confirms to the initial target set. The required degree of precision (80%) and recall (70%), for the Person name extractor, has been achieved with the hurricane evaluation. Some of the entries within the gazetteers were extracted from the same corpus used also for creating the reference corpus for evaluation. However, the results achieved are accurate since they indicated recognition of person entities not included in the gazetteers but being recognized by the grammar rules.

Table1 indicates the performance figures produced by 6 out of the 46 sets used for Hurricane evaluation.

The average Precision and Recall for the total 46 sets in recognizing person names is 85.5% and 89%, respectively. And the average f-measure is 87.5%.

Test Set	Precision	Recall	F-measure
Treebank set 1	91.2	90.3	90.7
Treebank set 2	94	96.3	95.1
Treebank set 3	84.2	84.7	84.4
ACE set 1	89.6	96.8	93.1
ACE set 2	88.4	94.2	91.2
ACE set 3	86.7	89	87.8

Table 1: Evaluation result for 6 test sets.

The missing accuracy can be overcome in the following ways:

- Expanding the dictionary of person names further.
- More Arabic text/corpus can be analyzed to identify strings that act as person indicators.
- Reducing negative effects on evaluation results (true positive being treated as false positives) caused due to incomplete annotation of the test corpus. The reference corpus can be further fine tuned to tag all person entities completely.
- Enhancing quality of transliterated names used.
- Using Arabic text with error free spelling.
- Including all possible spelling variations used for names in Arabic written text.

7 Conclusion and Future Work

The work done in this project is an attempt to broaden the coverage for entity extraction by incorporating the Arabic language, thereby paving the path towards enabling search solutions to the Arabian market.

Various data collection techniques were used for acquiring gazetteer name lists. The rule-based approach employed with great linguistic expertise provided a successful implementation of the PERA system. Rules are capable of recognizing inflected forms by breaking them down into stems and affixes. A filtration mechanism is employed in the form of a rejecter within the grammar configuration that helps in deciding where a name ends and the non-name context begins. We have evaluated our system performance using a reference corpus that is tagged in a semi-automated way. The average Precision and Recall achieved for recognizing person names was 85.5% and 89%, respectively. Suggestions for improving the system performance were provided.

This work is part of a new system for Arabic NER. It has several ongoing activities, all concerned with extending our research to recognize and categorize other entity Arabic named entities such as locations, organization.

Acknowledgement

This work is funded by the "Named Entity Recognition for Arabic" joint project between The British Univ. in Duabi, Dubai, UAE and FAST search & Transfer Inc., Oslo, Norway. We thank the FAST team. In particular, we would like to thank Dr. Petra Maier and Dr. Jürgen Oesterle for their technical support.

Any opinions, findings and conclusions or recommendations expressed in this material are the authors, and do not necessarily reflect those of the sponsor.

References

Saleem Abuleil 2004. Extracting Names from Arabic Text for Question-Answering Systems, *In Proceedings of Coupling approaches, coupling media and coupling languages for information retrieval (RIAO 2004)*, Avignon, France. pp. 638- 647.

Da'ud Ibn Auda. 2003. Period Arabic Names and Naming Practices, *In Proceedings of the Known World Heraldic Symposium* (SCA: KWHS Proceedings, 2003), pp. 42-56, St. Louis, USA.

FAST ESP http://www.fastsearch.com/thesolution.aspx?m=376

Nancy Chinchor 1998. Overview of MUC-7. *In Proceedings of the Seventh Message Understanding Conference (MUC-7).* Available at: http://www.itl.nist.gov/iaui/894.02/related_projects/muc/

Leah S. Larkey, Nasreen Abdul Jaleel, Margaret Connell. 2003. *What's in a Name?: Proper Names in Arabic Cross Language Information Retrieval* CIIR Technical Report IR-278. Available at http://ciir.cs.umass.edu/pubfiles/ir-278.pdf

John Maloney and Michael Niv. 1998. TAGARAB: A Fast, Accurate Arabic Name Recogniser Using High Precision Morphological Analysis. *In Proceedings of the Workshop on Computational Approaches to Semitic Languages.* Montreal, Canada. August, pp. 8-15.

Bruno Pouliquen, Ralf Steinberger, Camelia Ignat, Irina Temnikova, Anna Widiger, Wajdi Zaghouani, and Jan Zizka. 2005. Multilingual person name recognition and transliteration. Journal CORELA-Cognition, Représentation, Langage, Vol. 2, ISSN 1638-5748. Available at http://edel.univ-poitiers.fr/corela/

Doaa Samy, Antonio Moreno and Jose M. Guirao. 2005. *A Proposal for an Arabic Named Entity Tagger Leveraging a Parallel Corpus*, International Conference RANLP, Borovets, Bulgaria, pp. 459-465.

An De Sitter, Toon Calders, and Walter Daelemans. 2004. A Formal Framework for Evaluation of Information Extraction, University of Antwerp, Dept. of Mathematics and Computer Science, Technical Report, TR 2004-0. Available at http://www.cnts.ua.ac.be/Publications/2004/DCD04

Antonio Toral. 2005. DRAMNERI: a free knowledge based tool to Named Entity Recognition. *In Proceedings of the 1st Free Software Technologies Conference.* A Coruña, Spain. pp. 27-32.

Imed Zitouni, Jeffrey Sorensen, Xiaoqiang Luo and Radu Florian, 2005 The Impact of Morphological Stemming on Arabic Mention Detection and Coreference Resolution, *In the Proceedings of the ACL workshop on Computational Approaches to Semitic Languages,* 43rd Annual Meeting of the Association of Computational Linguistics (ACL05). June, Ann Arbor, Michigan, USA, pp. 63-70.

Arabic Cross-Document Person Name Normalization

Walid Magdy, Kareem Darwish, Ossama Emam, and Hany Hassan

Human Language Technologies Group
IBM Cairo Technology Development Center
P.O. Box 166 El-Ahram, Giza, Egypt
{wmagdy, darwishk, emam, hanyh}@eg.ibm.com

Abstract

This paper presents a machine learning approach based on an SVM classifier coupled with preprocessing rules for cross-document named entity normalization. The classifier uses lexical, orthographic, phonetic, and morphological features. The process involves disambiguating different entities with shared name mentions and normalizing identical entities with different name mentions. In evaluating the quality of the clusters, the reported approach achieves a cluster F-measure of 0.93. The approach is significantly better than the two baseline approaches in which none of the entities are normalized or entities with exact name mentions are normalized. The two baseline approaches achieve cluster F-measures of 0.62 and 0.74 respectively. The classifier properly normalizes the vast majority of entities that are misnormalized by the baseline system.

1. Introduction:

Much recent attention has focused on the extraction of salient information from unstructured text. One of the enabling technologies for information extraction is Named Entity Recognition (NER), which is concerned with identifying the names of persons, organizations, locations, expressions of times, quantities, ... etc. (Chinchor, 1999; Maynard et al., 2001; Sekine, 2004; Joachims, 2002). The NER task is challenging due to the ambiguity of natural language and to the lack of uniformity in writing styles and vocabulary used across documents (Solorio, 2004).

Beyond NER, considerable work has focused on the tracking and normalization of entities that could be mentioned using different names (e.g. *George Bush, Bush*) or nominals (e.g. *the president, Mr., the son*) (Florian et al., 2004). Most of the named entity tracking work has focused on intra-document normalization with very limited work on cross-documents normalization.

Recognizing and tracking entities of type "Person Name" are particularly important for information extraction. Yet they pose interesting challenges that require special attention. The problems can result from:

1. A Person's name having many variant spellings (especially when it is transliterated into a foreign language). These variations are typically limited in the same document, but are very common across different documents from different sources (e.g. *Mahmoud Abbas = Mahmod Abas, Mohamed El-Baradei = Muhammad AlBaradey ... etc)*.
2. A person having more than one name (e.g. *Mahmoud Abbas = Abu Mazen*).
3. Some names having very similar or identical names but refer to completely different persons (*George H. W. Bush ≠ George W. Bush*).
4. Single token names (e.g. *Bill Clinton = Clinton ≠ Hillary Clinton*).

This paper will focus on Arabic cross-document normalization of named entities of type "person name," which would involve resolving the aforementioned problems. As illustrated in Figure 1, the task involves normalizing a set of person entities into a set of classes each of which is

Proceedings of the 5th Workshop on Important Unresolved Matters, pages 25–32,
Prague, Czech Republic, June 2007. ©2007 Association for Computational Linguistics

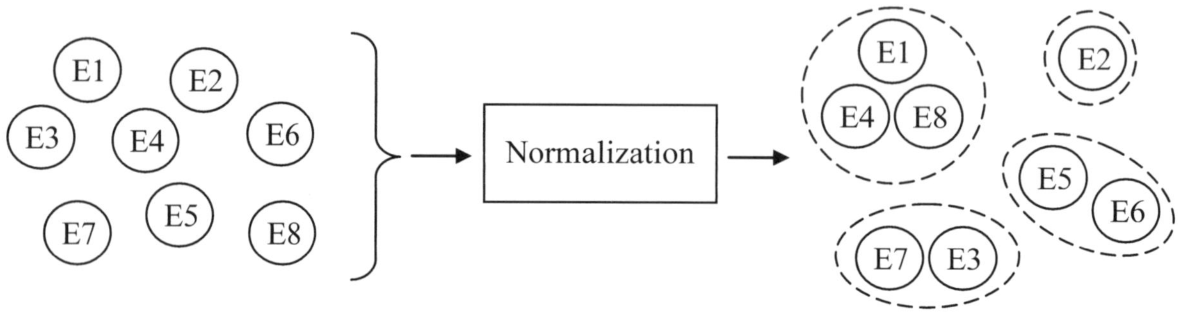

Figure 1 Normalization Model

formed of at least one entity. For N input entities, the output of normalization process will be M classes, where $M \leq N$. Each class would refer to only one person and each class would contain all entities referring to that person.

For this work, intra-document normalization is assumed and an entity refers to a normalized set of name mentions and nominals referring to a single person in a single document. Florian et al. (2004) were kind enough to provide the authors access to an updated version of their state-of-the-art Named Entity Recognition and Tracking (NERT) system, which achieves an F-measure of 0.77 for NER, and an F-measure of 0.88 for intra-document normalization assuming perfect NER. Although the NERT systems is efficient for relatively short documents, it is computational impractical for large documents, which precludes using the NERT system for cross-document normalization through combining the documents into one large document. The main challenges of this work stem from large variations in the spelling of transliterated foreign names and the presence of many common Arabic names (such as Muhammad, Abdullah, Ahmed …etc.), which increases the ambiguity in identifying the person referred to by the mentioned name. Further, the NERT system output system contains many NER errors and intra-document normalization errors.

In this paper, cross-document normalization system employs a two-step approach. In the first step, preprocessing rules are used to remove errant named entities. In the second step, a support vector machine (SVM) classifier is used to determine if two entities from two different documents need to be normalized. The classifier is trained on lexical, orthographic, phonetic, and morphological features.

The paper is organized as follows: Section 2 provides a background on cross-document NE normalization; Section 3 describes the preprocessing steps and data used for training and testing; Section 4 describes the normalization methodology; Section 5 describes the experimental setup; Section 6 reports and discusses experimental results; and Section 7 concludes the paper and provides possible future directions.

2. Background

While considerable work has focused on named entity normalization within a single document, little work has focused on the challenges associated with resolving person name references across multiple documents. Most of the work done in cross-document normalization focused on the problem of determining if two instances with the same name from different documents referring to the same person (Fleischman and Hovy, 2004). Fleischman and Hovy (2004) focused on distinguishing between individuals having identical names, but they did not extend normalization to different names referring to the same individual. Their task is a subtask of what is examined in this paper. They used a large number of features to accomplish their work, depending mostly on language specific dictionaries and wordnet. Some these resources are not available for Arabic and many other languages. Mann and Yarowsky (Mann and Yarowsky, 2003) examined the same problem but they treated it as a clustering task. They focused on information extraction to build biographical profiles (date of birth, place of birth, etc.), and they wanted to disambiguate biographies belonging to different authors with identical names.

Dozier and Zielund (Dozier and Zielund, 2004) reported on cross-document person name normalization in the legal domain. They used a finite state machine that identifies paragraphs in a document containing the names of attorneys, judges, or experts and a semantic parser that extracts from the paragraphs template information about each named individual. They relied on reliable biographies for each individual. A biography would typically contain a person's first name, middle name, last name, firm, city, state, court, and other information. They used a Bayesian network to match the name mentions to the biographical records.

Bhattacharya and Getoor (Bhattacharya and Getoor, 2006) introduced a collective decision algorithm for author name entity resolution, where decisions are not considered on an independent pairwise basis. They focused on using relational links among the references and co-author relationships to infer collaboration groups, which would disambiguate entity names. Such explicit links between co-authors can be extracted directly. However, implicit links can be useful when looking at completely unstructured text. Other work has extended beyond entities of type "person name" to include the normalization of location names (Li et al., 2002) and organizations (Ji and Grishman. 2004).

3. Preprocessing and the Data Set

For this work, a set of 7,184 person name entities was constructed. Building new training and test sets is warranted, because the task at hand is sufficiently different from previously reported tasks in the literature. The entities were recognized from 2,931 topically related documents (relating to the situation in the Gaza and Lebanon during July of 2006) from different Arabic news

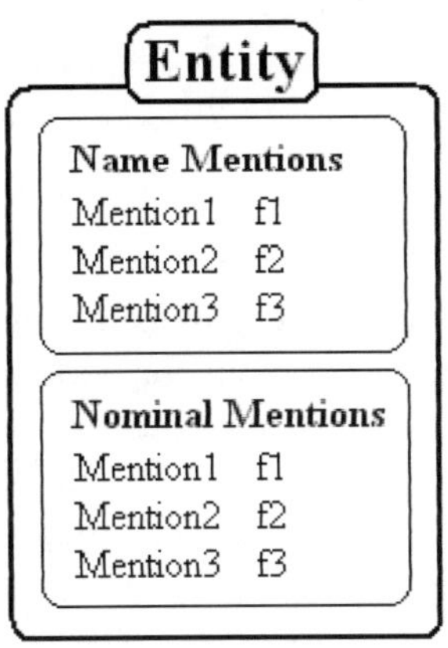

Figure 2 Entity Description

sources (obtained from searching the Arabic version of news.google.com). The entities were recognized and normalized (within document) using the NERT system of Florian et al (2004). As shown in Figure 2, each entity is composed of a set of name mentions (one or more) and a set of nominal mentions (zero or more).

The NERT system achieves an F-score of 0.77 with precision of 0.82 and recall of 0.73 for person name mention and nominal recognition and an F-score of 0.88 for tracking (assuming 100% recognition accuracy). The produced entities may suffer from the following:

1. Errant name mentions: Two name mentions referring to two different entities are concatenated into an errant name mention (e.g. "*Bush Blair*", "*Ahmadinejad Bush*"). These types of errors stem from phrases such as "*The meeting of Bush Blair*" and generally due to lack of sufficient punctuation marks.
2. NE misrecognitions: Regular words are recognized as person name mentions and are embedded into person entities (e.g. *Bush = George Bush = said*).
3. Errant entity tracking: name mentions of different entities are recognized as different mentions of the same entity (e.g. *Bush = Clinton = Ahmadinejad*).
4. Lack of nominal mentions: Many entities do not contain any nominal mentions, which increases the entity ambiguity (especially when there is only one name mention composed of a single token).

To overcome these problems, entities were preprocessed as follows:

1. Errant name mentions such as "*Bush Blair*" were automatically removed. In this step, a dictionary of person name mentions was built from the 2,931 documents collection from which the entities were recognized and normalized along with the frequency of appearance in the collection. For each entity, all its name mentions are checked in the dictionary and their frequencies are compared to each other. Any name mention with a frequency less than 1/30 of the frequency of the name mention with the highest frequency is automatically removed (1/30 was picked based on manual examination of the training set).

2. Name mentions formed of a single token consisting of less than 3 characters are removed. Such names are almost always misrecognized name entities.
3. Name entities with 10 or more different name mentions are automatically removed. The NERT system often produces entities that include many different name mentions referring to different persons as one. Such entities are errant because they over normalize name mentions. Persons are referred to using a limited number of name mentions.
4. Nominal mentions are stemmed using a context sensitive Arabic stemmer (Lee et al. 2003) to overcome the morphological complexity of Arabic. For example, "رئيس" = "president", "الرئيس" = "the president", "والرئيس" = "and the president", "رئيسها" = "its presidents" … etc are stemmed to "رئيس" = "president".

Cross-document entities are compared in a pairwise manner and binary decision is taken on whether they are the same. Therefore, the available 7,184 entities lead to nearly 26 million pairwise comparisons (For N entities, the number of pair wise comparisons $= \frac{N(N-1)}{2}$).

Entity pairs were chosen to be included in the training set if they match any of the following criteria:

1. Both entities have one shared name mention.
2. Both entities have shared nominal mentions.
3. A name mention in one of the entities is a substring of a name mention in the other entity.
4. Both entities have nearly identical name mentions (small edit distance between both mentions).

The resulting set was composed of 19,825 pairs, which were manually judged to determine if they should be normalized or not. These criteria skew the selection of pairs towards more ambiguous cases, which would be better candidates to train the intended SVM classifier, where the items near the boundary dividing the hyperplane are the most important. For the training set, 18,503 pairs were normalized, and 1,322 pairs were judged as different. Unfortunately, the training set selection criteria skewed the distribution of training examples heavily in favor of positive examples. It would interesting to examine other training sets where the distribution of positives and negatives is balanced or skewed in favor of negatives.

The test set was composed of 470 entities that were manually normalized into 253 classes, of which 304 entities were normalized to 87 classes and 166 entities remained unnormalized (forming single-entity classes). Using 470 entities leads to 110,215 pairwise comparisons. The test set, which was distinct from the training set, was chosen using the same criteria as the training set. Further, all duplicate (identical) entities were removed from the test set. The selection criteria insure that the test set is skewed more towards ambiguous cases. Randomly choosing entities would have made the normalization too easy.

4. Normalization Methodology

SVMLight, an SVM classifier (Joachims, 2002), was used for classification with a linear kernel and default parameters. The following training features were employed:

1. The percentage of shared name mentions between two entities calculated as:
   Name Commonality =
   $$\sum_{\text{<common names>}} \min\left(\frac{f_{1i}}{\sum f_{1j}}, \frac{f_{2i}}{\sum f_{2j}}\right)$$
   where f_{1i} is the frequency of the shared name mention in first entity, and f_{2i} is the frequency of the shared name mention in the second entity. $\sum f_{1i}$ is the number of name mentions appearing in the entity.
2. The maximum number of tokens in the shared name mentions, i.e. if there exists more than one shared name mention then this feature is the number of tokens in the longest shared name mention.
3. The percentage of shared nominal mentions between two entities, and it is calculated as the name commonality but for nominal mentions.
4. The smallest minimum edit distance (Levenshtein distance with uniform weights) between any two name mentions in both entities (Cohen et al., 2003) and this feature is only enabled when name commonality between both entities equals to zero.

5. Phonetic edit distance, which is similar to edit distance except that phonetically similar characters, namely {(ت – t, ط – T), (ك – k, ق – q),(د – d, ض – D),(ث – v, س – s, ص – S), (ذ – *, ز – z, ظ – Z),(ج – j, غ – g),(ة – p, ه – h),(إ – <, آ – |, أ – >, ا – A)[1]}, are normalized, vowels are removed, and spaces between tokens are removed.
6. The number of tokens in the pair of name mentions that lead to the minimum edit distance.

Some of the features might seem duplicative. However, the edit distance and phonetic edit distance are often necessary when names are transliterated into Arabic and hence may have different spellings and consequently no shared name mentions. Conversely, given a shared name mention between a pair of entities will lead to zero edit distance, but the name commonality may also be very low indicating two different persons may have a shared name mention. For example "Abdullah the second" and "Abdullah bin Hussein" have the shared name mention "Abdullah" that leads to zero edit distance, but they are in fact two different persons. In this case, the name commonality feature can be indicative of the difference. Further, nominals are important in differentiating between identical name mentions that in fact refer to different persons (Fleischman and Hovy, 2004). The number of tokens feature indicates the importance of the presence of similarity between two name mentions, as the similarity between name mentions formed of one token cannot be indicative for similarity when the number of tokens is more than one.

Further, it is assumed that entities are transitive and are not available all at once, but rather the system has to normalize entities incrementally as they appear. Therefore, for a given set of entity pairs, if the classifier deems that $Entity_i = Entity_j$ and $Entity_j = Entity_k$, then $Entity_i$ is set to equal $Entity_k$ even if the classifier indicates that $Entity_i \neq Entity_k$, and all entities (i, j, and k) are merged into one class.

[1] Buckwalter transliteration scheme is used throughout the paper

5. Experimental Setup

Two baselines were established for the normalization process. In the first, no entities are normalized, which produces single entity classes ("no normalization" condition). In the second, any two entities having two identical name mentions in common are normalized ("surface normalization" condition). For the rest of the experiments, focus was given to two main issues:

1. Determining the effect of the different features used for classification.
2. Determining the effect of varying the number of training examples.

To determine the effect of different features, multiple classifiers were trained using different features, namely:

- All features: all the features mentioned above are used,
- Edit distance removed: edit distance features (features 4, 5, and 6) are removed,
- Number of tokens per name mention removed: the number of shared tokens and the number of tokens leading to the least edit distance (features 2 and 6) are removed.

To determine the effect of training examples, the classifier was trained using all features but with a varying number of training example pairs, namely all 19,825 pairs, a set of randomly picked 5,000 pairs, and a set of randomly picked 2,000 pairs.

For evaluation, 470 entities in test set were normalized into set of classes with different thresholds for the SVM classifier. The quality of the clusters was evaluated using purity, entropy, and Cluster F-measure (CF-measure) in the manner suggested by Rosell et al. (2004). For the cluster quality measures, given cluster i (formed using automatic normalization) and each cluster j (reference normalization formed manually), cluster precision (p) and recall (r) are computed as follows:

$p_{ij} = \frac{n_{ij}}{n_i}$, and $r_{ij} = \frac{n_{ij}}{n_j}$, where n_i number of entities in cluster i, n_j number of entities in cluster j, and n_{ij} number of shared entities between cluster i and j.

The CF-measure for an automatic cluster i against a manually formed reference cluster j is:

$CF_{ij} = \dfrac{2 \cdot r_{ij} \cdot p_{ij}}{r_{ij} + p_{ij}}$, and the CF-measure for a reference cluster j is:

$CF_j = \max_i \{CF_{ij}\}$.

The final CF-measure is computed over all the reference clusters as follows: $CF = \sum_j \frac{n_{ij}}{n} CF_j$.

Purity of (ρ_i) of an automatically produced cluster i is the maximum cluster precision obtained when comparing it with all the reference clusters as follows: $\rho_i = \max_j \{p_{ij}\}$, and the weighted average purity over all clusters is:

$\rho = \sum_i \frac{n_{ij}}{n_i} \rho_i$, where n is the total number of entities in the set to be normalized (470 in this case).

As for entropy of a cluster, it is calculated as: $E_i = -\sum_j p_{ij} \log p_{ij}$, and the average entropy as:

$E = \sum_i \frac{n_i}{n_i} E_i$.

The CF-measure captures both precision and recall while purity and entropy are precision oriented measures (Rosell et al., 2004).

6. Results and Discussion

Figure 3 shows the purity and CF-measure for the two baseline conditions (no normalization, and surface normalization) and for the normalization system with different SVM thresholds. Since purity is a precision measure, purity is 100% when no normalization is done. The CF-measure is 62% and 74% for baseline runs with no normalization and surface normalization respectively. As can be seen from the results, the baseline run based on exact matching of name mentions in entities achieves low CF-measure and low purity. Low CF-measure values stem from the inability to match identical entities with different name mentions, and the low purity value stems from not disambiguating different entities with shared name mentions. Some notable examples where the surface normalization baseline failed include:

1. The normalization of the different entities referring to the Israeli soldier who is imprisoned in Gaza with different Arabic spellings for his name, namely "جلعاد شليط" (jlEAd $lyT), "جلعاد شاليط" (jlEAd $AlyT), "الجندي شليت" (the soldier $lyt), and so forth.
2. The separation between "الملك عبد الله الثاني" (King Abdullah the Second) and "الملك عبد الله بن عبد العزيز" (King Abdullah ibn Abdul-Aziz) that have a shared name mention "الملك عبدالله" (King Abdullah).
3. The normalization of the different entities representing the president of Palestinian Authority with different name mentions, namely "أبو مازن" (Abu Mazen) and "محمود عباس" (Mahmoud Abbas).

The proposed normalization technique properly normalized the aforementioned examples. Given different SVM thresholds, Figure 3 shows that the purity of resultant classes increases as the SVM threshold increases since the number of normalized entities decreases as the threshold increases. The best CF-measure of 93.1% is obtained at a threshold of 1.4 and as show in Table 1 the corresponding purity and entropy are 97.2% and 0.056 respectively. The results confirm the success of the approach.

Table 1 highlights the effect of removing different training feature and the highest CF-measures (at different SVM thresholds) as a result. The table shows that using all 6 features produced the best results and the removal of the shared names and tokens (features 2 and 6) had the most adverse effect on normalization effectiveness. The adverse effect is reasonable especially given that some single token names such as "*Muhammad*" and "*Abdullah*" are very common and matching one of these names across entities is an insufficient indicator that they are the same. Meanwhile, the exclusion of edit distance features (features 4, 5, and 6) had a lesser but significant adverse impact on normalization effectiveness. Table 1 reports the best results obtained using different thresholds. Perhaps, a separate development set should be used for ascertaining the best threshold.

Table 2 shows that decreasing the number of training examples (all six features are used) has a noticeable but less pronounced effect on normalization effectiveness compared to removing training features.

Table 1 Quality of clusters as measured by purity (higher values are better), entropy (lower values are better), and CF-measure (higher values are better) for different feature sets. Values are shown for max CF-measure. Thresholds were tuned for max CF-measure for each feature configuration separately

Training Data	Purity	Maximum CF-Measure	Entropy	Threshold
No Normalization	100.0%	62.6%	0.000	-
Baseline	83.4%	74.7%	0.151	-
All Features	97.2%	93.1%	0.056	1.4
Edit Distance removed	99.4%	85.5%	0.010	1.0
# of tokens/name removed	96.6%	77.8%	0.071	1.5

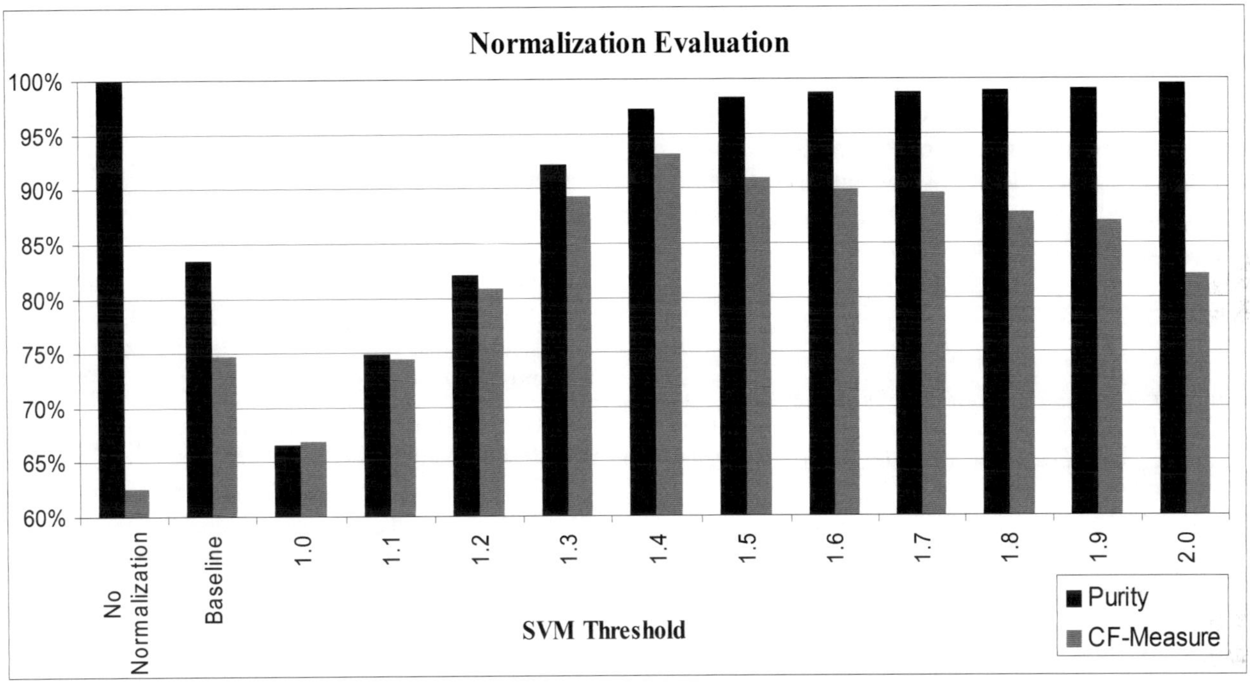

Figure 3 Purity and cluster F-measure versus SVM Threshold

Table 2 Effect of number of training examples on normalization effectiveness

Training Data	Purity	Maximum CF-Measure	Entropy	Threshold
20k training pairs	97.2%	93.1%	0.056	1.4
5k training pairs	97.4%	90.5%	0.053	1.5
2k training pairs	98.5%	90.3%	0.031	1.6

7. Conclusion:

This paper presented a two-step approach to cross-document named entity normalization. In the first step, preprocessing rules are used to remove errant named entities. In the second step, a machine learning approach based on an SVM classifier to disambiguate different entities with matching name mentions and to normalize identical entities with different name mentions. The classifier was trained on features that capture name mentions and nominals overlap between entities, edit distance, and phonetic similarity. In evaluating the quality of the clusters, the reported approach achieved a cluster F-measure of 0.93. The approach outperformed that two baseline approaches in which no normalization was done or normalization was done when two entities had matching name mentions. The two approaches achieved cluster F-measures of 0.62 and 0.74 respectively.

For future work, implicit links between entities in the text can serve as the relational links that would enable the use of entity attributes in conjunction with relationships between entities. An important problem that has not been sufficiently explored is cross-lingual cross-document normalization. This problem would pose unique and interesting challenges. The described approach could be generalized to perform normalization of entities of different types across multilingual documents. Also, the normalization problem was treated as a classification problem. Examining the problem as a clustering (or alternatively an incremental clustering) problem might prove useful. Lastly, the effect of cross-document normalization should be examined on applications such as information extraction, information retrieval, and relationship and social network visualization.

References:

Bhattacharya I. and Getoor L. "A Latent Dirichlet Allocation Model for Entity Resolution." 6th SIAM Conference on Data Mining (SDM), Bethesda, USA, April 2006.

Chinchor N., Brown E., Ferro L., and Robinson P. "Named Entity Recognition Task Definition." MITRE, 1999.

Cohen W., Ravikumar P., and Fienberg S. E. "A Comparison of String Distance Metrics for Name-Matching Tasks." In Proceedings of the International Joint Conference on Artificial Intelligence, 2003.

Dozier C. and Zielund T. "Cross-document Co-Reference Resolution Applications for People in the Legal Domain." In 42nd Annual Meeting of the Association for Computational Linguistics, Reference Resolution Workshop, Barcelona, Spain. July 2004.

Fleischman M. B. and Hovy E. "Multi-Document Person Name Resolution." In 42nd Annual Meeting of the Association for Computational Linguistics, Reference Resolution Workshop, Barcelona, Spain. July 2004.

Ji H. and Grishman R. "Applying Coreference to Improve Name Recognition". In 42nd Annual Meeting of the Association for Computational Linguistics, Reference Resolution Workshop, Barcelona, Spain. July (2004).

Ji H. and Grishman R. "Improving Name Tagging by Reference Resolution and Relation Detection." ACL 2005

Joachims T. "Learning to Classify Text Using Support Vector Machines." Ph.D. Dissertation, Kluwer, (2002).

Joachims T. "Optimizing Search Engines Using Click-through Data." Proceedings of the ACM Conference on Knowledge Discovery and Data Mining (KDD), (2002).

Lee Y. S., Papineni K., Roukos S., Emam O., Hassan H. "Language Model Based Arabic Word Segmentation." In ACL 2003, pp. 399-406, (2003).

Li H., Srihari R. K., Niu C., and Li W. "Location Normalization for Information Extraction." Proceedings of the 19th international conference on Computational linguistics, pp. 1-7, 2002

Li H., Srihari R. K., Niu C., and Li W. "Location Normalization for Information Extraction." Proceedings of the sixth conference on applied natural language processing, 2000. pp. 247 – 254.

Mann G. S. and Yarowsky D. "Unsupervised Personal Name Disambiguation." Proceedings of the seventh conference on Natural language learning at HLT-NAACL 2003. pp. 33-40.

Maynard D., Tablan V., Ursu C., Cunningham H., and Wilks Y. "Named Entity Recognition from Diverse Text Types." Recent Advances in Natural Language Processing Conference, (2001).

Palmer D. D. and Day D. S. "A statistical Profile of the Named Entity Task". Proceedings of the fifth conference on Applied natural language processing, pp. 190-193, (1997).

R. Florian R., Hassan H., Ittycheriah A., Jing H., Kambhatla N., Luo X., Nicolov N., and Roukos S. "A Statistical Model for Multilingual Entity Detection and Tracking." In HLT-NAACL, 2004.

Rosell M., Kann V., and Litton J. E. "Comparing Comparisons: Document Clustering Evaluation Using Two Manual Classifications." In ICON 2004

Sekine S. "Named Entity: History and Future". Project notes, New York University, (2004).

Solorio T. "Improvement of Named Entity Tagging by Machine Learning." Ph.D. thesis, National Institute of Astrophysics, Optics and Electronics, Puebla, Mexico, September 2005.

Syllable-Based Speech Recognition for Amharic

Solomon Teferra Abate
solomon_teferra_7@yahoo.com

Wolfgang Menzel
menzel@informatik.uni-hamburg.de

Uniformity of Hamburg, Department of Informatik Natural Language Systems Groups
Vogt-Kölln-Strasse. 30, D-22527 Hamburg, Germany

Abstract

Amharic is the Semitic language that has the second large number of speakers after Arabic (Hayward and Richard 1999). Its writing system is syllabic with Consonant-Vowel (CV) syllable structure. Amharic orthography has more or less a one to one correspondence with syllabic sounds. We have used this feature of Amharic to develop a CV syllable-based speech recognizer, using Hidden Markov Modeling (HMM), and achieved 90.43% word recognition accuracy.

1 Introduction

Most of the Semitic languages are technologically unfavored. Amharic is one of these languages that are looking for technological considerations of researchers and developers in the area of natural language processing (NLP). Automatic Speech Recognition (ASR) is one of the major areas of NLP that is understudied in Amharic. Only few attempts (Solomon, 2001; Kinfe, 2002; Zegaye, 2003; Martha, 2003; Hussien and Gambäck, 2005; Solomon et al., 2005; Solomon, 2006) have been made.

We have developed an ASR for the language using CV syllables as recognition units. In this paper we present the development and the recognition performance of the recognizer following a brief description of the Amharic language and speech recognition technology.

2 The Amharic Language

Amharic, which belongs to the Semitic language family, is the official language of Ethiopia. In this family, Amharic stands second in its number of speakers after Arabic (Hayward and Richard 1999). Amharic has five dialectical variations (Addis Ababa, Gojjam, Gonder, Wollo, and Menz) spoken in different regions of the country (Cowley, et.al. 1976). The speech of Addis Ababa has emerged as the standard dialect and has wide currency across all Amharic-speaking communities (Hayward and Richard 1999).

As with all of the other languages, Amharic has its own characterizing phonetic, phonological and morphological properties. For example, it has a set of speech sounds that is not found in other languages. For example the following sounds are not found in English: [p`], [tS`], [s`], [t`], and [q].

Amharic also has its own inventory of speech sounds. It has thirty one consonants and seven vowels. The consonants are generally classified as stops, fricatives, nasals, liquids, and semi-vowels (Leslau 2000). Tables 1 and 2 show the classification of Amharic consonants and vowels[1].

Man of Art	Voicing	Place of Articulation				
		Lab	Den	Pal	Vel	Glot
Stops	Vs	[p]	[t]	[tS]	[k]	[?]
	Vd	[b]	[d]	[d3]	[g]	
	Glott	[p`]	[t`]	[tS`]	[q]	
	Rd				$[k^w]$ $[g^w]$ $[q^w]$	
Fric	Vs	[f]	[s]	[S]		[h]
	Vd		[z]	[3]		
	Glott		[s`]			
	Rd					$[h^w]$
Nasals	Vd	[m]	[n]	[ɳ]		
Liq	Vd		[l] [r]			
Sv	Vd	[w]			[j]	

Table 1: Amharic Consonants

Key: Lab = Labials; Den = Dentals; Pal = Palatals; Vel = Velars; Glot = Glottal; Vs = Voiceless;

[1] International Phonetic Association's (IPA) standard has been used for representation.

Proceedings of the 5th Workshop on Important Unresolved Matters, pages 33–40,
Prague, Czech Republic, June 2007.

Vd = Voiced; Rd = Rounded; Fric = Fricatives; Liq = Liquids; Sv = Semi-Vowels.

Positions	front	center	back
high	[i]	ɨ	[u]
mid	[e]	[ə]	[o]
low		[a]	

Table 2: Amharic Vowels

Amharic is one of the languages that have their own writing system, which is used across all Amharic dialects. Getachew (1967) stated that the Amharic writing system is phonetic. It allows any one to write Amharic texts if s/he can speak Amharic and has knowledge of the Amharic alphabet. Unlike most known languages, no one needs to learn how to spell Amharic words. In support of the above point, Leslaw (1995) noted that no real problems exist in Amharic orthography, as there is more or less, a one-to-one correspondence between the sounds and the graphic symbols, except for the gemination of consonants and some redundant symbols.

Many (Bender 1976; Cowley 1976; Baye 1986) have claimed the Amharic orthography as a syllabary for a relatively long period of time. Recently, however, Taddesse (1994) and Baye (1997), who apparently modified his view, have argued it is not. Both of these arguments are based on the special feature of the orthography; the possibility of representing speech using either isolated phoneme symbols or concatenated symbols.

In the concatenated feature, commonly known to most of the population, each orthographic symbol represents a consonant and a vowel, except for the sixth order[2], which is sometimes realized as a consonant without a vowel and at other times a consonant with a vowel. This representation of concatenated speech sounds by a single symbol has been the basis for the claim made of the writing system, as syllabary.

Amharic orthography does not indicate gemination, but since there are relatively few minimal pairs of geminations, Amharic readers do not find this to be a problem. This property of the writing system is analogous to the vowels of Arabic and Hebrew, which are not normally indicated in writing.

The Amharic orthography, as represented in the Amharic Character set - also called [fidəll] consists of 276 distinct symbols. In addition, there are twenty numerals and eight punctuation marks. A sample of the orthographic symbols is given in Table 3.

	ə	*u*	*i*	*a*	*e*	ɨ	*o*
h	ሀ	ሁ	ሂ	ሃ	ሄ	ህ	ሆ
l	ለ	ሉ	ሊ	ላ	ሌ	ል	ሎ
m	መ	ሙ	ሚ	ማ	ሜ	ም	ሞ
r	ረ	ሩ	ሪ	ራ	ሬ	ር	ሮ

Table 3: Some Orthographic Symbols of Amharic

However, research in speech recognition should only consider distinct sounds instead of all the orthographic symbols, unless there is a need to develop a dictation machine that includes all of the orthographic symbols. Therefore, redundant orthographic symbols that represent the same syllabic sounds can be eliminated. Thus, by eliminating redundant graphemes, we are left with a total of 233 distinct CV syllable characters. In our work, an HMM model has been developed for each of these CV syllables.

3 HMM-Based Speech Recognition

The most well known and well performing approach for speech recognition are Hidden Markov Models (HMM). An HMM can be classified on the basis of the type of its observation distributions, the structure in its transition matrix and the number of states.

The observation distributions of HMMs can be either discrete, or continuous. In discrete HMMs, distributions are defined on finite spaces while in continuous HMMs, distributions are defined as probability densities on continuous observation spaces, usually as a mixture of several Gaussian distributions.

The model topology that is generally adopted for speech recognition is a left-to-right or Bakis model

[2]An order in Amharic writing system is a combination of a consonant with a vowel represented by a symbol. A consonant has therefore, 7 orders or different symbols that represent its combination with 7 Amharic vowels.

because the speech signal varies in time from left to right (Deller, Proakis and Hansen 1993).

An HMM is flexible in its size, type, or architecture to model words as well as any sub-word unit.

3.1 Sub-word Units of Speech Recognition

Large Vocabulary Automatic Speech Recognition Systems (LVASRSs) require modeling of speech in smaller units than words because the acoustic samples of most words will never be seen during training, and therefore, can not be trained. Moreover, in LVASRSs there are thousands of words and most of them occur very rarely, consequently training of models for whole words is generally impractical. That is why LVASRSs require a segmentation of each word in the vocabulary into sub-word units that occur more frequently and can be trained more robustly than words. Using sub-word based models enables us to deal with words which have not been seen during training since they can just be decomposed into the sub-word units. As a word can be decomposed in sub-word units of different granularities, there is a need to choose the most suitable sub-word unit that fits the purpose of the system.

Lee et al. (1992) pointed out that there are two alternatives for choosing the fundamental sub-word units, namely acoustically-based and linguistically-based units . The acoustic units are the labels assigned to acoustic segment models, which are defined on the basis of procuring a set of segment models that spans the acoustic space determined by the given, unlabeled training data. The linguistically-based units include the linguistic units, e.g. phones, demi-syllables, syllables and morphemes.

It should be clear that there is no ideal (perfect) set of sub-word units. Although phones are very small in number and relatively easy to train, they are much more sensitive to contextual influences than larger units. The use of triphones, which model both the right and left context of a phone, has become the dominant solution to the problem of the context sensitivity of phones.

Triphones are also relatively inefficient sub-word units due to their large number. Moreover, since a triphone unit spans a short time-interval, it is not suitable for the integration of spectral and temporal dependencies.

An other alternative is the syllable. Syllables are longer and less context sensitive than phones and capable of exploiting both the spectral and temporal characteristics of continuous speech (Ganapathiraju et al. 1997). Moreover, the syllable has a close connection to articulation, integrates some co-articulation phenomena, and has the potential for a relatively compact representation of conversational speech.

Therefore, different attempts have been made to use syllables as a unit of recognition for the development of ASR. To mention a few: Ganapathiraju et al. (1997) have explored techniques to accentuate the strengths of syllable-based modeling with a primary interest of integrating finite-duration modeling and monosyllabic word modeling. Wu et al. (1998) tried to extract the features of speech over the syllabic duration (250ms), considering syllable-length interval to be 100-250ms. Hu et al. (1996) used a pronunciation dictionary of syllable-like units that are created from sequences of phones for which the boundary is difficult to detect. Kanokphara (2003) used syllable-structure-based triphones as speech recognition units for Thai.

However, syllables are too many in a number of languages, such as English, to be trained properly. Thus ASR researchers in languages like English are led to choose phones where as for Amharic it seems promising to consider syllables as an alternative, because Amharic has only 233 distinct CV syllables.

4 Syllable-Based Speech Recognition for Amharic

In the development of syllable-based LVASRSs for Amharic we need to deal with a language model, pronunciation dictionary, initialization and training of the HMM models, and identification of the proper HMM topologies that can be properly trained with the available data. This section presents the development and the performance of syllable based speech recognizers.

4.1 The Language Model

One of the required elements in the development of LVASRSs is the language model. As there is no usable language model for Amharic, we have trained bigram language models using the HTK statistical language model development modules. Due to the inflectional and derivativational morphological feature of Amharic our language models have relatively high perplexities.

4.2 The Pronunciation Dictionary

The development of a large vocabulary speaker independent recognition system requires the availability of an appropriate pronunciation dictionary. It specifies the finite set of words that may be output by the speech recognizer and gives, at least, one pronunciation for each. A pronunciation dictionary can be classified as a canonical or alternative on the basis of the pronunciations it includes.

A canonical pronunciation dictionary includes only the standard phone (or other sub-word) sequence assumed to be pronounced in read speech. It does not consider pronunciation variations such as speaker variability, dialect, or co-articulation in conversational speech. On the other hand, an alternative pronunciation dictionary uses the actual phone (or other sub-word) sequences pronounced in speech. In an alternative pronunciation dictionary, various pronunciation variations can be included (Fukada et al. 1999).

We have used the pronunciation dictionary that has been developed by Solomon et al. (2005). They have developed a canonical and an alternative pronunciation dictionaries. Their canonical dictionary transcribes 50,000 words and the alternative one transcribes 25,000 words in terms of CV syllables.

Both these pronunciation dictionaries do not handle the difference between geminated and non-geminated consonants; the variation of the pronunciation of the sixth order grapheme, with or without vowel; and the absence or presence of the glottal stop consonant. Gemination of Amharic consonants range from a slight lengthening to much more than doubling. In the dictionary, however, they are represented with the same transcription symbols.

The sixth order grapheme may be realized with or without vowel but the pronunciation dictionaries do not indicate this difference. For example, the dictionaries used the same symbol for the syllable [rI] in the word [d3əmərInI] 'we started', whose vowel part may not be realized, and in the word [bərIzo] 'he diluted with water' that is always realized with its vowel sound. That forces a syllable model to capture two different sounds: a sound of a consonant followed by a vowel, and a sound of the consonant only. A similar problem occurs with the glottal stop consonant [?] which may be uttered or not.

A sample of pronunciations in the canonical and alternative pronunciation dictionaries is given in Table 4[3]. The alternative pronunciation dictionary contains up to 25 pronunciation variants per word form. Table 5 illustrates some cases of the variation.

Words	Canonical Pronunciation	Alternative Pronunciation
CAmA	CA mA sp	CA mA sp
		Ca mA sp
Hitey-oPeyA	Hi te yo Pe yA sp	Hi te yo Pe yA sp
		Hi te yo Pi yA sp
		Hi to Pe yA sp
		te yo Pe yA sp
		to Pe yA sp

Table 4: Canonical and Alternative Pronunciation

Words	Number of pronunciation variants
HiteyoPeyAweyAne	25
HiheHadEge	16
yaHiteyoPeyAne	7
miniseteru	7
yaganezabe	6
HegeziHabehEre	6
yehenene	5

Table 5: Number of Pronunciation variants

Although it does not handle gemination and pronunciation variabilities, the canonical pronunciation dictionary contains all 233 distinct CV syllables of Amharic, which is 100% syllable coverage.

Pronunciation dictionaries of development and evaluation test sets have been extracted from the canonical pronunciation dictionary. These test dictionaries have 5,000 and 20,000 words each.

4.3 The Acoustic Model

For training and evaluation of our recognizers, we have used the Amharic read speech corpus that has been developed by Solomon et al. (2005).

The speech corpus consists of a training set, a speaker adaptation set, development test sets (for 5,000 and 20,000 vocabularies), and evaluation test sets (for 5,000 and 20,000 vocabularies). It is a medium size speech corpus of 20 hours of training speech that has been read by 100 training speakers who read a total of 10850 different sentences. Eighty of the training speakers are from the Addis

[3]In tables 4 and 5, we used our own transcription

Ababa dialect while the other twenty are from the other four dialects.

Test and speaker adaptation sets were read by twenty other speakers of the Addis Ababa dialect and four speakers of the other four dialects. Each speaker read 18 different sentences for the 5,000 vocabulary (development and evaluation sets each) and 20 different sentences for the 20,000 vocabulary (development and evaluation sets each) test sets. For the adaptation set all of these readers read 53 adaptation sentences that consist of all Amharic CV syllables.

Initialization: Training HMM models starts with initialization. Initialization of the model for a set of sub-word HMMs prior to re-estimation can be achieved in two different ways: bootstrapping and flat start. The latter implies that during the first cycle of embedded re-estimation, each training utterance will be uniformly segmented. The hope of using such a procedure is that in the second and subsequent iterations, the models align as intended.

We have initialized HMMs with both methods and trained them in the same way. The HMMs that have been initialized with the flat start method performed better (40% word recognition accuracy) on development test set of 5,000 words.

The problem with the bootstrapping approach is that any error of the labeler strongly affects the performance of the resulting model because consecutive training steps are influenced by the initial value of the model. As a result, we did not benefit from the use of the segmented speech, which has been transcribed with a speech recognizer that has low word recognition accuracy, and edited by non-linguist listeners. We have, therefore, continued our subsequent experiments with the flat start initialization method.

Training: We have used the Baum-Welch re-estimation procedure for the training. In training sub-word HMMs that are initialized using the flat-start procedure, this re-estimation procedure uses the parameters of continuously spoken utterances as an input source. A transcription, in terms of sub-word units, is also needed for each input utterance. Using the speech parameters and their transcription, the complete set of sub-word HMMs are re-estimated simultaneously. Then all of the sub-word HMMs corresponding to the sub-word list are joined together to make a single composite HMM. It is important to emphasize that in this process the transcriptions are only needed to identify the sequence of sub-word units in each utterance. No boundary information is required (Young et al. 2002).

The major problem with HMM training is that it requires a great amount of speech data. To overcome the problem of training with insufficient speech data, a variety of sharing mechanisms can be implemented. For example, HMM parameters are tied together so that the training data is pooled and more robust estimates result. It is also possible to restrict the model to a variance vector for the description of output probabilities, instead of a full covariance matrix. Rabiner and Juang(1993) pointed out that for the continuous HMM models, it is preferable to use diagonal covariance matrices with several mixtures, rather than fewer mixtures with full covariance matrices to perform reliable re-estimation of the components of the model from limited training data. The diagonal covariance matrices have been used in our work.

HMM Topologies: To our knowledge, there is no topology of HMM model that can be taken as a rule of thumb for modeling syllable HMMs, especially, for Amharic CV syllables. To have a good HMM model for Amharic CV syllables, one needs to conduct experiments to select the optimal model topology. Designing an HMM topology has to be done with proper consideration of the size of the unit of recognition and the amount of the training speech data. This is because as the size of the recognition unit increases and the size of the model (in terms of the number of parameters to be re-estimated) grows, the model requires more training data.

We, therefore, carried out a series of experiments using a left-to-right HMM with and without jumps and skips, with a different number of emitting states (3, 5, 6, 7, 8, 9, 10 and 11) and different number of Gaussian mixtures (from 2 to 98). By jump we mean skips from the first non-emitting state to the middle state and/or from the middle state to the last non-emitting state. Figure 1 shows a left-to-right HMM of 5 emitting states with jumps and skips.

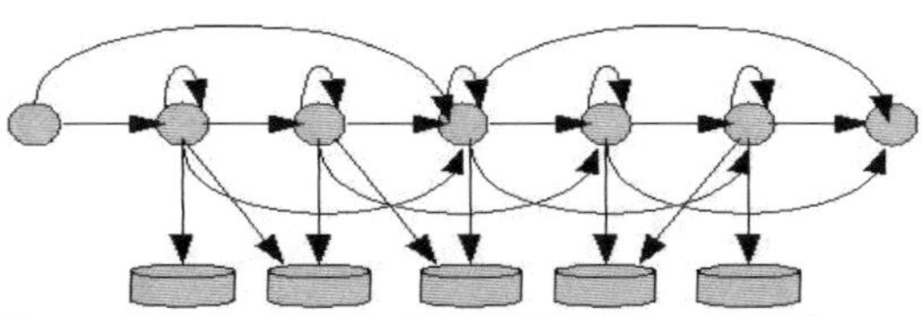

Figure 1: An example of HMM topologies

We have assumed that the problem of gemination may be compensated by the looping state transitions of the HMM. Accordingly, CV syllables containing geminated consonants should have a higher loop probability than those with the non-geminated consonants.

To develop a solution for the problem of the irregularities in the realization of the sixth order vowel [I] and the glottal stop consonant [?], HMM topologies with jumps have been used.

We conducted an experiment using HMMs with a jump from the middle state to the last (non-emitting) state for all of the CV syllables with the sixth order vowel, and a jump from the first emitting state to the middle state for all of the CV syllables with the glottal stop consonant. The CV syllable with the glottal stop consonant and the 6th order vowel have both jumps. These topologies have been chosen so that the models recognize the absence of the vowel and the glottal stop consonant of CV syllables. This assumption was confirmed by the observation that the trained models favor such a jump. A model, which has 5 emitting states, of the glottal stop consonant with the sixth order vowel tends to start emitting with the 3rd emitting state with a probability of 0.72. The model also has accumulated a considerable probability (0.38) to jump from the 3rd emitting state to the last (non-emitting) state.

A similar model of this consonant with the other vowels (our example is the 5th order vowel) tend to start emitting with the 3rd emitting state with a probability of 0.68. This is two times the probability (0.32) of its transition from the starting (non-emitting state) to the 1st emitting state.

The models of the other consonants with the sixth order vowel, which are exemplified by the model of the syllable [jI], tend to jump from the 3rd emitting state to the last (non-emitting) state with a probability of 0.39, which is considerably greater than that of continuing with the next state (0.09).

Since the amount of available training speech is not enough to train transition probabilities for skipping two or more states, the number of states to be skipped have been limited to one.

To determine the optimal number of Gaussian mixtures for the syllable models, we have conducted a series of experiments by adding two Gaussian mixtures for all the models until the performance of the model starts to degrade. Considering the difference in the frequency of the CV syllables, a hybrid number of Gaussian mixtures has been tried. By hybrid, we mean that Gaussian mixtures are assigned to different syllables based on their frequency. For example: the frequent syllables, like [nI], are assigned up to fifty-eight while rare syllables, like [p`i], are assigned not more than two Gaussian mixtures.

4.4 Performance of the Recognizers

We present recognition results of only those recognizers which have competitive performance to the best performing models. For example: the performance of the model with 11 emitting states with skips and hybrid Gaussian mixtures is more competitive than those with 7, 8, 9, and 10 emitting states. We have also systematically left out test results which are worse than those presented in Table 6. Table 6[4] shows evaluation results made on the 5k development test set.

States	Transition Topologies	Mix.	Models		
			AM	AM + LM	AM + LM + SA
3	No skip and jump	18	62.85	88.82	
		Hy	60.87	87.63	88.50
	skip	12		69.20	
	jump	12	43.74	79.94	
5	No skip and jump	12	69.29	88.99	**89.80**
		Hy	60.04		
	skip	12		85.77	
	jump	12	54.53	84.60	
11	skip	12	55.04		
		Hy	71.83	89.21	**89.04**

Table 6: Recognition Performance on 5k Development test set

From Table 6, we can see that the models with five emitting states, with twelve Gaussian mixtures, without skips and jumps has the best (89.80%) word recognition accuracy. It has 87.69% word recognition accuracy on the 20k development test set.

Since the most commonly used number of HMM states for phone-based speech recognizers is three emitting states, one may expect a model of six emitting states to be the best for an HMM of

[4]In tables 6 and 7, States refers to the number of emitting states; Mix refers to the number of Gaussian mixtures per state; Hy refers to hybrid; AM refers to acoustic model; LM refers to language model; and SA refers to speaker adaptation.

concatenated consonant and vowel. But the result of our experiment shows that a CV syllable-based recognizer with only five emitting states performed better than all the other recognizers.

As we can see from Table 6, models with three emitting states do have a competitive performance with 18 and hybrid Gaussian mixtures. They have the least number of states of all our models. Nevertheless, they require more storage space (33MB with 18 Gaussian mixtures and 34MB with hybrid Gaussian mixtures) than the best performing models (32MB). Models with three emitting states also have larger number of total Gaussian mixtures[5] (30,401 with 18 Gaussian mixtures and 31,384 with hybrid Gaussian mixtures) than the best performing models (13,626 Gaussian mixtures).

The other model topology that is competitive in word recognition performance is the model with eleven emitting states, with skip and hybrid Gaussian mixtures, which has a word recognition accuracy of 89.21%. It requires the biggest memory space (40MB) and uses the largest number of total Gaussian mixtures (36,619) of all the models we have developed.

We have evaluated the top two models with regard to their word recognition accuracy on the evaluation test sets. Their performance is presented in Table 7. As it can be seen from the table, the models with the better performance on the development test sets also showed better results with the evaluation test sets. We can, therefore, say that the model with five emitting states without skips and twelve Gaussian mixtures is preferable not only with regard to its word recognition accuracy, but also with regard to its memory requirements.

Sta tes	Mix.	Models			
		AM + LM		AM + LM + SA	
		5k	20k	5k	20k
5	12			**90.43**	87.26
11	Hy	89.36	87.13		

Table 7: Recognition Performance on 5k and 20k Evaluation test sets

For a comparison purpose, we have developed a baseline word-internal triphone-based recognizer using the same corpus. The models of 3 emitting states, 12 Gaussian mixtures, with skips have the best word recognition accuracy (91.31%) of all the other triphone-based recognizers that we have developed. This recognizer also has better word recognition accuracy than that of our syllable-based recognizer (90.43%). But tying is applied only for the triphone-based recognizers.

However the triphone-based recognizer requires much more storage space (38MB) than the syllable-based recognizer that requires only 15MB space. With regard to their speed of processing, the syllable-based model was 37% faster than triphone-based one.

These are encouraging results as compared to the performance reported by Afify et al. (2005) for Arabic speech recognition (14.2% word error rate). They have used a trigram language model with a lexicon of 60k vocabulary.

4.5 Conclusions and Research Areas in the Future

We conclude that the use of CV syllables is a promising alternative in the development of ASRSs for Amharic. Although there are still possibilities of performance improvement, we have got an encouraging word recognition accuracy (90.43%). Some of the possibilities of performance improvement are:

- The pronunciation dictionary that we have used does not handle the problem of gemination of consonants and the irregular realization of the sixth order vowel and the glottal stop consonant, which has a direct effect on the quality of the sub-word transcriptions. Proper editing (use of phonetic transcription) of the pronunciation dictionaries which, however, requires a considerable amount of work, certainly will result in a higher quality of sub-word transcription and consequently in the improvement of the recognizers' performance. By switching from the grapheme-based recognizer to phonetic-based recognizer in Arabic, Afif et al. (2005) gained relative word error rate reduction of 10% to 14%.
- Since tying is one way of minimizing the problem of shortage of training speech, tying the syllable-based models would possibly result in a gain of some degree of performance improvement.

[5]We counted the Gaussian mixtures that are physically saved, instead of what should actually be.

5 References

Afif, Mohamed, Long Nguyen, Bing Xiang, Sherif Abdou, and John Makhoul. 2005. Recent progress in Arabic broadcast news transcription at BBN. In *INTERSPEECH-2005*, 1637-1640

Baye Yimam and TEAM 503 students. 1997. "ፊደል እንደገና" Ethiopian Journal of Languages and Literature 7(1997): 1-32.

Baye Yimam. 1986. "የአማርኛ ሰዋሰው". Addis Ababa. ት.መ.ማ.ማ.ድ.

Bender, L.M. and Ferguson C. 1976. The Ethiopian Writing System. In Language in Ethiopia. Edited by M.L. Bender, J.D. Bowen, R.L. Cooper, and C.A. Ferguson. London: Oxford University press.

Cowley, Roger, Marvin L. Bender and Charles A. Fergusone. 1976. The Amharic Language-Description. In Language in Ethiopia. Edited by M.L. Bender, J.D. Bowen, R.L. Cooper, and C.A. Ferguson. London: Oxford University press.

Deller, J.R. Jr., Hansen, J.H.L. and Proakis, J.G., Discrete-time Processing of Speech Signals. Macmillan Publishing Company, New York, 2000.

Fukada, Toshiaki, Takayoshi Yoshimura and Yoshinori Sagisa. 1999. Automatic generation of multiple pronunciations based on neural networks. Speech Communication 27:63—73 http://citeseer.ist.psu.edu/fukada99automatic.html.

Ganapathiraju, Aravind; Jonathan Hamaker; Mark Ordowski; and George R. Doddington. 1997. Joseph Picone. Syllable-based Large Vocabulary Continuous Speech Recognition.

Getachew Haile. 1967. The Problems of the Amharic Writing System. A paper presented in advance for the interdisciplinary seminar of the Faculty of Arts and Education. HSIU.

Hayward, Katrina and Richard J. Hayward. 1999. Amharic. In Handbook of the International Phonetic Association: A guide to the use of the International Phonetic Alphabet. Cambridge: the University Press.

Hu, Zhihong; Johan Schalkwyk; Etienne Barnard; and Ronald Cole. 1996. Speech recognition using syllable like units. Proc. Int'l Conf. on Spoken Language Processing (ICSLP), 2:426-429.

Kanokphara, Supphanat; Virongrong Tesprasit and Rachod Thongprasirt. 2003. Pronunciation Variation Speech Recognition Without Dictionary Modification on Sparse Database, IEEE International Conference on Acoustics, Speech, and Signal Processing (ICASSP 2003, Hong Kong).

Kinfe Tadesse. 2002. Sub-word Based Amharic Word Recognition: An Experiment Using Hidden Markov Model (HMM), M.Sc Thesis. Addis Ababa University Faculty of Informatics. Addis Ababa.

Lee, C-H., Gauvain, J-L., Pieraccini, R. and Rabiner, L. R.. 1992. Large vocabulary speech recognition using subword units. Proc. ICSST-92, Brisbane, Australia, pp. 342-353.

Leslau, W. 2000. Introductory Grammar of Amharic, Wiesbaden: Harrassowitz.

Martha Yifiru. 2003. Application of Amharic speech recognition system to command and control computer: An experiment with Microsoft Word, M.Sc Thesis. Addis Ababa University Faculty of Informatics. Addis Ababa.

Rabiner, L. and Juang, B. 1993. Fundamentals of speech recognition. Englewood Cliffs, NJ.

Hussien Seid and Björn. Gambäck 2005. A Speaker Independent Continuous Speech Recognizer for Amharic. In: INTERSPEECH 2005, 9th European Conference on Speech Communication and Technology. Lisbon, September 4-9.

Solomon Birihanu. 2001. Isolated Amharic Consonant-Vowel (CV) Syllable Recognition, M.Sc Thesis. Addis Ababa University Faculty of Informatics. Addis Ababa.

Solomon Teferra Abate. 2006. Automatic Speech Recognition for Amharic. Ph.D. Thesis. University of Hamburg. Hamburg.

Solomon Teferra Abate, Wolfgang Menzel and Bairu Tafla. 2005. An Amharic Speech Corpus for Large Vocabulary Continuous Speech Recognition. In: INTERSPEECH 2005, 9th European Conference on Speech Communication and Technology. Lisbon, September 4-9.

Tadesse Beyene. 1994. The Ethiopian Writing System. Paper presented at the 12th International Conference of Ethiopian Studies, Michigan State University.

Wu, Su-Lin. 1998. Incorporating Information from Syllable-length Time Scales into Automatic Speech Recognition. PhD thesis, University of California, Berkeley, CA.

Young, Steve; Dan Kershaw; Julian Odell and Dave Ollason. 2002. The HTK Book.

Zegaye Seyifu. 2003. Large vocabulary, speaker independent, continuous Amharic speech recognition, M.Sc Thesis. Addis Ababa University Faculty of Informatics. Addis Ababa.

Adapting a Medical Speech to Speech Translation System (MedSLT) to Arabic

Pierrette Bouillon
University of Geneva, TIM/ISSCO, ETI
40, Bd. Du Pont d'Arve
CH-1211 Geneva 4, Switzerland
Pierrette.Bouillon@issco.unige.ch

Sonia Halimi
University of Geneva, TIM/ISSCO, ETI
40, Bd. Du Pont d'Arve
CH-1211 Geneva 4, Switzerland
Sonia.Halimi@eti.unige.ch

Manny Rayner
Powerset Inc
475 Brannan Str.
San Francisco
CA 94107, USA
manny@powerset.com

Beth Ann Hockey
Mail Stop 19-26, UCSC UARC, NASA
Ames Research Center, Moffett Field,
CA 94035-1000
bahockey@ucsc.edu

Abstract

We describe the adaptation for Arabic of the grammar-based MedSLT medical speech system. The system supports simple medical diagnosis questions about headaches using vocabulary of 322 words. We show that the MedSLT architecture based on motivated general grammars produces very good results, with a limited effort. Based on the grammars for other languages covered by the system, it is in fact very easy to develop an Arabic grammar and to specialize it efficiently for the different system tasks. In this paper, we focus on generation.

1 Introduction

MedSLT is a medical speech translation system. It allows a doctor to ask diagnosis questions in medical subdomains, such as headaches, abdominal pain, etc, covering a wide range of questions that doctors generally ask their patients. The grammar-based architecture, built using specialization from reusable general grammars, is designed to allow a rapid development of different domains and languages. Presently, it supports English, French, Japanese, Spanish and Catalan. This article focuses on the system development for Arabic.

In general, translation in this context raises two specific questions: 1) how to achieve recognition quality that is good enough for translation, and 2) how to get translations to be as idiomatic as possible so they can be understood by the patient. For close languages and domains where accuracy is not very important (e.g. information requests), it may be possible to combine a statistical recognizer with a commercial translation system as it is often done in commercial tools such as *SpokenTranslation* (Seligman and Dillinger, 2006). However, for this specific application in a multilingual context, this solution is not applicable at all: even if perfect recognition were possible (which is far from being the case), current commercial tools for translating to Arabic do not guarantee good quality. The domain dealt with here contains, in fact, many structures specific to this type of oral dialogue that can not be handled by these systems. For example, all the doctor's interactions with the MedSLT system consist of questions whose structures differ from one language to another, with each language having its own constraints. Consequently, two types of errors occur in Arabic translation systems. Either they do not recognize the interrogative structure as in example (1), or they produce ungrammatical sentences by copying the original structure as in example (2):

Proceedings of the 5th Workshop on Important Unresolved Matters, pages 41–48,
Prague, Czech Republic, June 2007.

(1) was the pain severe?
كان الألم الشديد (***Google***)
(*kana al alam chadid*)
'have-past-3 the pain severe'

is the pain aggravated by exertion?
الألم يفاقم بجهد (***Systran***)
(*al alam yufaqim bi juhd*)
'the pain escalate-3 with effort'

(2) is the headache aggravated by bright light?
لا يضيء بشكل ساطع صداعين سبب (***Cimos***)
(*la yudhi' bi chakl sathi' suda'ayn sabab*)
'not light in manner bright-3 headache-plur cause'

is the headache aggravated by bright light?
يتم ساطعة خفيفة سبب صداعات (***Systran***)
(*yatim sathia khafifa sabab suda'at*)
'finish-3 bright-fem not-heavy-fem cause headache-plur'

are your headaches accompanied by nausea?
إن ترافق صداعاتك بواسطة غثيان
(***1-800-translate***)
(*in turafiq suda'atik bi wasithat rhathayan*)
'if you-accompany your headache-plur using nausea'

Ellipsis is another problem for MT systems. Many elliptical structures cannot be translated without context. In example 3, the context is needed to guarantee adjective agreement.

(3) Doctor: is the pain severe?
Trad: هل الألم شديد؟ (MedSLT)
(*hal al alam chadid*)
'Q the pain severe'

Doctor: moderate?
Trad: محتمل؟ محتملا؟ محتملة؟
(*muhtamala, muhtamalan, muhtamal*)
'moderate_fem_attributive_adj, moderate_vocalized-predicative_adj, moderate_attributive_adj'.

It is also essential for rules of translation to be applied consistently. For instance, in MedSLT, *onset* is translated by the verb ظهر (*dhahara*). In this context, the adjective *sudden* has to be translated by an adverb فجأة (*fajatan*) (example 4). This implies that the translation of the ellipsis in the second utterance needs to change syntactic category too. We can wonder to what extent the word-for-word translation of the elliptical sentence in (4) can be understood by the patient.

4) Doctor: was the onset of headaches sudden?
Trad: هل ظهر الصداع فجأة؟ (MedSLT)
(*hal dhahara al sudaa fajatan?*)
(Q appear-past-3 the headache suddenly?)

Doctor: acute?
Trad: مفاجئ؟
(*mufaji?*)
(acute)

In addition to that ellipsis can not always be translated by the same type of ellipsis. Arabic grammar (Amin, 1982) allows the use of elliptical structures in cases where there is a semantic link (قرينة) referring to the omitted part of the sentence otherwise the elliptical construction is ambiguous. In example (3), the use of an adjective alone presents an ambiguity introducing, therefore, a difficulty in comprehension which can be problematic. Thus, it is necessary to resort to a more sophisticated approach. We will describe, in the following part, the architecture on which MedSLT is based. Then, we will show how it has been adapted to Arabic.

2 The Architecture

MedSLT is a grammar-based medical speech translation system which uses the commercial *Nuance* speech recognition platform. It has two main features (Bouillon et *al.*, 2005). First, all the language models (for recognition, analysis, generation) are produced from linguistically motivated, general unification grammars using the *Regulus* platform (Rayner, et *al.*, 2006). First, domain specific unification grammars are created from the general grammar for the different domains of medical diagnosis through a trainable corpus-based automatic grammar specialization process. They are, next, compiled into Context Free Grammars (CFGs) in a format suitable for use with the *Nuance* speech recognition platform, and into a form needed for a variant of Semantic Head-driven generation (Shieber et *al.,* 1990). Therefore, the different grammars needed by the system under this approach are easy to build and maintain.

This leads us to the second feature. Because grammar-based speech recognition only produces competitive results for the sentences covered by the grammar, the user will need to learn the coverage of the system. In order to assist in this, a help system is included in the system (Starlander et *al.*, 2005 and Chatzichrisafis et *al.*, 2006). The help system suggests, after each user utterance, similar utterances covered by the grammar which can be taken as a model. In order to derive the help sentences, the system performs, in parallel, a statistical recognition of the input speech. It then compares the recognition result using an N-gram based metric, against a set of known correct in-coverage questions to extract the most similar ones. It is in that way that we introduce some of the robustness of the statistical systems in the controlled application.

Once the sentence recognized, the translation is interlingua-based. *Regulus* allows different types of source representations (Rayner, et *al.*, 2006), but we have chosen to use the simplest one in order to facilitate the translation process. It is a flat semantic structure built up by concatenation of word meanings. For instance, هل يشتد الصداع عند القلق؟ (*hal yachtaddou al soudaa inda al qalaq?* 'Q aggravate-3 the headache in the stress') would be represented as follows:

```
[[cause,qalaq],[event,yachtaddou],
[prep_cause,inda],[symptom,soudaa],
[tense,present],[utterance_type,ynq],
[voice,active]]
```

The same formalism is used for the interlingua which is a standardized version of the most explicit source English representation. For example, the interlingua representation of the previous sentence corresponds to the following structure that can be paraphrased as follows: « does the pain become worse when you experience anxiety?»:

```
[[sc,when],[clause,
        [[pronoun,you],
        [secondary_symptom,anxiety],
        [state,experience],
        [tense,present],
        [utterance_type,dcl],
        [voice,active]]],
[event,become_worse],[symtom,headache],
[tense,present],[utterance_type,ynq],
[voice,active]].
```

Under this approach the translation process only involves mapping simple structures. This facilitates the process of translation and the resolution of divergences. This process goes through five stages: 1) source language analysis in order to extract source representation; 2) ellipsis resolution if necessary; 3) mapping the source structure into the interlingua; 4) mapping the interlingua into the target structure and 5) generation of the target language in accordance with its own grammar.

We will show next the adequacy of this architecture for translation in Arabic. On the basis of the grammars already implemented for some languages covered by the system (French, English, Spanish, Catalan), it is, in fact, easy to develop a general Arabic grammar that meets the constraints of the MedSLT project and to specialize it for the purposes of speech recognition and generation. This method produces very good results when compared to commercial systems.

3 General MedSLT grammar for Arabic

Writing unification grammars for speech presents two requirements. Since it has to be transformed into context–free grammar (CFG) for recognition, features must have a finite number of values, as limited as possible. In practice, this means that attributes can not take complex values and the lexicalist approach used in LFG or HPSG cannot be applied here. For example, subcategorization is not represented with general rule schemata as in HPSG. Therefore, syntagmatic rules must be multiplied for each type of verb (transitive, intransitive, etc.). Even if this first constraint results in a less elegant and more repetitive grammar, it is not a limitation to the development of grammars with the complexity required for such applications.

The grammar is used to constrain the recognition process, so it needs to include all information that could improve recognition. For instance, evaluation has shown that the quality of recognition decreases considerably when selection restrictions are omitted (Rayner, et *al.*, 2006). Thus, in practice, this means that all *Regulus* general grammars include many features for managing this type of constraint. For example, nouns are semantically typed; verbal entries contain features to determine the type of complements according to their subcategorization, etc. These types are difficult to define coherently for the general vocabulary but are not problematic when the domain is very controlled and the vocabulary very limited. In addition, they do not have any effect on the whole structure of the general grammar since they come from specialized lexica of various domains.

As with all Regulus grammars, the Arabic grammar and lexicon are bound by these two restrictions. At the present time, they cover only questions in relation to headaches. The vocabulary contains 322 different forms. Nouns are semantically typed and verbs specify the type of complements. For instance, the entry أجريت (*ajrayta,* 'carry out') indicates that the verb selects a subject which is an agent (**subj_np_type=agent**) and an object of **thera** type (therapeutic) (**obj_np_type=thera**):

```
v:[sem=[[state,tajri],[tense,passé]],
   subcat=trans, agr=2/\sing/\masc,
   vform=finite, subj_np_type=agent,
   obj_np_type=thera] -->
         @a('أجريت', ajrayta).
```

It is interesting to note that features and values are the same in Arabic as in other languages except for some differences such as the **agr**(eement) feature which can take a "dual" value, *inter alia.* To avoid the multiplication of entries, particles such as ال (*al*), بـ (*bi*), كـ (*ka*), were separated from words to which they are normally attached. For recognition, this does not seem to pose a problem. For generation, they are joined to their heads according to specific orthography rules after the generation of sentences. Since the word is synthesized, it appears only in its non-vocalic form.

The grammar contains 38 rules that describe yes-no questions introduced by هل (*hal*), for example : هل يمتد الألم إلى الكتفين؟ (*hal yamtad al alam ila al katifayn,* 'Q irradiate-3 the pain to the shoulders') and some wh-questions, for example : متى يظهر الألم؟ (*mata yadhar al alam,* 'when appear-3 the pain'). The grammar structure is, in the end, quite close to romance languages. As it can happen in Spanish or Catalan, the subject of yes-no questions in Arabic comes conventionally after the verb (*hal yamtad* [*al alam*]_sujet [الألم]) if not elided when it is agentive (*hal* [*tahus*] *bi al alam* [تحس], 'Q you-feel with the pain'). Thus, we can use similar rules applied to *Prodrop* and *inversion* in these languages. Inversion is not dealt with as a type of movement otherwise it would have obliged us to multiply the number of features in the grammar. Instead, we use the constituent **vbar**, which is also convenient for Arabic. We consider a yes-no question (**yn_question**) to be made up of a particle, which is هل (*hal*), and a sentence (**s**) where the subject is either elided (**inv=prodrop**), or comes after the verb (**inv=inverted**), namely:

```
yn_question:[sem=...] -->
         @a('هل', hal),
         optional_adverb:[...],
         s:[...inv=inverted\/prodrop].
```

The **s** is rewritten in a **vp** which is itself constituted of a **vbar** and its complements according to the type of the verb (transitive, intransitive, etc.) as is a standard grammar structure:

```
s:[sem=] -->
         vp:[inv=INV, …].

vp:[sem=…, inv=INV, …] -->
         vbar:[subcat=trans, inv=INV, ….],
         optional_adverb:[….],
         np:[….],
         optional_adverb:[…],
         optional_pp:[….],
         optional_adverb:[….].
```

The **vbar** is itself composed of a single verb (if the subject is elided; in this case it has an **inv=prodrop** feature), or a verb followed by a subject (in such instance, it has a **inv=inverted** feature) as in rules shown above. We note that the elision will only be possible here if the verb takes a subject of **agent** type:

```
vbar:[sem=…,inv=prodrop] -->
         optional_v:[agr=2/\masc/\sing,
         subj_np_type=agent].
```

```
vbar:[sem=..,inv=inverted] -->
         optional_v:[],
         np:[].
```

The treatment of *wh*-questions is more conventional in all languages because it is not possible to handle them without simulating movement. We consider that the interrogative pronoun moved from its initial place (PP, etc.), which becomes empty, to an initial position (*ayna_i tahus bi al alam [i]*, أين تحس بـالألم, 'where you-feel with the pain'). To deal with the movement, we use the standard mechanism of gap threading, introduced by Pereira (1981). The link between the empty constituent [i] and the constituent which has been moved (*ayna_i* in our example) is possible using two attributes which are **gapsin** and **gapsout**, included in all categories related to the movement. For example, in the following rule, such attributes indicate that the interrogative element (**wh_pp**) is only possible if the sentence (**s**) contains an empty pp (indicated by the attribute **gapsin=pp_gap**):

```
wh_question:[sem=...] -->
        wh_pp:[sem=..],
        s:[…, gapsin=pp_gap, gapsout=B].
```

In comparison with the rest of languages previously processed by the system, the Arabic grammar does not have a lot of special cases. One rule specifies that some verb such as "to be" (كان (*kana*), يكون (*yakun*), with the feature subcat=pred(icatif)) can be optional – they can be rewritten in an empty constituent indicated as []:

```
optional_v:
        [sem=[[state,be],[tense,present]],
        subcat=pred] --> [].
```

Rules for numbers are also very complex in order to represent the dual form in addition to the position of numbers which can change depending on whether the number is singular: one, for example : more than one day أكثر من يوم واحد (*akthar min yawm wahid,* 'more than day one') and, the third day اليوم الثالث (*al yawm al thalith,* 'the day the third'), or plural, for example : more than 3 days, أكثر من ثلاثة أيام (*akthar min thalathat ayam,* 'more than three days').

4 Grammar specialization

One of the most important advantages of the approach adopted here is that the general grammar can be specialized for use in different tasks and domains, to obtain a useful grammar in each case. In the case of Arabic, it is possible to perform generation and recognition directly using the general grammar described above, since it is not yet very elaborate. The general grammar is however already large enough to cause serious efficiency problems, When compiled for generation, the general grammar overgenerates, as the target structures are flat and underspecified (they do not include, for example, information on numbers or determiners, cf. examples above). It would be possible to insert preference rules to force the intended structure, but this solution is extremely unattractive from a software engineering point of view. When compiling the grammar for recognition, the situation is even worse. All our experiments on other languages show that recognizers compiled from general grammars either perform very poorly (Bouillon et al 2007), or fail to recognize at all (Rayner et al 2006, section 11.7). As in previous work, we have attacked these problems by creating specialized versions of the general Arabic grammar.

In our approach to grammar specialization, domain-specific unification grammars are derived from general ones using the Explanation Based Learning (EBL) technique (Rayner, et *al.*, 2006). This corpus-based specialization process is parameterized by a training corpus and a set of operationality criteria. The training corpus, which can be relatively small, consists of examples of utterances that should be covered by the domain grammar. (For Arabic, the current training corpus is about 450 sentences). The sentences of the corpus are parsed using the general grammar, then those parses are partitioned into phrases based on the operationality criteria. Each phrase defined by the operationality criteria is flattened, producing rules of a phrasal grammar for the application domain. The resulting domain-specific grammar has a subset of the coverage of the general grammar and reduced structural ambiguity. In a generation grammar, over-generation is virtually eliminated; specialized recognition grammars typically have greatly superior recognition due to the reduction in search space that they provide. In the case of the Arabic grammar described here, the training corpus is a set of Arabic sentences based on the English reference corpus for the headaches domain. The operationality criteria are a slightly modified version of those used for the Romance grammars discussed in Bouillon et al., 2007.

In previous work, we have described at length the structural relationships between general grammars, and specialized grammars for recognition and generation; here, we will briefly summarize the main points and show a simple example of how they apply to our Arabic grammar. Figures (1) to (3) present parse trees for the sentence هل الألم دائم؟ (*hal al alam daym* 'Q the pain permanent'):

```
.MAIN
   utterance
      yn_question
      /  lex(hal)
      |  optional_adverb null
      |  s
      |     vp
      |     /  vbar
      |     |  /  optional_v null
      |     |  |  np
      |     |  |  /  spec lex(al)
      |     |  |  |  nbar
      |     |  \  \     noun lex(alam)
      |     |  adj lex(daym)
      |     |  optional_adverb null
      |     |  optional_pp null
      \     \  optional_adverb null
```

Figure (1): Parse tree for *'hal al alam daym'* with the general grammar

```
.MAIN
   utterance
   /  lex(hal)
   |  vp
   |  /  vbar
   |  |     np
   |  |     /  spec lex(al)
   |  |     \  noun lex(alam)
   |  |  adj lex(daym)
   \  \  optional_pp null
```

Figure (2): Parse tree for *'hal al alam daym'* with the specialized recognition grammar

```
.MAIN
   utterance
   /  lex(hal)
   |  vp
   |  /  vbar
   |  |     np lex(al) lex(alam)
   |  |  adj lex(daym)
   \  \  optional_pp null
```

Figure (3): Parse tree for *'hal al alam daym'* with the specialized generation grammar

It is immediately apparent that (1), the parse tree for the general grammar, is structurally much more complex than (2) and (3), the trees for the specialized grammars. In particular, (1) has several nodes filled by optional modifiers of various kinds, all of which are here null; if this grammar is compiled into a recognizer, all these nodes result in extra paths in the search space, with a corresponding loss of efficiency. Both the specialized grammars flatten out the modifier structure, for example using learning a set of vp rules which instantiate only those combinations of modifiers that have actually been seen in the training corpus.

The difference between the specialized recognition grammar (2) and the specialized generation grammar (3) is more subtle. The first thing to consider is that the recognition version needs to contain all the rules required for recognition and analysis of multiple syntactic variants of the diagnosis questions, while the generation one only has to contain sufficient rules to generate one variant (ideally, the most correct and idiomatic one) for each question. An important consequence of this general principle relates to the treatment of NPs. The general grammar includes a rule that forms an NP in a conventional manner from a specifier (*iddat, koul* and *al*, which has been separated from the noun), potentially optional, and a noun. This rule permits a compositional analysis of all the grammatical combinations of nouns and articles, which is also appropriate for the recognition grammar. For generation, however, the system learns generally complete (lexicalized) NPs, in order to attach the appropriate article for each noun on the basis of the corpus (there is an exception for NPs containing a number because it is obviously undesirable to include in the corpus one example of every number/noun combination). Contrasting (2) and (3), we see that in (2), the phrase الألم (*al alam*, 'the pain') is treated compositionally; in (3), it is a lexicalized phrase produced by the rule

```
np --> الألم          (al alam)
```

Our previous experience with French, English and Spanish has shown that this method is a good solution for specialized and limited domains like the one under study. Articles are difficult to recognize (they are usually short unstressed words) and to translate, but the right combinations can easily be learnt according to the context and subdomain. In the next section, we show that the specialization method yields good results in practice when applied to Arabic.

5 Evaluation

Our initial evaluation only tests the specialized Arabic generation grammar. We used an English corpus of 522 diagnostic questions gathered with MedSLT, which has previously been used to compare linguistic and statistical recognition (Rayner et *al.*, 2004). Translation were judged by four Arabic translators from the Geneva Translation School on the following three-point scale:

- **Good** : translation respects completely the meaning and the grammatical form;
- **OK** : translation is not completely idiomatic but understandable;
- **Bad** : translation does not keep the meaning, is non understandable or it is agrammatical.

The results are as follows:

Evaluation	T1	T2	T3	T4
Good	365 (69.9%)	318 (60%)	323 (61%)	281 (53%)
Ok	16 (3.1%)	63 (12%)	56 (10%)	86 (16%)
Bad	3 (0.6%)	3 (0.6%)	5 (0.9%)	17 (3%)
Not analyzed sentences	114 (21.8%)			
Not translated sentences	21 (4%)			
Not generated sentences	3 (0.6%)			
Total	**522 (100.0%)**			

We clearly can see that translations are good (**Good** or **Ok**) if the sentences are well recognized/analyzed in English, which is very important for our application (381/408 for **T1** (93%), 381/408 for **T2** (93%), 379/408 for **T3** (92%), 367/408 for **T4**, (89.9%)). **Not analyzed sentences** (21.8%) are those which are not covered by the English grammar but had to be reformulated in an existent structure with the help system (see above; Chatzichrisafis, et *al.*, 2006).

Three sentences only (0.6%) failed at the level of generation (**Not generated sentences),** which shows that the specialized generation grammar is robust enough for the domain. These sentences have now to be added in the corpus to be generated correctly. In other languages, we have indeed noticed that this kind of error disappears after one or two cycles of evaluation on new data. **Not translated sentences** (4%) are mostly caused by specialized medical terms describing pain (*pounding, throbbing*, etc.) that we did not introduce yet because they need to be validated by Arabic medical specialists. Here are some examples of **Good** translations:

does chocolate cause your headaches
هل يظهر الصداع عندما تأكل الشوكولا؟
(*hal yadhharou al soudaa indama takoul al chocolat*)
(Q appear-3 the headache when you-eat the chocolate)

do headaches usually occur in the morning
هل كثيرا ما تحس بالصداع في الصباح؟
(*hal kathiran ma tahus bi al soudaa fi al sabah*)
(Q often ma-you-feel-bi the headache in the morning)

is the headache in the front of your head
هل تحس بالصداع في الجبهة؟
(*hal tahus bi al soudaa fi al jabha*)
(Q you-feel-bi the headache in the front)

does stress cause your headaches
هل يظهر الصداع عند الإرهاق؟
(*hal yadhharou al soudaa inda al irhaq*)
(Q appear-3 the headache in the stress)

is it a stabbing pain
هل الألم مثل طعنة سكين؟
(*hal al alam mithl taanat sikin*)
(Q the pain like stabbing knive)

In order to compare our results with commercial MT systems output, we submitted the first 124 well analyzed sentences to *Systran.* Among these translations, 98 were judged as **Bad**, 6 as **Good** and 20 as **Ok**. What the translator has considered as bad are the translations that are not in the interrogative form and neither grammatical nor idiomatic. Consequently they are not understandable. Here are the first ten translations we have obtained:

Original sentence (English)	Translation (Arabic)	Evaluation
is the pain relieved by stress removal?	يكون الألم خففت بإجهاد إزالة ؟ *(yakun al alam khafafat bi ijhad izalat)* 'be-3 the pain relieve-	Bad

	past-fem with stress removal'	
does the pain extend to your neck?	الألم يمدّد إلى عنقك ؟ *(al alam yumadid ila ounoukika)* 'the pain make-longer-3 to neck-yours'	Ok
is the pain severe?	يكون الألم قاسية ؟ *(yakun al alam qassiya)* be-3 the pain harsh-fem'	Ok
is caused by bright light?	سبّبت بضوء ساطعة ؟ *(sababat bi dhaw sathia)* 'cause-she with light bright-she'	Bad
is the pain made better by coffee?	يكون الألم يجعل جيّدة بقهوة ؟ *(yakun al alam yajaal jayida bi qahwa)* 'be-3 the pain make good-fem-3 with coffee'	Bad
does it sometimes last more than two hours?	هو أحيانا يدوم أكثر من اثنان ساعات ؟ *(howa ahyan yadum akthan min ithnan saat)* 'he sometimes do-last-3 more than two hours'	Bad
do you have headaches in the morning?	أنت تتلقى صداعات في الصباح ؟ *(anta tatalaqa sudaaat fi al sabah)* 'you do-receive headache-plur in the morning'	Bad
how long do your headaches last?	[هوو لونغ] يتمّ صداعاتك يدوم ؟ *([how long] yatim sudaatik yadum)* 'how long finish-3 headache-plur- yours long'	Bad
thirteen minutes to a few hours?	ثلاثة عشر دقائق إلى [ا فو] ساعات ؟ *(thalatat achar daqaiq ila [fu] saat)* 'thirteen minutes to saat'	Bad
how long does the headache last?	[هوو لونغ] الصداع يدوم ؟ *([how long] al sudaa yadum)* '[how long] the headache last-3'	Bad

6 Conclusion

At the present time, it would have been difficult to use a commercial machine translation system for Arabic in the context of our application where accuracy is very important. One possibility is thus to use a more linguistic approach that takes advantage of the subdomain constraints. This approach is usually very costly. However we have shown in this paper that the MedSLT architecture based on motivated general grammars produces very good results, with a limited effort. The general grammar can be developed very easily on the basis of other languages. The experiments described here show good results for the Arabic generation grammar. Our initial anecdotal results with the Arabic recognizer are promising, and we hope to begin evaluation of this component in the near future.

References

P. Bouillon, F. Ehsani, R. Frederking and M. Rayner (Eds.) 2006. *Medical Speech Translation.* Proceedings of the Workshop. HLT/NAACL-06, New York, NY, USA.

P. Bouillon, M. Rayner, B. Novellas, M. Starlander, M. Santaholma, Y. Nakao and N. Chatzichrisafis. 2007. Une grammaire partagée multi-tâche pour le traitement de la parole : application aux langues romanes. *TAL.*

P. Bouillon, M. Rayner, N. Chatzichrisafis, B.A. Hockey, B.A., M. Santaholma, M. Starlander, H. Isahara, K. Kanzaki, and Y. Nakao. 2005. A generic Multi-Lingual Open Source Platform for Limited-Domain Medical Speech Translation. *Proc. 10th EAMT.* Budapest, Hungary.

N. Chatzichrisafis, P. Bouillon, M. Rayner, M. Santaholma, M. Starlander, B. A. Hockey. 2006. Evaluating Task Performance for a Unidirectional Controlled Language Medical Speech Translation System. In (Bouillon et al, 2006)

M. Rayner, B. A. Hockey and P. Bouillon. 2006. *Putting Linguistics into Speech Recognition: The Regulus Grammar Compiler.* Stanford University Center for the Study of language and information, Stanford, California.

S. Shieber and G. van Noord and F.C.N. Pereira and R.C. Moore. 1990. Semantic-Head-Driven Generation. *Computational Linguistics*, 16(1).

M. Seligman and M. Dillinger. 2006. Usability Issues in an Interactive Speech-to-Speech Translation System for Healthcare. In (Bouillon et al, 2006).

M. Starlander, P. Bouillon, N. Chatzichrisafis, M. Santaholma, M. Rayner, B.A. Hockey, H. Isahara, K. Kanzaki, Y. Nakao. 2005. Practising Controlled Language through a Help System integrated into the Medical Speech Translation System (MedSLT). *Proceedings of the MT Summit X*, Phuket, Thailand.

B. Amin. 1982. *Al-Balagha Al-Arabia. 'ilm Al-Ma'ani. Dar Al-'ilm Li-Almalayeen.* Beirut, Lebanon.

Finding Variants of Out-of-Vocabulary Words in Arabic

Abdusalam F.A. Nwesri   S.M.M. Tahaghoghi   Falk Scholer
School of Computer Science and Information Technology
RMIT University, GPO Box 2476V, Melbourne 3001, Australia
{nwesri,saied,fscholer}@cs.rmit.edu.au

Abstract

Transliteration of a word into another language often leads to multiple spellings. Unless an information retrieval system recognises different forms of transliterated words, a significant number of documents will be missed when users specify only one spelling variant. Using two different datasets, we evaluate several approaches to finding variants of foreign words in Arabic, and show that the longest common subsequence (LCS) technique is the best overall.

1 Introduction

The pronunciation of a word in one language is converted into the phonemes of another language through transliteration. This is particularly common with proper nouns. However, phonetics differ across languages, and transliteration usually results in many spellings for the same word. This is an issue even across languages that use substantially the same character set; simple examples would be "colour" and "color" across British and American usage, and "ambience" and "ambiance" across French and English.

A change in character sets compounds the problem: for instance, there are at least 32 English forms for the Arabic name of the Libyan leader "Kaddafi",[1] and Nwesri et al. (2006) have identified 28 different spellings for the name of the former Serbian president Milosevic in the eleventh Text REtrieval Conference (TREC) Arabic newswire collection. Users typically submit only one spelling variant in their query, and current Arabic text retrieval systems return only documents that contain that variant (Abdelali et al., 2004). We apply techniques used to identify similar strings in other languages such as English, and present a novel approach to identify and retrieve different variants of foreign words in Arabic.

2 The Arabic Language

Arabic is a Semitic language written from right to left, with most words derived from three-character root words. The Arabic alphabet has 28 characters, each with a distinct sound. Short vowels do not have any associated characters, but are instead indicated by diacritics attached to other characters. For example, the letter ف /f/ with the diacritic Fatha فَ is pronounced /fa/,[2] with the diacritic Kasra فِ is pronounced /fɪ/, and with the diacritic Damma فُ is pronounced /fʊ/.

In general written Arabic, diacritics are not indicated; readers must rely on context to determine implicit diacritics, and so how the word should be pronounced. For example, some of the variants of the word كتب are كَتَبَ /kataba/ ⟨he wrote⟩, كُتُب /kʊtʊb/ ⟨books⟩, or كُتِبَ /kʊtɪba/ ⟨is written⟩.

There are also three long vowels — represented by the letters {و ي ا} — that are more pronounced than short vowels. For instance, the letter ف can be followed by the long vowel ا /aː/ to form فا /faː/, by و /uː/ to form فو /fuː/, and by ي /iː/ to form في /fiː/.

2.1 Foreign Words

From an information retrieval (IR) perspective, foreign words in Arabic can be classified into two general categories: translated and transliterated (Nwesri et al., 2006). Translated words, sometimes referred to as Arabised words, are foreign words that are modified or remodelled to conform to Arabic word

[1] http://www.geocities.com/Athens/8744/spelling.htm

[2] We use the International Phonetic Alphabet.

Proceedings of the 5th Workshop on Important Unresolved Matters, pages 49–56,
Prague, Czech Republic, June 2007.

paradigms, and are well assimilated into the language. The assimilation process includes changes in the structure of the borrowed word, including segmental and vowel changes, addition or deletion of syllables, and modification of stress patterns (Al-Qinal, 2002). Foreign words of this category usually have a single consistent spelling variant, for example فيروس ⟨virus⟩, ارشيف ⟨archive⟩, and راديو ⟨radio⟩.

Where equivalent native terms are not available early enough for widespread adoption, foreign terms are used directly with their original pronunciation represented using Arabic letters. As these do not appear in standard Arabic lexicons — that may include adopted words — they are considered to be Out-Of-Vocabulary (OOV) words.

With transliterated words, the phonemes of a foreign word are replaced with their nearest Arabic equivalents. Since Arabic phonemes cannot represent all phonemes found in other languages, the original phonemes are usually not represented uniformly by different transliterators, resulting in multiple spelling variants for the same foreign word (Stalls and Knight, 1998).

Faced with the need to use new foreign terms, native speakers often cannot wait for formal equivalents to be defined. This is particularly true for news agencies, which encounter new foreign nouns and technical terms daily. This urgency leads to more transliteration than translation, with the associated problem of multiple spellings.

2.2 Spelling Variants

In Arabic, short vowels must be indicated using diacritics, but these are rarely used in general text, and there are no standard rules on when and where diacritics must be indicated. Context does not help in predicting diacritics for foreign words such as proper nouns or technical terms, and so long vowels are often used to make the pronunciation explicit in the spelling of the word without relying on diacritics. This, too, is subject to variation; some transliterators add a long vowel after each consonant in the word, while others add just enough long vowels to clarify word segments with ambiguous pronunciation.

The absence of certain sounds in Arabic, and varying pronunciations across dialects, also contributes to the multiplicity of spellings. For instance, the sound /g/ has no standard equivalent in Arabic, since transliterators represent it according to how they pronounce it. For instance, the English letter G /g/ is at times mapped to the Arabic letters غـ /ɣ/, قـ /q/, or جـ /ʒ/ (Abduljaleel and Larkey, 2003); we have also observed it mapped to the letter ک /k/: كورباتشوف, غورباتشوف, جورباتشوف, and قورباتشوف are transliterations of ⟨Gorbachev⟩ we have found on the Web.

Similarly, the interpretation of character combinations varies between transliterators. Moreover, Typographical and phonetic errors during transliteration may add even more variants (Borgman and Siegfried, 1992).

2.3 Retrieval of Variants

When different variants of a word exist, only a subset of related documents can be found when the search uses only one variant. Typical search engine users are unlikely to recognise the problem and hence do not add other variants to their query. Currently, major search engines such as Google, Yahoo, and MSN search use exact match for Arabic search, and no publicly available Arabic Information Retrieval (AIR) system has been reported to retrieve different spelling variants (Abdelali et al., 2004).

In this paper we explore how the different variants of a foreign word may be captured. We test existing similarity techniques, and introduce three techniques to search for variants of foreign words in Arabic. In the first technique, we convert different variants to a single normalised form by removing vowels and conflating homophones. In the second technique, we extend the well-known Soundex technique — commonly used to identify variants of names in English — to the OOV problem in Arabic, and in the third technique, we modify the English Editex algorithm to identify similar foreign words in Arabic.

3 Related Work

Approaches to identify similar-sounding but differently spelt words have been heavily investigated in English; among these are techniques that make use of string or phonetic similarity.

String similarity approaches include the Edit Distance (Hall and Dowling, 1980), used to measure the similarity of two strings by counting the minimal number of character insertions, deletions, or replacements needed to transform one string into another. To transpose a string s of length n into a string t of length m, $edit(m, n)$ computes the minimal steps required as follows:

$$\begin{aligned} &edit(0,0) = 0 \\ &edit(i,0) = i \\ &edit(0,j) = j \\ &edit(i,j) = min[edit(i-1,j)+1, \\ &\qquad edit(i,j-1)+1, \\ &\qquad edit(i-1,j-1)+d(s_i,t_i)] \end{aligned}$$

where $d(s_i, t_i) = 1$ if $s_i = t_i$, 0 otherwise.

This measure can be used to rank words in the collection with respect to a query word. Zobel and Dart (1995) showed that Edit Distance performed the best among the techniques they evaluated for matching English names. It is not known how this technique will perform with Arabic words.

Another candidate approach that can be used to identify similar foreign words in Arabic is n-grams (Hall and Dowling, 1980). This approach is language independent; the strings are divided into grams (substrings) of length n, and the similarity of the strings is computed on the basis of the similarity of their n-grams. Pfeifer et al. (1996) compute the similarity as the number of shared grams divided by the total number of distinct grams in the two strings.

$$gramCount = \frac{\mid G_s \cap G_t \mid}{\mid G_s \cup G_t \mid}$$

where G_s is the set of grams in string s. For example, with n=2, the similarity of "ahmed" and "ahmmed" using this measure is 0.8 because both strings contain the four 2-grams `ah`, `hm`, `me`, and `ed`, while there are five distinct 2-grams across the two strings.

Gram distance (Ukkonen, 1992) is another string similarity technique. When grams are not repeated – which is the case in names — the similarity is computed as (Zobel and Dart, 1996):

$$gramDist(s,t) = \mid G_s \mid + \mid G_t \mid - 2 \mid G_s \cap G_t \mid$$

According to this measure, the similarity between "ahmed" and "ahmmed" is 1.

With the Dice (1945) measure, the similarity of strings s and t is computed as twice the number of common n-grams between s and t, divided by the total number of n-grams in the two strings:

$$Dice(s,t) = \frac{2\times \mid G_s \cap G_t \mid}{\mid G_s \mid + \mid G_t \mid}$$

where G_s denotes the set of n-grams in s, and G_t denotes the set of n-grams in t.

The longest common subsequence (LCS) algorithm measures the similarity between two strings based on the common characters in the two strings (Wagner and Fischer, 1974; Stephen, 1992). Similarity is normalised by dividing the length of the common subsequence by the length of the longer string (Melamed, 1995). The similarity between between "ahmed" and "ahmmed" is (5/6=0.833).

Phonetic approaches to determine similarity between two words include the well-known Soundex algorithm developed by Odell and Russell, patented in 1918 and 1922 (Hall and Dowling, 1980). This has predefined codes for the sounds in a language, with similar-sounding letters grouped under one code. During comparisons, all letters in a word bar the first one are encoded, and the resulting representation is truncated to be at most four characters long. A variant of Soundex is the Phonix algorithm (Gadd, 1990), which transforms letter groups to letters and then to codes; the actual mappings are different from Soundex. Both Soundex and Phonix have been reported to have poorer precision in identifying variants of English names than both Edit Distance and n-grams (Zobel and Dart, 1995).

Aqeel et al. (2006) propose an Arabic version of English Soundex (Asoundex-final). They include diacritics in a list of Arabic names, and created queries by altering some of these names by adding, deleting, or inserting characters.

Most Arabic names are meaningful words — for example, محمد ⟨the praised one⟩ — and rarely do have spelling variants. This leads to morphological ambiguity as names may match verbs, pronouns and other categories of the language. We have found that using Asoundex-final with the misspelt query تهصين on an Arabic collection with 35 949 unique words returns تحجيم ⟨exaggeration⟩, تحزن ⟨she becomes sad⟩, تحسم ⟨she resolves⟩, تحسن ⟨she helps⟩, تحسين ⟨improvement⟩, تحصين ⟨immunisation⟩, تحكم ⟨she governs⟩, تهزم ⟨she defeats⟩. Moreover, it is not clear when and how diacritics are removed, nor where the long vowel ي belongs in their implementation.

Editex, developed by Zobel and Dart (1996), enhances the Edit Distance technique by incorporating the letter-grouping strategy used by Soundex and Phonix, and has been shown to have better performance than these two algorithms, as well as Edit Distance, on a collection of 30 000 distinct English names. The similarity between two strings s and t is computed as:

$edit(0, 0) = 0$
$edit(i, 0) = edit(i-1, 0) + d(s_i - 1, s_1)$
$edit(0.j) = edit(0, j-1) + d(t_j - 1, t_j)$
$edit(i.j) = min[edit(i-1, j) + d(s_i - 1, s_i),$
$\quad edit(i, j-1) + d(t_j - 1, t_j),$
$\quad edit(i-1, j-1) + r(s_i, t_j)]$

where: $r(s_i, t_j)$ is 0 if s_i=t_j, 1 if $group(s_i)$=$group(t_j)$, and 2 otherwise; and $d(s_i, t_j)$ is 1 if $s_i \neq t_j$ and s_i is "h" or "w", and $r(s_i, t_j)$ otherwise.

4 Data

We used two different data sets. The first set is generated from text crawled from the Web, and the second is prepared by manual transliteration of foreign words from English to Arabic.

4.1 Crawled Data

This set is derived from a one-gigabyte crawl of Arabic web pages from twelve different online news sites. From this data we extracted 18 873 073 Arabic words, 383 649 of them unique. We used the Microsoft Office 2003 Arabic spellchecker to build a reference list of OOV words. To avoid duplicates in the 40 514 OOV words returned by the spellchecker, we removed the first character if it is an Arabic preposition, and if the string remaining after that character exists in the collectionWe also removed the definite article "Al" to obtain a list of 32 583 words. Through manual inspection, we identified 2 039 foreign words.

To evaluate alternative techniques, we use a reference list of foreign words and their variants. To identify variants, we generated all possible spelling variants of each word according to the patterns we describe in Section 4.1.1, and kept only the patterns that exist in our collection; 556 clusters of foreign words remain.

Table 1: Variants of the word "Beckham" generated by adding vowels

بكم	باكم	بوكم	بيكم
بكوم	باكوم	بوكوم	بيكوم
بكام	باكام	بوكام	بيكام
بكيم	باكيم	بوكيم	بيكيم

4.1.1 Generation of Variants

To generate foreing words variants, we first remove any vowels and then reinsert vowel combinations of the three long vowels {و ي ا} between the consonants that remain. For a word of length n, this process generates $4^{(n-1)}$ variants. Consider the word بيكام ⟨Beckham⟩. We remove vowels to obtain بكم, and then add all possible vowels to obtain the variants shown in Table 1.

As discussed in Section 2.2, inconsistent representation of sounds between transliterators adds to the variations in spelling. Thus, the number of possible transliterations for a foreign word is given by $4^{(n-1)}$ multiplied by the number of possible transliterations for each of its consonants. In our example, the letter ق /q/ may also be used in place of ك /k/, and so we generate another set; since the representation tends to be consistent within a given word, we need to create only as many sets as there are Arabic representations for the sound.

We validate the generated variants against our collection and keep only those that appear in the crawled text. For our example word "Beckham", we found only two correct variants: بيكام and بيكم. Some of the generated variants could be correct Arabic words that would be valid when checked against the collection. Many of the generated clusters were found to be noisy – that is, they included many native Arabic words. We manually corrected these clusters by removing unrelated Arabic words. The average cluster length is 2.8 words; the smallest cluster has two variants, and the largest has nine, with a total of 1 718 words.

4.2 Transliterated Data

Our second collection reflects one pattern in which OOV words are introduced by ordinary users transliterating English words into Arabic. We extracted a list of 1 134 foreign words from the TREC 2002 Arabic collection, and passed these to the Google translation engine to obtain their English equivalents. We manually inspected these and corrected any incorrect translations. We also removed the 57 words mapped by Google to multiple English words. These are usually a word and a possible conjunction or preposition. For example the word لوكسمبرج ⟨Luxembourg⟩ is transliterated to ⟨For June⟩. We passed the English list to seven Arabic native speakers and asked them to transliterate each word in the list back into Arabic, even if the word has an Arabic equivalent. Four of the translators are PhD candidates in the sciences or engineering, and have finished an advanced-level English course; the other three are currently enrolled in an intermediate-level English course. Participants were asked to type in their transliteration next to each English word. We noticed that some transliterators had only basic computing skills, and made many spelling mistakes. For example, instead of typing the character ا, we found that transliterators sometimes mistakenly type لـ.

We clustered transliterations by the original English words, removed duplicates from each cluster, and also removed 103 clusters where all transliterators agreed on the same version of transliteration. This left 3 582 words in 207 clusters of size 2, 252 clusters of size 3, 192 clusters of size 4, 149 clusters of size 5, 93 clusters of size 6, and 47 clusters of size 7. Finally, we incorporated these transliterations into a list with 35 949 unique Arabic native words prepared by Nwesri et al. (2006).

5 Algorithms

We propose three algorithms to identify foreign words in Arabic text. The first is normalisation, which aims to handle different types of typographical errors described in Section 2.1. The second and third techniques are extensions to the English Soundex and Editex techniques.

5.1 Normalisation

To deal with different typographical styles in writing foreign words, we first remove vowels from every foreign term. We keep vowels unchanged if they

Table 2: Normalisation of equivalent consonants to a single form

Original	Normalised
ص ز ش س	س
ت ط	ط
ق ك غ ج	غ
ث	ت

are the first or the last characters of the word, since they are generally pronounced in Arabic. The long vowel letters are sometimes used as consonants, and these may be followed immediately by another long vowel. For example, the vowel letter ي /i/ may be followed by the long vowel و /u:/ to form يو /ju:/. For such cases, we keep the first vowel and remove the second. Two vowels can also be used together as diphthongs, as in او /aw/ and اي /aj/. We retain vowels that are followed by another vowel or preceded by a vowel that forms a diphthong. We also conflate similar consonants based on statistical analysis of letter mappings between English and Arabic (Abduljaleel and Larkey, 2003; Stalls and Knight, 1998), and confirming through a web search that these consonants are used interchangeably in web documents.[3] Table 2 shows all consonants we consider to be equivalent.

Our process may lead to ambiguity where a similar native word exists; for instance, the spelling variants بيكام and بيكم for ⟨Beckham⟩ are normalised to بكم, which is identical to the Arabic word meaning either ⟨how much⟩ or ⟨in you⟩. Adding a custom prefix to the normalised form is one way to address this issue; we add the letter "ة" to the beginning of each normalised word. For example, variants for Beckham are thus normalised to ةبكم. Since the letter ة never occurs at the beginning of any Arabic word, no ambiguity remains.

5.2 Phonetic Approach

Our phonetic algorithm aims to replace similar sounds with a single code. As noted earlier, we do not envisage that this algorithm has use for native Arabic words, as these are usually distinct, and pro-

[3] All phonetic groups are created based on transliteration mapping between English and Arabic letters

Table 3: Mappings for our phonetic approach

Characters						Code
ا	و	ي				0
ة	ت	ط	ث	ظ	ض	1
س	ش	ز	ص			2
د	ذ					3
ج	غ	ك	ق			4
ع	ه	ح				5
ن						6
م						7
ف						8
ل						9
ب						A
ر						B
خ						C

nunciation is rarely ambiguous. Table 3 shows Arabic letters and their corresponding codes. To normalise foreign words, we replace each letter but the first by its phonetic code, and drop any vowels. We have found — as have (Aqeel et al., 2006) and (Zobel and Dart, 1996) — that it is better to encode all letters, rather than only the first four characters; for brevity, we show only the results for coding all characters, under the label "Soutex".

5.3 Arabic Editex

Based on groups identified in Table 4, we have modified the Editex algorithm of Zobel and Dart (1996). It works as in English except that we drop the functionality used to consider the two silent characters in the English version as silent characters in Arabic are rare and usually occur at the beginning or at the end of the word. Specifically, we replace $d(s_i, t_j)$ by $r(s_i, t_j)$. We call the Arabic version of this algorithm "AEditex".

6 Evaluation

To evaluate the effectiveness of our approaches, we consider each word in the list to be a query, and pose this to the entire collection. The query result should be other words in the same cluster. We consider every word to be a query to avoid any bias towards string similarity techniques as phonetic based techniques fail to capture misspelled words whereas string similarity techniques do.

Table 4: AEditex letter groups

Characters				Group
ا	و	ي		0
ت	ث			1
ت	ط			2
ظ	ض			3
س	ش			4
س	ص			5
ز	س			6
د	ذ			7
ج	غ	ك	ق	8

The results returned by the different algorithms described in the previous section are not directly comparable, as some algorithms return ranked results and others return unranked results. Ranked results could also form a weak ordering in which multiple results belong to the same rank (Raghavan et al., 1989). Standard information retrieval measures are not appropriate for evaluating such techniques. Zobel and Dart (1996) address this by using standard precision and recall, but randomly permute results of equal ranks and calculate the average of recall and precision over ten different permutations. Raghavan et al (1989) propose a different measure called *Probability of Relevance* (PRR). This measure assumes that the user randomly selects a document from the topmost ranks. At any point the precision is defined as the probability that the random examined document is relevant. Recall is the number of relevant documents that the user has seen so far. If we require NR relevant documents — in our case, words — from a ranked result, we start by looking at the top answer and continue until we get to the $NRth$ relevant word at rank k. The PRR measure is calculated as (Raghavan et al., 1989):

$$PRR = \frac{NR}{NR + j + (i.s)/(r+1)}$$

Where j is the number of non-relevant words found in ranks before k, s is the number of remaining relevant words still to be retrieved in rank k, i is the number of non-relevant words in rank k, and r is the

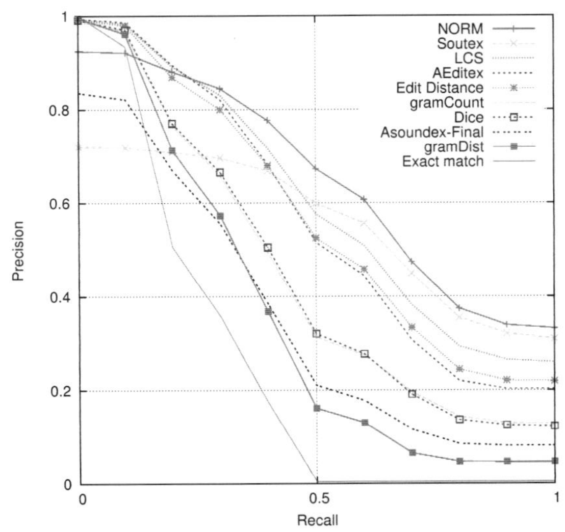

Figure 1: Results on the crawled data

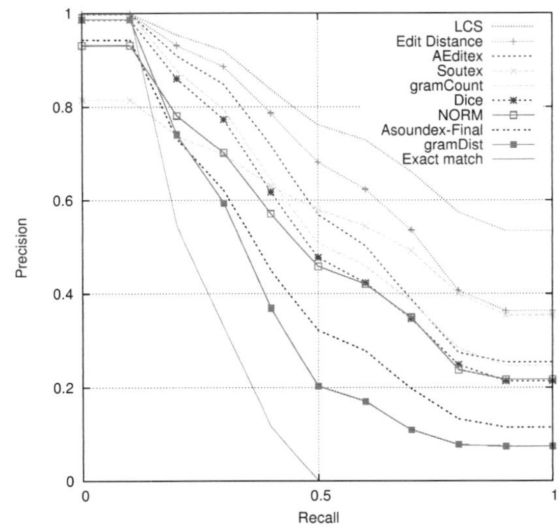

Figure 2: Results on the transliterated data

number of relevant words in rank k. Interpolation is used to smooth results and calculate an average across all queries.

6.1 Results and Discussion

Results from running algorithms using queries in both datasets against their respective collection are shown in Figure 1 and Figure 2. The average precision (average PRR in our case) for each algorithm is shown in Table 5. The algorithms produce significantly better results than exact match (p<0.0001).

On the first data set, NORM performs the best. LCS is the second best algorithm, followed by AEditex and Edit Distance. Soutex shows better performance than all other algorithms except NORM after 50% recall, but performs poorly at lower recall levels. Both the gramCount and Dice algorithms have similar performance with average precision at around 46%. Asoundex-final and gramDist show poorer performance than other algorithms, with average precision at 38%.

Asoundex-final performs poorly; As mentioned earlier, the absence of diacritics in typical Arabic text makes it hard to generalise this technique to retrieve names.

Results from the transliterated dataset generally favour the string similarity algorithms. LCS outperforms all other techniques with an average precision of 78%, followed by Edit Distance at 70%, and then AEditex at 62%. Soutex performs better than both

Table 5: Average precision results

	Data set	
Algorithm	First	Second
NORM	0.660	0.536
LCS	0.619	0.782
Edit Distance	0.572	0.700
AEditex	0.576	0.624
Soutex	0.530	0.590
gramCount	0.451	0.595
Dice	0.457	0.568
Asoundex-final	0.368	0.446
gramDist	0.376	0.401
Exact Match	0.300	0.261

the gramCount and Dice algorithms. It performs better than AEditex at 50% and higher recall levels. NORM performs better than the Asoundex-final and gramDist algorithms. The gramDist algorithm is again the worst. All algorithms showed significant improvements above the baseline (p<0.0001).

Although NORM and Soutex algorithms do not produce the best performance, they have the advantage of being run at index time to encode foreign words which can be later used in retrieval. The alternative algorithms such as Edit Distance are more computationally expensive and can only be used at query time.

7 Conclusion

Foreign words transliterated into Arabic can appear with multiple spellings, hindering effective recall in a text-retrieval system. In this work, we have evaluated nine techniques to find such variants. Edit Distance, Gram Count, Dice, Asoundex-final, Gram Distance, and Longest Common Subsequence are language independent techniques used to find variant names in other languages; Soutex and AEditex are extended techniques to accommodate Arabic Words; and NORM is a novel technique to find OOV variants in Arabic. We show that these techniques are effective for finding foreign word variants. The phonetic approaches generally perform better on a collection of newswire text than on a manually transliterated word list, although our Soutex algorithm performs well on both datasets. LCS was the best of the string-similarity techniques, especially with the manually transliterated dataset, and is the most robust choice overall.

The way the transliterated dataset was created affected the results of phonetic approaches; the dataset has many spelling mistakes, with words interpreted differently and often wrongly by users not fluent in English. Often users only hear these words in the news, and are not even familiar with the spelling of the word in the original language. To construct a more realistic data set, we could ask Arabic writers to transliterate words from a recording; this would allow pronunciation to be accurately captured by users not fluent in English.

Information retrieval systems must cater for common spelling variants; our results help understand how to identify these in Arabic text.

References

Ahmed Abdelali, Jim Cowie, and Hamdy S. Soliman. 2004. Arabic information retrieval perspectives. In *Proceedings of the 11th Conference on Natural Language Processing, Journes d'Etude sur la Parole - Traitement Automatique des Langues Naturelles (JEP-TALN)*, Fez, Morocco.

Nasreen Abduljaleel and Leah S. Larkey. 2003. Statistical transliteration for English-Arabic cross-language information retrieval. In *Proceedings of the International Conference on Information and Knowledge Management*, pages 139–146, New Orleans, LA, USA. ACM Press.

Jamal B. S. Al-Qinal. 2002. Morphophonemics of loanwords in translation. *Journal of King Saud University*, 13:1–132.

Syed Uzair Aqeel, Steve Beitzel, Eric Jensen, David Grossman, and Ophir Frieder. 2006. On the development of name search techniques for Arabic. *Journal of the American Society for Information Science and Technology*, 57(6):728–739.

Christine L. Borgman and Susan L. Siegfried. 1992. Getty's synoname and its cousins: A survey of applications of personal name-matching algorithms. *Journal of the American Society for Information Science*, 43(7):459–476.

Lee R. Dice. 1945. Measures of the amount of ecologic association between species. *Ecology*, 26(3):297–302, July.

T. Gadd. 1990. Phonix: the algorithm. *Program*, 24(4):363–369.

Patrick A. V. Hall and Geoff R. Dowling. 1980. Approximate string matching. *ACM Computing Surveys*, 12(4):381–402.

Dan Melamed. 1995. Automatic evaluation and uniform filter cascades for inducing N-best translation lexicons. In David Yarovsky and Kenneth Church, editors, *Proceedings of the Third Workshop on Very Large Corpora*, pages 184–198, Somerset, New Jersey. Association for Computational Linguistics.

Abdusalam F Ahmad Nwesri, S. M. M. Tahaghoghi, and Falk Scholer. 2006. Capturing out-of-vocabulary words in Arabic text. In *Proceedings of the 2006 Conference on Empirical Methods in Natural Language Processing (EMNLP 2006)*, pages 258–266, Sydney, Australia, 22–23 July. Association for Computational Linguistics.

Ulrich Pfeifer, Thomas Poersch, and Norbert Fuhr. 1996. Retrieval effectiveness of proper name search methods. *Inf. Process. Manage.*, 32(6):667–679.

Vijay Raghavan, Peter Bollmann, and Gwang S. Jung. 1989. A critical investigation of recall and precision as measures of retrieval system performance. *ACM Trans. Inf. Syst.*, 7(3):205–229.

Bonnie Glover Stalls and Kevin Knight. 1998. Translating names and technical terms in Arabic text. In *COLING/ACL Workshop on Computational Approaches to Semitic Languages*, pages 34–41, Montreal, Quebc, Canada.

Graham A Stephen. 1992. String search. Technical report, School of Electronic Engineering Science, University College of North Wales.

Esko Ukkonen. 1992. Approximate string-matching with q-grams and maximal matches. *Theor. Comput. Sci.*, 92(1):191–211.

Robert A. Wagner and Michael J. Fischer. 1974. The string-to-string correction problem. *J. ACM*, 21(1):168–173.

Justin Zobel and Philip Dart. 1995. Finding approximate matches in large lexicons. *Software - Practice and Experience*, 25(3):331–345.

Justin Zobel and Philip Dart. 1996. Phonetic string matching: lessons from information retrieval. In *The 19th annual international ACM SIGIR conference on Research and development in information retrieval*, pages 166–172, New York, NY, USA. ACM Press.

Can You Tag the Modal? You Should.

Yael Netzer and **Meni Adler** and **David Gabay** and **Michael Elhadad**
Ben Gurion University of the Negev
Department of Computer Science
POB 653 Be'er Sheva, 84105, Israel
{yaeln,adlerm,gabayd,elhadad}@cs.bgu.ac.il

Abstract

Computational linguistics methods are typically first developed and tested in English. When applied to other languages, assumptions from English data are often applied to the target language. One of the most common such assumptions is that a "standard" part-of-speech (POS) tagset can be used across languages with only slight variations. We discuss in this paper a specific issue related to the definition of a POS tagset for Modern Hebrew, as an example to clarify the method through which such variations can be defined. It is widely assumed that Hebrew has no syntactic category of modals. There is, however, an identified class of words which are modal-like in their semantics, and can be characterized through distinct syntactic and morphologic criteria. We have found wide disagreement among traditional dictionaries on the POS tag attributed to such words. We describe three main approaches when deciding how to tag such words in Hebrew. We illustrate the impact of selecting each of these approaches on agreement among human taggers, and on the accuracy of automatic POS taggers induced for each method. We finally recommend the use of a "modal" tag in Hebrew and provide detailed guidelines for this tag. Our overall conclusion is that tagset definition is a complex task which deserves appropriate methodology.

1 Introduction

In this paper we address one linguistic issue that was raised while tagging a Hebrew corpus for part of speech (POS) and morphological information. Our corpus is comprised of short news stories. It includes roughly 1,000,000 tokens, in articles of typical length between 200 to 1000 tokens. The articles are written in a relatively simple style, with a high token/word ratio. Of the full corpus, a sample of articles comprising altogether 100,000 tokens was assembled at random and manually tagged for part of speech. We employed four students as taggers. An initial set of guidelines was first composed, relying on the categories found in several dictionaries and on the Penn treebank POS guidelines (Santorini, 1995). Tagging was done using an automatic tool[1]. We relied on existing computational lexicons (Segal, 2000; Yona, 2004) to generate candidate tags for each word. As many words from the corpus were either missing or tagged in a non uniform manner in the lexicons, we recommended looking up missing words in traditional dictionaries. Disagreement was also found among copyrighted dictionaries, both for open and closed set categories. Given the lack of a reliable lexicon, the taggers were not given a list of options to choose from, but were free to tag with whatever tag they found suitable. The process, although slower and bound to produce unintentional mistakes, was used for building a lexicon, and to refine the guidelines and on occasion modify the POS tagset. When constructing and then amending the guidelines we sought the best trade-off between

[1] http://wordfreak.sourceforge.net

Proceedings of the 5th Workshop on Important Unresolved Matters, pages 57–64,
Prague, Czech Republic, June 2007.

accuracy and meaningfulness of the categorization, and simplicity of the guidelines, which is important for consistent tagging.

Initially, each text was tagged by four different people, and the guidelines were revised according to questions or disagreements that were raised. As the guidelines became more stable, the disagreement rate decreased, each text was tagged by three people only and eventually two taggers and a referee that reviewed disagreements between the two. The disagreement rate between any two taggers was initially as high as 20%, and dropped to 3% after a few rounds of tagging and revising the guidelines.

Major sources of disagreements that were identified, include:

Prepositional phrases vs. prepositions In Hebrew, formative letters – ב,כ,ל,מ *b,c,l,m*[2] – can be attached to a noun to create a short prepositional phrase. In some cases, such phrases function as a preposition and the original meaning of the noun is not clearly felt. Some taggers would tag the word as a prepositional prefix + noun, while others tagged it as a preposition, *e.g.*, בעקבות *b'iqbot* (following), that can be tagged as ב-עקבות *b-iqbot* (in the footsteps of).

Adverbial phrases vs. Adverbs the problem is similar to the one above, *e.g.*, בדיוק *bdiyuq* (exactly), can be tagged as *b-diyuq* (with accuracy).

Participles vs. Adjectives as both categories can modify nouns, it is hard to distinguish between them, *e.g*, מבט מאיים *mabaṭ m'ayem* (a threatening stare) - the category of מאיים *m'ayem* is unclear.

Another problem, on which the remainder of the article focuses, was a set of words that express modality, and commonly appear before verbs in the infinitive. Such words were tagged as adjectives or adverbs, and the taggers were systematically uncertain about them.

Beside the disagreement among taggers, there was also significant disagreement among Modern Hebrew dictionaries we examined, as well as computational analyzers and annotated corpora. Table 1 lists the various selected POS tags for these words, as determined by: (1) Rav Milim (Choueka et al., 1997), (2) Sapir (Avneyon et al., 2002), (3) Even-Shoshan (Even-Shoshan, 2003), (4) Knaani (Knaani, 1960), (5) HMA (Carmel and Maarek, 1999), (6) Segal (Segal, 2000), (7) Yona (Yona, 2004), (8) Hebrew Treebank (Sima'an et al., 2001).

As can be seen, eight different POS tags were suggested by these dictionaries: ad**J**ective (29.6%), adve**R**b (25.9%), **V**erb (22.2%), **A**uxilary verb (8.2%), **N**oun (4.4%), par**T**icle (3.7%), **P**reposition (1.5%), and **U**nknown (4.5%). The average number of options per word is about 3.3, which is about 60% agreement. For none of the words there was a comprehensive agreement, and the PoS of only seven words (43.75%) can be determinded by voting (*i.e.*, there is one major option).

In the remainder of the paper, we investigate the existence of a *modal* category in Modern Hebrew, by analyzing the characteristic of these words, from a morphological, syntactic, semantic and practical point of view. The decision whether to introduce a modal tag in a Hebrew tagset has practical consequences: we counted that over 3% of the tokens in our 1M token corpus can potentially be tagged as modals. Beyond this practical impact, the decision process illustrates the relevant method through which a tagset can be derived and fine tuned.

2 Modality in Hebrew

Semantically, *Modus* is considered to be the *attitude on the part of the speaking subject with regard to its content* (Ducrot and Todorov, 1972), as opposed to the *Dictum* which is the linguistic realization of a predicate. While a predicate is most commonly represented with a verb, modality can be uttered in various manners: adjectives and adverbs (*definitely, probable*), using thought/belief verbs, mood, intonation, or with modal verbs. The latter are recognized as a grammatical category in many languages (modals), *e.g.*, *can, should* and *must* in English.

From the semantic perspective, modality is coarsely divided into *epistemic modality* (the amount of confidence the speaker holds with reference to the truth of the proposition) and *deontic modality* (the degree of force exerted on the subject of the sentence to perform the action) views (de Haan, 2005).

Modal expressions do not constitute a syntactic class in Modern Hebrew (Kopelovich, 1982). In her work, Kopelovich reviews classic descriptive

[2]Transcription according to (Ornan, 2002)

Word	Example	1	2	3	4	5	6	7	8
יש ***yeš*** **should**	יש לשים לב לניסוח *yeš laśim leb lanisuḥ* Attention should be paid to the wording	R	N	N	R	N	A	R	V
אין ***’ein*** **shouldn’t**	אין לשים לב לניסוח *’ein laśim leb lanisuḥ* Attention should not be paid to the wording	R	U	N R	U	P	P	R	V
חייב ***ḥayab*** **must**	הציבור חייב להבין את העניין *hacibur ḥayab lhabin ’et ha‘inyan* The public should be made aware of this issue	J	J	J	J	J	J	J	V
מותר ***mutar*** **allowed**	מותר לה לצאת לטיול *mutar lah lacet lṭiyul* She is allowed to go on a trip	R	N	J	R	J	A	V	J
אסור ***’asur*** **forbidden**	אסור לה לצאת לטיול ביום ראשון *’asur lah lacet lṭiyul byom rišon* She is not allowed to go on a trip on Sunday	R	R	R	R	J	A	J	J V
אפשר ***’epšr*** **may**	אפשר לרמוז רמזים *’epšr lirmoz rmazim* Giving hints is allowed	U	R	R	R	T	A	R	V
אמור ***’amur*** **supposed**	נשים אמורות ללבוש רעלות *našim ’amurot lilboš r‘alot* Women are supposed to wear veils	J	A	J	J	J	A	J	V
צריך ***carik*** **should**	במו"מ צריך לעמוד על שלך *bmw”m carik la‘amod ‘al šelka* In negotiation you should keep strong	J	J	R	J	J	A	J	V
ניתן ***nitan*** **can**	ניתן לפתור בעיה מכאיבה זו *nitan liptor b‘ayah mak’ibah zo* This troublesome problem can be solved	U	V	V	V	V	V	V	V
עלול ***‘alul*** **may**	הכלב עלול לנשוך *hakeleb ‘alul linšok* The dog may bite	J	J	J	J N	J	A	J	V
כדאי ***kda’y*** **worthwhile**	כדאי לשאול האם הדלת עשויה היטב *kda’y liš’ol ha’im hadelet ‘aśuyah heiṭeb* It is worth asking whether the door is well built	R	R	R	R	J	A	R	J
מוטב ***mutab*** **better**	מוטב להיות בשקט ולהנות *mutab lihyot bešeqeṭ wulhnot* Better to keep quiet and enjoy	R	R	R	R	T	T	V	V
מסוגל ***msugal*** **able**	הוא היה מסוגל לראותו בבית הלבן *hu’ hayah msugal lir’oto babait halaban* He could envision him sitting in the White House	J	R	J	J	J V	A	J	V
יכול ***yakol*** **can**	אנשים יכולים לתרום תרומות *’anašim ykolim litrom trumot* People can make contributions	V	V	V	J	V	A	V	V
אכפת ***’ikpat*** **care/mind**	אכפת לך ללכת? *’ikpat lka laleket?* Do you mind going	U	V R	V R	U	T	T	R	V
ראוי ***ra’uy*** **should**	ראוי לשלם על שרות זה *ra’uy lšalem ‘al šerut zeh* This service deserves to be paid for	R	R	R	R	J	V J	R	J

Table 1: Parts of speech of selected words

publications on the syntax of Hebrew and claims that these works (Ornan, Rubinstein, Azar, Rosen, Aronson-Berman and Maschler)[3] do not provide a satisfying description or explanation of the matter. In this section we review three major approaches to modality in Hebrew - the first is semantic (Kopelovich), the second is semantic-syntactic (Zadka) and the third is purely morphologico-syntactic (Rosen).

Kopelovich provides three binary dimensions that describe the modal system in Hebrew: Personal - Impersonal, Modality - Modulation and Objective - Subjective plane. The Personal-Impersonal system is connected to the absence or presence of a surface subject in the clause. A personal modal has a grammatical subject:

(1) דוד צריך להסיע את אמו
dawid carik lhasi' 'et 'imo
David should to-drive ACC mother-POSS
David should drive his mother

An impersonal modal has no grammatical subject, and modality predicates the entire clause.

(2) צריך להסיע את אמו לעבודה
carik lhasi' 'et 'imo la'abodah
should to-drive ACC mother-POSS to-the-work
His mother should be driven to work

Kopelovich makes no distinction between the various syntactic categories that the words may belong to, and interchangeably uses examples of words like מותר, יש, אפשר *mutar, yeš, 'epšar* [adverb, existential, participle respectively].

The Modality-Modulation plane, according to the functional school of Halliday (Halliday, 1985), refers to the interpersonal and ideational functions of language: Modality expresses the speaker's own mind (epistemic modality - possibility, probability and certainty) עלול לרדת גשם מחר *'alul laredet gešem mahar* (it may rain tomorrow). Modulation participates in the content clause expressing external conditions in the world (deontic modality - permission, obligation, ability and inclination): אתה יכול להתחיל עכשיו *'ata yakol lhathil 'akšaw* (you can start now). Modality does not carry tense and cannot be negated, while modulation can be modified by tense and can be negative.

The Objective-Subjective plane is what Kopelovich calls the *perception of the world*. Objectivity is achieved using different tenses of *to-be* in conjunction with the modal (including tense of modal if it is a verb), and their order subjective vs. objective:

(3) דוד היה צריך לנסוע לתל אביב
dawid haya carik lisw' ltel 'abib
David was have to-drive to-Tel Aviv
David had to drive to Tel Aviv

(4) כדי להעביר את ההחלטה, צריך היה לכנס את כל העובדים
kdei lha'abir 'et hahahlata,
carik haya lkanes 'et kol ha'obdim
In-order to-pass ACC the-decision,
should to-assemble ACC all the-employees
In order to obtain a favorable vote on this decision,
all of the employees had to be assembled.

Zadka (1995) defines the class of *single-argument bridge verbs*[4], *i.e.*, any verb or pro-verb that can have an infinitive as a subject or object, and that does not accept a subordinate clause as subject or object:

(5) אסור לעשן **[subject]**
'sur l'ašen
Forbidden to-smoke
It is forbidden to smoke

(6) הוא רצה/התחיל לשחק **[object]**
hua racah/hthil lšaheq
He wanted/started to-play
He wanted/started to play

(7) יוסף התחיל/עמד/מסוגל לקרוא את הדו"ח במלואו
Yosep hithil/'amad/msugal liqro'
'et hado"h bimlo'o.
Yosef began/is-about/is-capable to-read
ACC the report entirely.
Yosef began/is-about/(is-capable) to read (of reading)
the report entirely.

(8) *יוסף התחיל/עמד/מסוגל שיקרא את הדו"ח במלואו
**Yosep hithil/'amad/msugal šiqra'*
'et hado"h bimlo'o.
*Yosef started/was-about/is-capable that-he-read
ACC the report entirely.

Zadka classifies these verbs into seven semantic categories: (1) Will (2) Manner (3) Aspect (4) Ability (5) Possibility/Certainty (6) Necessity/Obligation

[3] For reference see (Kopelovich, 1982), see below for Rosen's analysis

[4] "Ride Verb" in Zadka's terminology, פועל רוכב חד-מושאי

and (7) Negation. Categories 1, 4, 5, 6 and 7 are considered by Zadka to include *pure modal verbs*, *e.g.*, *alethic* and *deontic* verbs.

In his paper, Zadka defines classification criteria that refer to syntactic-semantic properties such as: can the infinitive verb be realized as a relative clause, are the subject of the verb and its complement the same, can the infinitive be converted to a gerund, animacy of subject; deep semantic properties – argument structure and selectional restrictions, the ability to drop a common subject of the verb and its complement, factuality level (factual, non-factual, counter-factual); and morphological properties.

Will, Manner and Aspectual verbs as Zadka defines are not considered modals by Kopelovich since they can be inflected by tense (with the exceptions of אמור *'amur* (supposed),עתיד *'atid* (should). Ability verbs are יכול *yakol* (can), מסוגל *msugal* (can,capable) [participle]. They have both an animate actor as a subject and an infinitive as a complement, with the same deep subject. These verbs are counter-factual.

Certainty verbs include מוכרח *mukrak* (must), צריך *carik* (should), נאלץ *ne'elac* (be forced to), יכול *yakol* (can), הכרחי *hekreḥi* (necessary), עשוי *'aśuy* (may), עלול *'alul* (might), צפוי *capuy* (expected). They represent the alethic and epistemic necessity or possibility of the process realized in the clause. All of them cannot be inflected morphologically. The modal predicates the whole situation in the proposition, and may be subjective (epistemic) or objective (alethic). The subject of these verbs coreferences with the subject of the modal:

(9) אני מוכרח לקנות מכונית
'ani mukrak liqnot mkonit
I must to-buy car
I must buy a car

Necessity/Obligation includes adjectives – *e.g.*, חייב *ḥayab* (must), רשאי *raša'y* (allowed), gerunds – מוכרח *mukraḥ* (must), אסור *'asur* (forbidden), מותר *mutar* (allowed) and the verb יכול *yakwl* (can) [5]. Necessity verbs/proverbs present deontic modality, and all clauses share, in Zadka's view - a causing participant that is not always realized in the surface.

[5]as well as nouns and prepositions - among them יש and אין *yeš* and *'ein* - according to Zadka

From the morphological point of view, one may characterize impersonals by a non-inflectional behavior, *e.g.*, יש *yeš*, אין *'ein*, מותר *mutar*, אסור *'asur*, אפשר *'epšar*,אכפת *'ikpat*. All of these words do not inflect in number and gender with their argument. But this criterion leaves out all of the gender-quantity inflected words, *e.g.*, ראוי *ra'uy*, מסוגל *msugal*, עלול *'alul*, אמור *'amur*, צריך *carik*, יכול *yakol*, which are all classified as modals by Zadka. On the other hand, including all the gender-quantity inflected words with infinite or relative clause complements as modals, will include certain adjectives, *e.g.*, מוסמך *musmak* (certified), nouns, *e.g.*, זכות *zkut* (credit), and participles, *e.g.*, נמנע *nimna'* (avoid), as well. It appears that Zadka's classification relies primarily on semantic criteria.

Rosen (1977, pp. 113-115) defines a syntactic category he calls *impersonals*. Words in this category occur only as the predicative constituent of a sentence with an infinitive or a subordinate clause argument. Past and future tense is marked with the auxilary verb היה *hayah* (to-be). In addition, impersonals cannot function as predicative adjectives: כדאי *kda'i* (worthwhile), מוטב *mutab* (better), אכפת *'ikpat* (care/mind).

Personal reference can be added to the clause (governed by the infinitive) with the ל *l* dative preposition:

(10)כדאי לי לשתות
kda'y li lištot
worthwhile to-me to-drink
It is worthwhile for me to drink

2.1 Criteria to Identify Modal-like Words in Hebrew

We have reviewed three major approaches to categorizing modals in Hebrew:
Semantic - represented mostly in Kopelovich's work, modality is categorized by three dimensions of semantic attributes. Since her claim is that there is no syntactic category of modality at all, this approach 'over-generates' modals and includes words that from any other syntactic or morphologic view fall into other parts of speech.
Syntactic-semantic - Zadka classifies seven sets of verbs and pro-verbs following syntactic and semantic criteria. His claim is that modality actually is marked by syntactic characteristics, which can be

identified by structural criteria. However, his evaluation mixes semantics with syntactic attributes.

Morphological-syntactic - Rosen's definition of *Impersonals* is strictly syntactic/morpholgical and does not try to characterize words with modality. Consequently, words that are usually considered modals, are not included in his definition אסור *'asur* (forbidden), מותר *mutar* (allowed), יכול *yakol* (can).

3 Proposed Modal Guidelines to Identify

The variety of criteria proposed by linguists reflects the disagreements we identified in lexicographic work about modal-like words in Hebrew. For a computational application, all words in a corpus must be tagged. Given the complex nature of modality in Hebrew, should we introduce a modal tag in our tagset, or instead, rely on other existing tags? We have decided to introduce a modal tag in our Hebrew tagset. Although there is no distinct syntactic category for modals in Hebrew, we propose the following criteria: (i) They have an infinitive complement or a clausal complement introduced by the binder ש *š*. (ii) They are NOT adjectives. (iii) They have irregular inflections in the past tense, *i.e.*, רציתי לדעת *raciti lada'at* (I wanted to know) is not a modal usage.

The tests to distinguish modal from non-modal usages are:

- יש and אין which can be also existential, are used as modals if they can be replaced with צריך.
- Adjectives are gradable and can be modified by מאוד *m'od* (very) or יותר *yoter* (more).
- Adjectives can become describers of the nominalized verb: קל להרוס ⇒ ההריסה קלה מאוד *qal laharos* ⇒ *haharisah qala m'od* (easy to destroy ⇒ the destruction is easy).
- In all other cases where a verb is serving in to convey modality, it is still tagged as a verb, *e.g.*, מובן שיוסי הוא המנצח *muban šyosi hu' hamnaceḥ* (it is clear that Yossi is the winner).

We first review how these guidelines help us address some of the most difficult tagging decisions we had to face while building the corpus, we then indicate quantitatively the impact of the modal tag on the practical problem of tagging.

3.1 "What do I care" מה אכפת לי

One of the words tagged as a modal in our corpus - the word אכפת *'ikpat* – is not considered thus far to be a modal. However, at least in some of its instances it fits our definition of modal, and it can also be interpreted as modality according to its sense. The only definition that is consistent with our observation is Rosen's *impersonals*.

Looking back at its origins, we checked the Historical Lexicon of the Hebrew Language[6], the word אכפת was used in the medieval period in the Talmud and the Mishna, where it only appears in the following construction:

(11) מה אכפת לך
mah 'ikpat lk
what care to-you
what do you care

Similarly, in the Ben Yehuda Project – an Israeli version of the Guttenberg project[7] which includes texts from the Middle Ages up to the beginning of the $20th$ century – we have found 28 instances of the word, with the very same usage as in older times. While trying to figure its part of speech, we do not identify אכפת as a NOUN - as it cannot have a definite marker ה[8], and is not an adjective[9].

Traditional Hebrew Dictionaries consider אכפת to be an intransitive verb (Kohut, 1926; Even-Shoshan, 2003; Avneyon et al., 2002) or an adverb. Some dictionaries from the middle of the 20th century (Gur, 1946; Knaani, 1960), as well as recent ones (Choueka et al., 1997) did not give it a part of speech at all.

In our corpus we found 130 occurences of the word אכפת of which 55 have an infinitive/relative clause complement, 35 have null complement, and 40 have מ *m* PP complement אכפת לו מהמדינה *'ikpat lo mehamdina* (he cares for the country). The latter has no modal interpretation. We claim that in this case it should be tagged as a participle (בינוני). The test to tell apart modal and participle is:

[6] http://hebrew-treasures.huji.ac.il/ an enterprise conducted by the Israeli Academy of the Hebrew Language.

[7] http://www.benyehuda.org, http://www.gutenberg.org

[8] Although we found in the internet clauses as נסתמו לי נקבוביות האכפת *nistmu li naqbubiyot ha'ikpat* (My caring pores got blocked).

[9] Only its derivatives אכפתי, אכפתיות *'ikpati, ikpatiyut* (caring, care) allows adjectival usage.

(12) אכפת לו לשטוף כלים ⇒

*הוא אכפתי כלפי שטיפת כלים

ikpat lo lištop kelim ⇒

**hu' 'ikpati klapei šṭipat kelim*

mind him to-wash dishes ⇒

*he concerned for washing dishes

He minds washing dishes ⇒

*He is concerned about washing dishes

(13) אכפת לו מהעניים ⇒

הוא אכפתי כלפי העניים

'ikpat lo meha'aniyim ⇒

hu' ikpati klapei ha'aniyim

care him of-the-poor-people ⇒

he caring for the-poor-people

He cares for the poor people ⇒

He is caring for the poor people

All other tests for modality hold in this case: (1) Infinitive/relative clause complement, (2) Not an adjective, (3) Irregular inflection (no inflection at all). To conclude this section, our proposed definition of modals allows us to tag this word in a systematic and complete manner and to avoid the confusion that characterizes this word.

3.2 "It's really hard" קשה לי

Some of the words tagged as modals are commonly referred to as *adjectives*, such as אסור, מותר *'asur, mutar* (allowed, forbidden), though everyone agrees - and tags these words as adverbs or participals (see table 1). However, questions are raised of how to tell apart modals as such from adjectives that show very similar properties: קשה לי ללכת *qaše li laleket* (it is hard for me to walk). Ambar (1995) analyzes the usage of adjectives in modal contexts, especially of *ability* and *possibility*. In sentences such as קשה לנו להסתגל לרעש *qaše lanu lhistagel lara'aš* (it is hard for us to get used to the noise) the adjective is used in a modal and not an adverbial meaning, in the sense that meaning of the adverbial בקושי *bqwši* (with difficulty) and the modal יכול *yakwl* (can) are unified into a single word קשה. Similarly, the *possibility* sense of קשה is unified with the modal אפשר *'epšar*. In any usage of the adjective as the modal, it is not possible to rephrase a clause in a way that the adjective modifies the noun, *i.e.*, the range is the action itself and not its subject.

(14) קשה לבצע את ההסכם

qaše lbace' 'et haheskem

hard to-perform PREP the-agreement

It is hard to perform the agreement

(15) *ההסכם קשה

haheskem kaše

the-agreement hard

The agreement is hard

However, following Ambar, there are cases where the usage of קשה ל *qaše le* is not modal, but an emotional adjective:

(16) קשה/נעים לשוחח איתו

qaše/na'im lšoḥeḥ 'ito

hard/pleasant to-chat with-him

It is hard/pleasant to chat with him

Berman (1980) classifies subjectless constructions in Modern Hebrew, and distinguishes what she calls *dative-marked experientials* where (mostly) adjective serves as a predicate followed by a dative-marked nominal

(17) קשה לרינה בחיים

qaše le-rinah baḥayim

hard for-Rina in-the-life

It is hard for Rina in life

Adjectives that allow this construction are circumstantial and do not describe an *inner state*: רינה עצובה *rina 'acuba* (Rina is sad) vs. עצוב לרינה *'acub lrina* (it is sad for Rina). Another recognized construction is the *modal expressions* that include sentences with dative marking on the individuals to whom the modality is imputed אסור לנו לדבר ככה *'asur lanu ldaber kakah* (we are not allowed to talk like this); Berman suggests that the similarity is due to the perception of the experiencer as recipient in both cases; This suggestion implies that Berman does not categorize the modals (*'asur, mutar*) as adjectives. Another possible criterion to allow these words to be tagged as modals (following Zadka) is the fact that for Necessary/Obligation modals there exists an 'outside force' which is the agent of the modal situation. Therefore, if אסור לנו לדבר ככה *'asur lanu ldaber kakah* (we are not allowed to talk like this), this is because someone forbids us from talking, while if קשה לרינה בחיים *qaše lrinah baḥayim* (It is hard for Rina in life) then no "outside force" is obliged to be the agent which makes her life hard. To conclude - we suggest tagging both *'asur* and *mutar* as modals, and we recommend allowing modal tagging for other possible adjectives in this syntactic structure.

4 Conclusion

We recommend the introduction of a modal POS tag in Hebrew, despite the fact that the set of criteria to identify modal usage is a complex combination of syntactic and morphological constraints. This class covers as many as 3% of the tokens observed in our corpus.

Our main motivation in introducing this tag in our tagset is that the alternative (no modal tag) creates confusion and disagreement: we have shown that both traditional dictionaries and previous computational resources had a high level of disagreement over the class of words we tag as modals. We have confirmed that our guidelines can be applied consistently by human taggers, with agreement level similar to the rest of the tokens (over 99% pairwise). We have checked that our guidelines stand the test of the most difficult disagreement types identified by taggers, such as "care to" and "difficult for".

Finally, the immediate context of modals includes a high proportion of infinitive words. Infinitive words in Hebrew are particularly ambiguous morphologically, because they begin with the letter ל *l* which is a formative letter, and often include the analysis le+ participle, *e.g.* לשמור can be interpreted, depending on context, as *lišmwr* (to guard), *le-šamur* (to a guarded), or *la-šamur* (to the guarded). Other ambiguities might occur too, *e.g.*, לשיר can be interpreted as *lašir* (to sing), *le-šir* (to a song), or as *la-šir* (to the song). We have measured that on average, infinitive verbs in our expanded corpus can be analyzed in 4.9 distinct manners, whereas the overall average for all word tokens is 2.65. The identification of modals can serve as an anchor which helps disambiguate neighboring infinitive words.

References

Ora Ambar. 1995. From modality to an emotional situation. *Te'udah*, 9:235–245. (in Hebrew).

Eitan Avneyon, Raphael Nir, and Idit Yosef. 2002. *Milon sapir: The Encyclopedic Sapphire Dictionary*. Hed Artsi, Tel Aviv. (in Hebrew).

Ruth Berman. 1980. The case of (s)vo language: Subjectless constructions in Modern Hebrew. *Language*, 56:759–776.

David Carmel and Yoelle S. Maarek. 1999. Morphological disambiguation for Hebrew search systems. In *Proceeding of NGITS-99*, pages 312–326.

Yaacov Choueka, Uzi Freidkin, Hayim A. Hakohen, , and Yael Zachi-Yannay. 1997. *Rav Milim: A Comprehensive Dictionary of Modern Hebrew*. Stimatski, Tel Aviv. (in Hebrew).

Ferdinand de Haan. 2005. Typological approaches to modality in approaches to modality. In William Frawley, editor, *Approaches to Modality*, pages 27–69. Mouton de Gruyter, Berlin.

Oswald Ducrot and Tzvetan Todorov. 1972. *Dictionnaire encyclopédique des sciences du langage*. Éditions de Seuil, Paris.

Avraham Even-Shoshan. 2003. *Even Shoshan's Dictionary - Renewed and Updated for the 2000s*. Am Oved, Kineret, Zmora-Bitan, Dvir and Yediot Aharonot. (in Hebrew).

Yehuda Gur. 1946. *The Hebrew Language Dictionary*. Dvir, Tel Aviv. (in Hebrew).

M. A. K. Halliday. 1985. *An introduction to functional grammar*. Edward Arnold, USA, second edition.

Yaakov Knaani. 1960. *The Hebrew Language Lexicon*. Masada, Jerusalem. (in Hebrew).

Alexander Kohut. 1926. *Aruch Completum auctore Nathane filio Jechielis*. Hebraischer Verlag - Menorah, Wien-Berlin. (in Hebrew).

Ziona Kopelovich. 1982. *Modality in Modern Hebrew*. Ph.D. thesis, University of Michigan.

Uzi Ornan. 2002. Hebrew in Latin script. *Lĕšonénu*, LXIV:137–151. (in Hebrew).

Haiim B. Rosen. 1977. *Contemporary Hebrew*. Mouton, The Hague, Paris.

Beatrice Santorini. 1995. Part-of-speech tagging guidelines for the Penn Treebank Project. 3rd revision;. Technical report, Department of Computer and Information Science, University of Pennsylvania.

Erel Segal. 2000. Hebrew morphological analyzer for Hebrew undotted texts. Master's thesis, Technion, Haifa, Israel. (in Hebrew).

Khalil Sima'an, Alon Itai, Alon Altman Yoad Winter, and Noa Nativ. 2001. Building a tree-bank of modern Hebrew text. *Journal Traitement Automatique des Langues (t.a.l.)*. Special Issue on NLP and Corpus Linguistics.

Shlomo Yona. 2004. A finite-state based morphological analyzer for Hebrew. Master's thesis, Haifa University.

Yitzhak Zadka. 1995. The single object "rider" verb in current Hebrew: Classification of modal, adverbial and aspectual verbs. *Te'udah*, 9:247–271. (in Hebrew).

Arabic Tokenization System

Mohammed A. Attia
School of Informatics / The University of Manchester, PO Box 88, Sackville Street, Manchester M60 1QD, UK
mohammed.attia@postgrad.manchester.ac.uk

Abstract

Tokenization is a necessary and non-trivial step in natural language processing. In the case of Arabic, where a single word can comprise up to four independent tokens, morphological knowledge needs to be incorporated into the tokenizer. In this paper we describe a rule-based tokenizer that handles tokenization as a full-rounded process with a preprocessing stage (white space normalizer), and a post-processing stage (token filter). We also show how it handles multiword expressions, and how ambiguity is resolved.

1 Introduction

Tokenization is a non-trivial problem as it is "closely related to the morphological analysis" (Chanod and Tapanainen 1994). This is even more the case with languages with rich and complex morphology such as Arabic. The function of a tokenizer is to split a running text into tokens, so that they can be fed into a morphological transducer or POS tagger for further processing. The tokenizer is responsible for defining word boundaries, demarcating clitics, multiword expressions, abbreviations and numbers.

Clitics are syntactic units that do not have free forms but are instead attached to other words. Deciding whether a morpheme is an affix or a clitic can be confusing. However, we can generally say that affixes carry morpho-syntactic features (such as tense, person, gender or number), while clitics serve syntactic functions (such as negation, definition, conjunction or preposition) that would otherwise be served by an independent lexical item. Therefore tokenization is a crucial step for a syntactic parser that needs to build a tree from syntactic units. An example of clitics in English is the genitive suffix "'s" in *the student's book.*

Arabic clitics, however, are not as easily recognizable. Clitics use the same alphabet as that of words with no demarcating mark as the English apostrophe, and they can be concatenated one after the other. Without sufficient morphological knowledge, it is impossible to detect and mark clitics. In this paper we will show different levels of implementation of the Arabic tokenizer, according to the levels of linguistic depth involved.

Arabic Tokenization has been described in various researches and implemented in many solutions as it is a required preliminary stage for further processing. These solutions include morphological analysis (Beesley 2001; Buckwalter 2002), diacritization (Nelken and Shieber 2005), Information Retrieval (Larkey and Connell 2002), and POS Tagging (Diab et al 2004; Habash and Rambow 2005). None of these projects, however, show how multiword expressions are treated, or how ambiguity is filtered out.

In our research, tokenization is handled in a rule-based system as an independent process. We show how the tokenizer interacts with other transducers, and how multiword expressions are identified and delimited. We also show how incorrect tokenizations are filtered out, and how undesired tokenizations are marked. All tools in this research are developed in Finite State Technology (Beesley and Karttunen 2003). These tools have been developed to serve an Arabic Lexical Functional Grammar parser using XLE (Xerox Linguistics Environment) platform as part of the ParGram Project (Butt et al 2002).

Proceedings of the 5th Workshop on Important Unresolved Matters, pages 65–72,
Prague, Czech Republic, June 2007.

2 Arabic Tokens

A *token* is the minimal syntactic unit; it can be a word, a part of a word (or a clitic), a multiword expression, or a punctuation mark. A tokenizer needs to know a list of all word boundaries, such as white spaces and punctuation marks, and also information about the token boundaries inside words when a word is composed of a stem and clitics. Throughout this research full form words, i.e. stems with or without clitics, as well as numbers will be termed *main tokens*. All main tokens are delimited either by a white space or a punctuation mark. Full form words can then be divided into *sub-tokens*, where clitics and stems are separated.

2.1 Main Tokens

A tokenizer relies mainly on white spaces and punctuation marks as delimiters of word boundaries (or main tokens). Additional punctuation marks are used in Arabic such as the comma '،', question mark '؟' and semicolon '؛'. Numbers are also considered as main tokens. A few Arab countries use the Arabic numerals as in English, while most Arab countries use the Hindi numerals such as '٢' (2) and '٣' (3). Therefore a list of all punctuation marks and number characters must be fed to the system to allow it to demarcate main tokens in the text.

2.2 Sub-Tokens

Arabic morphotactics allow words to be prefixed or suffixed with clitics (Attia 2006b). Clitics themselves can be concatenated one after the other. Furthermore, clitics undergo assimilation with word stems and with each other, which makes them even harder to handle in any superficial way. A verb can comprise up four sub-tokens (a conjunction, a complementizer, a verb stem and an object pronoun) as illustrated by Figure 1.

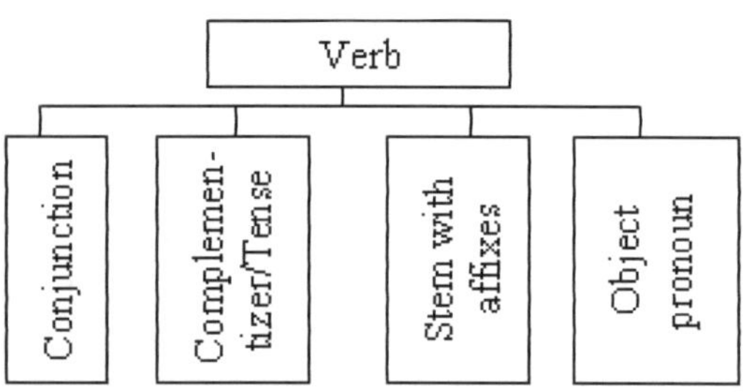

Figure 1: Possible sub-tokens in Arabic verbs

Similarly a noun can comprise up to four sub-tokens. Although Figure 2 shows five sub-tokens but we must note that the definite article and the genitive pronoun are mutually exclusive.

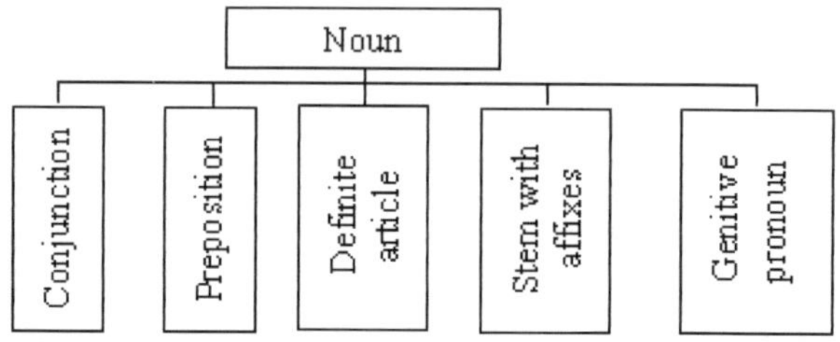

Figure 2: Possible sub-tokens in Arabic nouns

Moreover there are various rules that govern the combination of words with affixes and clitics. These rules are called grammar-lexis specifications (Abbès et al 2004; Dichy 2001; Dichy and Fargaly 2003). An example of these specifications is a rule that states that adjectives and proper nouns do not combine with possessive pronouns.

3 Development in Finite State Technology

Finite state technology has successfully been used in developing morphologies and text processing tools for many natural languages, including Semitic languages. We will explain briefly how finite state technology works, then we will proceed into showing how different tokenization models are implemented.

(1)
```
LEXICON Proclitic
al@U.Def.On@        Root;
                    Root;
LEXICON Root
kitab               Enclitic;
LEXICON Suffix
an                  Enclitic;
                    Enclitic;
LEXICON Enclitic
hi@U.Def.Off@       #;
```

In a standard finite state system, lexical entries along with all possible affixes and clitics are encoded in the lexc language which is a right recursive phrase structure grammar (Beesley and Karttunen 2003). A lexc file contains a number of lexicons connected through what is known as "continuation classes" which determine the path of concatenation. In example (1) above the lexicon *Proclitic* has a lexical form *al*, which is linked to a continuation class named *Root*. This means that the forms in *Root* will be appended to the right of *al*. The lexicon *Proclitic* also has an empty string, which means that *Proclitic* itself is optional and that the path can proceed without it. The bulk of all lexical entries are presumably listed under *Root* in the example.

Sometimes an affix or a clitic requires or forbids the existence of another affix or clitic. This is what is termed "long distance dependencies" (Beesley and Karttunen 2003). So Flag Diacritics are introduced to serve as filters on possible concatenations to a stem. As we want to prevent *Proclitic* and *Enclitic* from co-occurring, for the definite article and the possessive pronoun are mutually excusive, we add a Flag Diacritic to each of them with the same feature name "U.Def", but with different value "On/Off", as shown in (1) above. At the end we have a transducer with a binary relation between two sets of strings: the lower language that contains the surface forms, and the upper language that contains the analysis, as shown in (2) for the noun كتابان kitaban (two books).

(2) Lower Language: كتابان
Upper Language: كتاب+noun+dual+sg

4 Tokenization Solutions

There are different levels at which an Arabic tokenizer can be developed, depending on the depth of the linguistic analysis involved. During our work with the Arabic grammar we developed three different solutions, or three models, for Arabic tokenization. These models vary greatly in their robustness, compliance with the concept of modularity, and the ability to avoid unnecessary ambiguities.

The tokenizer relies on white spaces and punctuation marks to demarcate main tokens. In demarcating sub-tokens, however, the tokenizer needs more morphological information. This information is provided either deterministically by a morphological transducer, or indeterministically by a token guesser. Eventually both main tokens and sub-tokens are marked by the same token boundary, which is the sign '@' throughout this paper. The classification into main and sub-tokens is a conceptual idea that helps in assigning the task of identification to different components.

Identifying main tokens is considered a straightforward process that looks for white spaces and punctuation marks and divides the text accordingly. No further details of main tokens are given beyond this point. The three models described below are different ways to identify and divide sub-tokens, or clitics and stems within a full form word.

4.1 Model 1: Tokenization Combined with Morphological Analysis

In this implementation the tokenizer and the morphological analyzer are one and the same. A single transducer provides both morphological analysis and tokenization. Examples of the tokenizer/analyser output are shown in (3). The '+' sign precedes morphological features, while the '@' sign indicates token boundaries.

(3) وليشكر (waliyashkur: and to thank)
و+conj@ل+comp@+verb+pres+sgشكر@

This sort of implementation is the most linguistically motivated. This is also the most common form of implementation for Arabic tokenization (Habash and Rambow 2005). However, it violates the design concept of modularity which requires systems to have separate modules for undertaking separate tasks. For a syntactic parser that requires the existence of a tokenizer besides a morphological analyzer, this implementation is not workable, and either Model 2 or Model 3 is used instead.

4.2 Model 2: Tokenization Guesser

In this model tokenization is separated from morphological analysis. The tokenizer only detects and demarcates clitic boundaries. Yet information on what may constitute a clitic is still needed. This is why two additional components are required: a clitics guesser to be integrated with the tokenizer, and a clitics transducer to be integrated with the morphological transducer.

Clitics Guesser. We developed a guesser for Arabic words with all possible clitics and all possible assimilations. Please refer to (Beesley and Karttunen 2003) on how to create a basic guesser. The core idea of a guesser is to assume that a stem is composed of any arbitrary sequence of Arabic alphabets, and this stem can be prefixed or/and suffixed with a limited set of tokens. This guesser is then used by the tokenizer to mark clitic boundaries. Due to the nondeterministic nature of a guesser, there will be increased tokenization ambiguities.

(4) وللرجل (and to the man)
و@ل@ال@رجل@
و@ل@الرجل@
و@للرجل@
وللرجل@

Clitics Transducer. We must note that Arabic clitics do not occur individually in natural texts. They are always attached to words. Therefore a specialized small-scale morphological transducer is needed to handle these newly separated forms. We developed a lexc transducer for clitics only, treating them as separate words. The purpose of this transducer is to provide analysis for morphemes that do not occur independently.

(5) و+conj
ل+prep
ال+art+def

This small-scale specialized transducer is then unioned (or integrated) with the main morphological transducer. Before making the union it is necessary to remove all paths that contain any clitics in the main morphological transducer to eliminate redundancies.

In our opinion this is the best model, the advantages are robustness as it is able to deal with any words whether they are known to the morphological transducer or not, and abiding by the concept of modularity as it separates the process of tokenization from morphological analysis.

There are disadvantages, however, for this model, and among them is that the morphological analyzer and the syntactic parser have to deal with increased tokenization ambiguities. The tokenizer is highly non-deterministic as it depends on a guesser which, by definition, is non-deterministic. For a simple sentence of three words, we are faced with eight different tokenization solutions. Nonetheless, this can be handled as explained in subsection 5.1 on discarding spurious ambiguities.

4.3 Model 3: Tokenization Dependent on the Morphological Analyser

In the above solution, the tokenizer defines the possible Arabic stem as any arbitrary sequence of Arabic letters. In this solution, however, the word stem is not guessed, but taken as a list of actual words. A possible word in the tokenizer in this model is any word found in the morphological transducer. The morphological transducer here is the same as the one described in subsection 4.1 but with one difference, that is the output does not include any morphological features, but only token boundaries between clitics and stems.

This is a relatively deterministic tokenizer that handles clitics properly. The main downfall is that only words found in the morphological transducer are tokenized. It is not robust, yet it may be more convenient during grammar debugging, as it provides much fewer analyses than model 2. Here spurious ambiguities are successfully avoided.

(6) وللرجل (and to the man)
و@ل@ال@رجل@

One advantage of this implementation is that the tool becomes more deterministic and more manageable in debugging. Its lack of robustness, however, makes it mostly inapplicable as no single morphological transducer can claim to comprise all the words in a language. In our XLE grammar, this model is only 0.05% faster than Model 2. This is not statistically significant advantage compared to its limitations.

4.4 Tokenizing Multiword Expressions

Multiword Expressions (MWEs) are two or more words that behave like a single word syntactically and semantically. They are defined, more formally, as "idiosyncratic interpretations that cross word boundaries" (Sag et al 2001). MWEs cover expressions that are traditionally classified as idioms (e.g. *down the drain*), prepositional verbs (e.g. *rely on*), verbs with particles (e.g. *give up*), compound nouns (e.g. *traffic lights*) and collocations (e.g. *do a favour*).

With regard to syntactic and morphological flexibility, MWEs are classified into three types: fixed, semi-fixed and syntactically flexible expressions (Baldwin 2004; Oflazer et al 2004; Sag et al 2001).

a. Fixed Expressions. These expressions are lexically, syntactically and morphologically rigid. An expression of this type is considered as a word with spaces (a single word that happens to contain spaces), such as الشرق الأوسط al-sharq al-awsat (the Middle East) and بيت لحم bait lahem (Bethlehem).

b. Semi-Fixed Expressions. These expressions can undergo variations, but still the components of the expression are adjacent. The variations are of two types, morphological variations where lexical items can express person, number, tense, gender, etc., such as the examples in (7), and lexical variations, where one word can be replaced by another as in (8).

(7.a) فترة انتقالية
fatratah intiqaliyyah
translational.sg.fem period.sg.fem

(7.b) فترتان انتقاليتان
fatratan intiqaliyyatan
translational.dual.fem period.dual.fem

(8) على ظهر/وجه الأرض/البسيطة
ala zahr/wajh al-ard/al-basitah
on the face/surface of the land/earth
(on the face of the earth)

c. Syntactically Flexible Expressions. These are the expressions that can either undergo reordering, such as passivization (e.g. *the cat was let out of the bag*), or allow external elements to intervene between the components such as (9.b), where the adjacency of the MWE is disrupted.

(9.a) دراجة نارية
darrajah nariyyah
bike fiery (motorbike)

(9.b) دراجة الولد النارية
darrajat al-walad al-nariyyah
the-bike the-boy the-fiery (the boy's motorbike)

Fixed and semi-fixed expressions are identified and marked by the tokenizer, while syntactically flexible expressions can only be handled by a syntactic parser (Attia 2006a).

The tokenizer is responsible for treating MWEs in a special way. They should be marked as single tokens with the inner space(s) preserved. For this purpose, as well as for the purpose of morphological analysis, a specialized transducer is developed for MWEs that lists all variations of MWEs and provides analyses for them (Attia 2006a).

One way to allow the tokenizer to handle MWEs is to embed the MWEs in the Tokenizer (Beesley and Karttunen 2003). Yet a better approach, described by (Karttunen et al 1996), is to develop one or several multiword transducers or "staplers" that are composed on the tokenizer. We will explain here how this is implemented in our solution, where the list of MWEs is extracted from the MWE transducer and composed on the tokenizer. Let's look at the composition regular expression:

```
(10) 1  singleTokens.i
     2  .o. ?* 0:"[[[" (MweTokens.l) 0:"]]]" ?*
     3  .o. "@" -> " " || "[[[" [Alphabet* | "@"*] _
     4  .o. "[[[" -> [] .o. "]]]" -> []].i;
```

Single words separated by the '@' sign are defined in the variable *singleTokens* and the MWE transducer is defined in *MweTokens*. In the MWE transducer all spaces in the lower language are replaced by "@" so that the lower language can be matched against *singleTokens*. In line 1 the *singleTokens* is inverted (the upper language is shifted down) by the operator ".i" so that composition goes on the side that contains the relevant strings. From the MWE transducer we take only the lower language (or the surface form) by the operator ".l" in line 2. Single words are searched and if they contain any MWEs, the expressions will (optionally) be enclosed by three brackets on either side. Line 3 replaces all "@" signs with spaces in side MWEs only. The two compositions in line 4 remove the intermediary brackets.

Let's now show this with a working example. For the phrase in (11), the tokenizer first gives the output in (12). Then after the MWEs are composed with the tokenizer, we obtain the result in (13) with the MWE identified as a single token.

(11) ولوزير خارجيتها
wa-liwazir kharijiyatiha
and-to-foreign minister-its
(and to its foreign minister)

(12) و@ل@وزير@خارجية@ها@
(approx. and@to@foreign@minister@its@)

(13) و@ل@وزير خارجية@ها
(approx. and@to@foreign minister@its@)

4.5 Normalizing White Spaces

White space normalization is a preliminary stage to tokenization where redundant and misplaced white spaces are corrected, to enable the tokenizer to work on a clean and predictable text.

In real-life data spaces may not be as regularly and consistently used as expected. There may be two or more spaces, or even tabs, instead of a single space. Spaces might even be added before or after punctuation marks in the wrong manner. Therefore, there is a need for a tool that eliminates inconsistency in using white spaces, so that when the text is fed into a tokenizer or morphological analyzer, words and expressions can be correctly identified and analyzed. Table 1 shows where spaces are not expected before or after some punctuation marks.

No Space Before	No Space After
)	(
}	{
]	[
”	“

Table 1. Space distribution with some punctuation marks

We have developed a white space normalizer whose function is to go through real-life texts and correct mistakes related to the placement of white spaces. When it is fed an input such as the one in (14.a) in which additional spaces are inserted and some spaces are misplaced, it corrects the errors and gives the output in (14.b):

(14.a) نشر (الديمقراطية)سيقود إلى السلام .
(14.b) نشر (الديمقراطية) سيقود إلى السلام.

5 Resolving Ambiguity

There are different types of ambiguity. There are spurious ambiguities created by the guesser. There are also ambiguities which do not exist in the text before tokenization but are only created during the tokenization process. Finally there are real ambiguities, where a form can be read as a single word or two sub-tokens, or where an MWE has a compositional reading. These three types are treated by the following three subsections respectively.

5.1 Discarding Spurious Ambiguities

Tokenization Model 2 discussed above in subsection 4.2 is chosen as the optimal implementation due to its efficiency and robustness, yet it is highly nondeterministic and produces a large number of spurious ambiguities. Therefore, a morphological transducer is needed to filter out the tokenization paths that contain incorrect sub-tokens. Recall example (4) which contained the output of the nondeterministic tokenizer. In (15) below, after the output is fed into a morphological transducer, only one solution is accepted and the rest are discarded, as underlined words do not constitute valid stems.

(15) وللرجل (and to the man)
و@ل@ال@رجل@ - Passed.
و@ل@الرجل@ - Discarded.
و@للرجل@ - Discarded.
وللرجل@ - Discarded.

5.2 Handling Tokenization Ambiguities

Among the function of a tokenizer is separate clitics from stems. Some clitics, however, when separated, become ambiguous with other clitics and also with other free forms. For example the word كتابهم kitabahum has only one morphological reading (meaning *their book*), but after tokenization كتاب@هم there are three different readings, as the second token هم can either be a clitic genitive pronoun (the intended reading) or a free pronoun *they* (*a book, they*) or a noun meaning *worry* (forming the compound *book of worry*).

This problem is solved by inserting a mark that precedes enclitics and follows proclitics to distinguish them from each other as well as from free forms (Ron M. Kaplan and Martin Forst, personal communications, Oxford, UK, 20 September 2006). The mark we choose is the Arabic elongation short line called *cashida* which is originally used for graphical decorative purposes and looks natural with most clitics. To illustrate the usage, a two-word string (16.a) will be rendered without cashidas as in (16.b), and a single-word string that contains clitics (17.a) will be rendered with a distinctive cashida before the enclitic pronoun as in (17.b). This indicates that the pronoun is attached to the preceding word and not standing alone.

(16.a) كتاب هم
kitab hum/hamm (book of worry/a book, they)
(16.b) كتاب@هم
(17.a) كتابهم kitabuhum (their book)
(17.b) كتاب@ـهم

This implementation will also resolve a similar ambiguity, that is ambiguity arising between proclitics and enclitics. The proclitic preposition ك ka (as) always occurs initially. There is a homographic enclitic object pronoun ك ka (you) that always occurs in the final position. This can create ambiguity in instances such as the made-up sentence in (18.a). The sentence has the initial tokenization of (18.b) without a cashida, and therefore the central token becomes ambiguous as it can now be attached either to the preceding or following word leading either to the readings in (18.a) or (18.c). The cashida placement, however, resolves this ambiguity as in (18.d). The cashida is added after the token, indicating that it is attached to the following word and now only the reading in (18.a) is possible.

(18.a) أعطيت كالأمير
a'taitu ka-lamir (I gave like a prince)
(18.b) أعطيت@ك@الأمير
(18.c) أعطيتك الأمير
a'taitu-ka alamir (I gave you the prince)
(18.d) أعطيت@كـ@الأمير

5.3 Handling Real Ambiguities

Some tokenization readings are legal, yet highly infrequent and undesired in real-life data. These undesired readings create onerous ambiguities, as they are confused with more common and more acceptable forms. For example the Arabic preposition بعد ba'd (after) has the possible remote reading of being split into two tokens بـ@عد, which is made of two elements: بـ bi (with) and عد 'add (counting). Similarly بين baina (between) has the possible remote reading بـ@ين, which is made of two tokens as well: بـ bi (with) and ين yin (Yen).

The same problem occurs with MWEs. The optimal handling of MWEs is to treat them as single tokens and leave internal spaces intact. Yet a non-deterministic tokenizer allows MWEs to be analysed compositionally as individual words. So the MWE حظر التجول hazr al-tajawwul (curfew) has two analyses, as in (19), although the compositional reading in (19.b) is undesired.

(19.a) حظر التجول@ hazr al-tajawwul (curfew)
(19.b) حظر@التجول
hazr (forbidding) al-tajawwul (walking)

The solution to this problem is to mark the undesired readings. This is implemented by developing a filter, or a finite state transducer that contains all possible undesired tokenization possibilities and attaches the "+undesired" tag to each one of them.

Undesired tokens, such as بـ@ين and بـ@عد, explained above, can be included in a custom list in the token filter. As for MWEs, the token filter imports a list from the MWE transducer and replaces the spaces with the token delimiter '@' to denote the undesired tokenization solutions. The token filter then matches the lists against the output of the tokenizer. If the output contains a matching string a mark is added, giving the output in (20). Notice how (20.b) is marked with the "+undesired" tag.

(20.a) حظر التجول@ [hazr al-tajawwul (curfew)]
(20.b) حظر@التجول+undesired

This transducer or filter is composed on top of the core tokenizer. The overall design of the tokenizer and its interaction with other finite state components is shown in Figure 3. WE must note that the tokenizer, in its interaction with the morphological transducer and the MWE transducer, does not seek morpho-syntactic information, but it queries for lists and possible combinations.

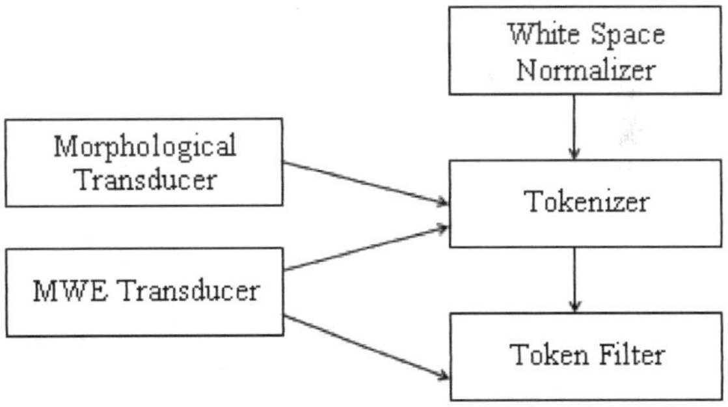

Figure 3: Design of the Arabic Tokenizer

6 Conclusion

Tokenization is a process that is closely connected to and dependent on morphological analysis. In our research we show how different models of tokenization are implemented at different levels of linguistic depth. We also explain how the tokenizer interacts with other components[1], and how it resolves complexity and filters ambiguity. By applying token filters we gain control over the tokenization output.

References

Abbès R, Dichy J, Hassoun M (2004): The Architecture of a Standard Arabic lexical database: some figures, ratios and categories from the DIINAR.1 source program, The Workshop on Computational Approaches to Arabic Script-based Languages, COLING 2004. Geneva, Switzerland.

Attia M (2006a): Accommodating Multiword Expressions in an Arabic LFG Grammar. In Salakoski T, Ginter F, Pyysalo S, Pahikkala T (eds), Advances in Natural Language Processing, 5th International Conference on NLP, FinTAL 2006, Turku, Finland, Vol 4139. Turku, Finland: Springer-Verlag Berlin Heidelberg, pp 87-98.

Attia M (2006b): An Ambiguity-Controlled Morphological Analyzer for Modern Standard Arabic Modelling Finite State Networks, The Challenge of Arabic for NLP/MT Conference. The British Computer Society, London, UK.

Baldwin T (2004): Multiword Expressions, an Advanced Course, The Australasian Language Technology Summer School (ALTSS 2004). Sydney, Australia.

Beesley KR (2001): Finite-State Morphological Analysis and Generation of Arabic at Xerox Research: Status and Plans in 2001, Proceedings of the Arabic Language Processing: Status and Prospect--39th Annual Meeting of the Association for Computational Linguistics. Toulouse, France.

Beesley KR, Karttunen L (2003): Finite State Morphology. Stanford, Calif.: CSLI.

Buckwalter T (2002): Buckwalter Arabic Morphological Analyzer Version 1.0., Linguistic Data Consortium. Catalog number LDC2002L49, and ISBN 1-58563-257-0.

Butt M, Dyvik H, King TH, Masuichi H, Rohrer C (2002): The Parallel Grammar Project, COLING-2002 Workshop on Grammar Engineering and Evaluation. Taipei, Taiwan.

Chanod J-P, Tapanainen P (1994): A Non-Deterministic Tokenizer for Finite-State Parsing, ECAI'96. Budapest, Hungary.

Diab M, Hacioglu K, Jurafsky D (2004): Automatic Tagging of Arabic Text: From Raw Text to Base Phrase Chunks, Proceedings of NAACL-HLT 2004. Boston.

Dichy J (2001): On lemmatization in Arabic. A formal definition of the Arabic entries of multilingual lexical databases, ACL 39th Annual Meeting. Workshop on Arabic Language Processing; Status and Prospect. Toulouse, pp 23-30.

Dichy J, Fargaly A (2003): Roots & Patterns vs. Stems plus Grammar-Lexis Specifications: on what basis should a multilingual lexical database centred on Arabic be built?, Proceedings of the MT-Summit IX workshop on Machine Translation for Semitic Languages. New-Orleans.

Habash N, Rambow O (2005): Arabic Tokenization, Part-of-Speech Tagging and Morphological Disambiguation in One Fell Swoop, Proceedings of ACL 2005. Michigan.

Karttunen L, Chanod J-P, Grefenstette G, Schiller A (1996): Regular expressions for language engineering. Natural Language Engineering 2:305-328.

Larkey LS, Connell ME (2002): Arabic Information Retrieval at UMass. In Voorhees EM, Harman DK (eds), The Tenth Text Retrieval Conference, TREC 2001. Maryland: NIST Special Publication, pp 562-570.

Nelken R, Shieber SM (2005): Arabic Diacritization Using Weighted Finite-State Transducers, Proceedings of the 2005 ACL Workshop on Computational Approaches to Semitic Languages. Michigan.

Oflazer K, Uglu ÖÇ, Say B (2004): Integrating Morphology with Multi-word Expression Processing in Turkish, Second ACL Workshop on Multiword Expressions: Integrating Processing. Spain, pp 64-71.

Sag IA, Baldwin T, Bond F, Copestake A, Flickinger D (2001): Multi-word Expressions: A Pain in the Neck for NLP, LinGO Working Papers. Stanford University, CA.

[1] The tokenizer along with a number of other Arabic finite state tools are made available for evaluation on the website: www.attiapace.com

Arabic to French Sentence Alignment: Exploration of A Cross-language Information Retrieval Approach

Nasredine Semmar
CEA, LIST
Laboratoire d'ingénierie de la connaissance multimédia multilingue
18 route du Panorama
BP6, FONTENAY AUX ROSES, F-92265 France
nasredine.semmar@cea.fr

Christian Fluhr
CEA, LIST
Service Réalite virtuelle, Cognitique et Interfaces
18 route du Panorama
BP6, FONTENAY AUX ROSES, F-92265 France
christian.fluhr@cea.fr

Abstract

Sentence alignment consists in estimating which sentence or sentences in the source language correspond with which sentence or sentences in a target language. We present in this paper a new approach to aligning sentences from a parallel corpus based on a cross-language information retrieval system. This approach consists in building a database of sentences of the target text and considering each sentence of the source text as a "query" to that database. The cross-language information retrieval system is a weighted Boolean search engine based on a deep linguistic analysis of the query and the documents to be indexed. This system is composed of a multilingual linguistic analyzer, a statistical analyzer, a reformulator, a comparator and a search engine. The multilingual linguistic analyzer includes a morphological analyzer, a part-of-speech tagger and a syntactic analyzer. The linguistic analyzer processes both documents to be indexed and queries to produce a set of normalized lemmas, a set of named entities and a set of nominal compounds with their morpho-syntactic tags. The statistical analyzer computes for documents to be indexed concept weights based on concept database frequencies. The comparator computes intersections between queries and documents and provides a relevance weight for each intersection. Before this comparison, the reformulator expands queries during the search. The expansion is used to infer from the original query words other words expressing the same concepts. The search engine retrieves the ranked, relevant documents from the indexes according to the corresponding reformulated query and then merges the results obtained for each language, taking into account the original words of the query and their weights in order to score the documents. The sentence aligner has been evaluated on the MD corpus of the ARCADE II project which is composed of news articles from the French newspaper "Le Monde Diplomatique". The part of the corpus used in evaluation consists of the same subset of sentences in Arabic and French. Arabic sentences are aligned to their French counterparts. Results showed that alignment has correct precision and recall even when the corpus is not completely parallel (changes in sentence order or missing sentences).

1 Introduction

Sentence alignment consists in mapping sentences of the source language with their translations in the target language. Automatic sentence alignment approaches face two kinds of difficulties: robustness and accuracy. A number of automatic sentence alignment techniques have been proposed (Kay and Röscheisen, 1993; Gale and Church, 1991; Brown et al., 1991; Debili and Samouda, 1992; Papageorgiou et al., 1994; Gaussier, 1995; Melamed, 1996; Fluhr et al., 2000).

Proceedings of the 5th Workshop on Important Unresolved Matters, pages 73–80,
Prague, Czech Republic, June 2007.

The method proposed in (Kay and Röscheisen, 1993) is based on the assumption that in order for the sentences in a translation to correspond, the words in them must correspond. In other words, all necessary information (and in particular, lexical mapping) is derived from the to-be-aligned texts themselves.

In (Gale and Church, 1991) and (Brown et al., 1991), the authors start from the fact that the length of a source text sentence is highly correlated with the length of its target text translation: short sentences tend to have short translations, and long sentences tend to have long translations.

The method proposed in (Debili and Sammouda, 1992) is based on the preliminary alignment of words using a conventional bilingual lexicon and the method described in (Papageorgiou et al., 1994) added grammatical labeling based on the assumption that the same parts of speech tend to be employed in the translation.

In this paper, we present a sentence aligner which is based on a cross-language information retrieval approach and combines different information sources (bilingual lexicon, sentence length and sentence position). This sentence aligner was first developed for aligning French-English parallel text. It is now ported to Arabic-French and Arabic-English language pairs.

We present in section 2 the main components of the cross-language search engine, in particular, we will focus on the linguistic processing. In section 3, the prototype of our sentence aligner is described. We discuss in section 4 results obtained after aligning sentences of the MD (Monde Diplomatique) corpus of the ARCADE II project. Section 5 concludes our study and presents our future work.

2 The Cross-language Search Engine

Information retrieval consists to find all relevant documents for a user query in a collection of documents. These documents are ordered by the probability of being relevant to the user's query. The highest ranked document is considered to be the most likely relevant document. Cross-language information retrieval consists in providing a query in one language and searching documents in different languages (Grefenstette, 1998). The cross-lingual search engine is a weighted Boolean search engine based on a deep linguistic analysis of the query and the documents to be indexed (Besançon et al., 2003). It is composed of a linguistic analyzer, a statistical analyzer, a reformulator and a comparator (Figure 1):

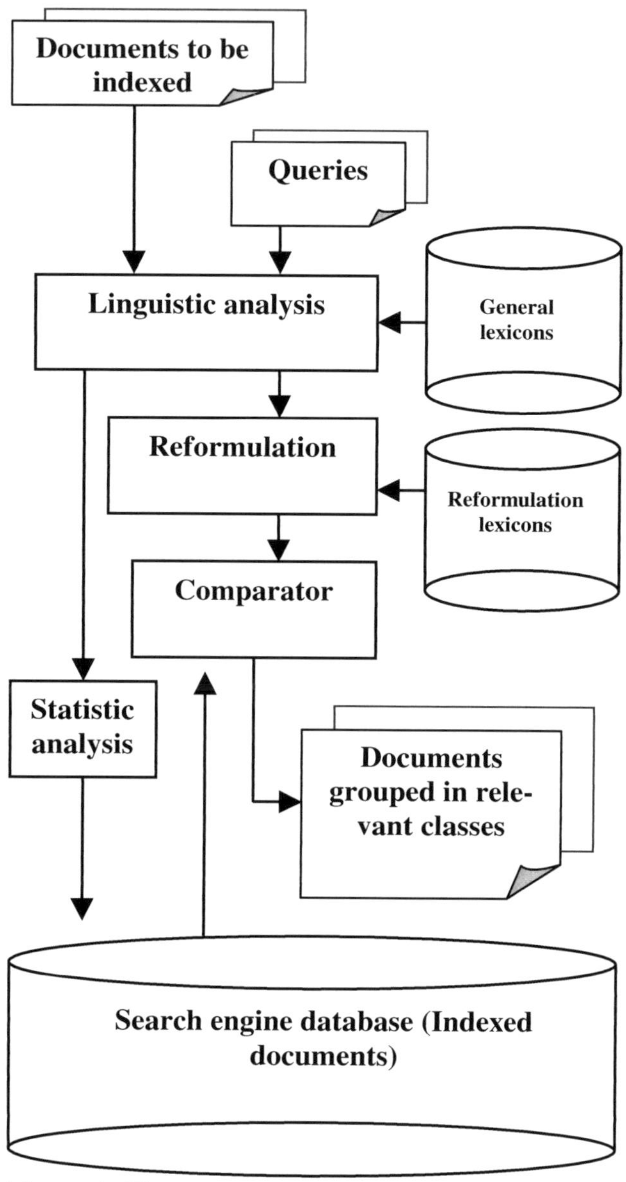

Figure 1. The cross-language search engine

2.1 Linguistic Analysis

The linguistic analyzer produces a set of normalized lemmas, a set of named entities and a set of nominal compounds. It is composed of several linguistic resources and processing modules.

Each language has its proper linguistic resources which are generally composed of:

- A full form dictionary, containing for each word form its possible part-of-speech tags and linguistic features (gender, number, etc). For languages such as Arabic which presents agglutination of articles, prepositions and conjunctions at the beginning of the word as well as pronouns at the ending of the word, we added two other dictionaries for proclitics and enclitics in order to split the input words into proclitics, simple forms and enclitics.

- A monolingual reformulation dictionary used in query expansion for expanding original query words to other words expressing the same concepts (synonyms, hyponyms, etc.).
- Bilingual dictionaries used in cross-language querying.
- A set of rules for tokenizing words.
- A set of part-of-speech n-grams (bigrams and trigrams from hand-tagged corpora) that are used for part-of-speech tagging.
- A set of rules for shallow parsing of sentences, extracting compounds from the input text.
- A set of rules for the identification of named entities: gazetteers and contextual rules that use special triggers to identify named entities and their type.

The processing modules are common for all the languages with some variations for some specific languages:

- A Tokenizer which separates the input stream into a graph of words. This separation is achieved by an automaton developed for each language and a set of segmentation rules.
- A Morphological analyzer which searches each word in a general dictionary (Debili and Zouari, 1985). If this word is found, it will be associated with its lemma and all its morpho-syntactic tags. If the word is not found in the general dictionary, it is given a default set of morpho-syntactic tags based on its typography. For Arabic, we added to the morphological analyzer a new processing step: a Clitic stemmer (Larkey et al., 2002) which splits agglutinated words into proclitics, simple forms and enclitics. If the simple form computed by the clitic stemmer does not exist in the general dictionary, re-write rules are applied (Darwish, 2002). For example, consider the token "بكرتهم" (with their ballon) and the included clitics "ب" (with) and "هم" (their), the computed simple form "كرت" does not exist in the general dictionary but after applying one of the dozen re-write rules, the modified simple form "كرة" (ballon) is found in the general dictionary and the input token is segmented as: هم + كرة + ب = بكـــرتهم.
- An Idiomatic Expressions recognizer which detects idiomatic expressions and considers them as single words for the rest of the processing. Idiomatic expressions are phrases or compound nouns that are listed in a specific dictionary. The detection of idiomatic expressions is performed by applying a set of rules that are triggered on specific words and tested on left and right contexts of the trigger. These rules can recognize contiguous expressions as the "white house" in English, la "maison blanche" in French or "البَيْت الأبْيَض" in Arabic. Non-contiguous expressions such as phrasal verbs in English: "switch…on" or "tomber vaguement dans les pommes" in French are recognized too.
- A Part-Of-Speech (POS) tagger which searches valid paths through all the possible tags paths using attested trigrams and bigrams sequences. The trigram and bigram matrices are generated from a manually annotated training corpus (Grefenstette et al., 2005). They are extracted from a hand-tagged corpora of 13 200 words for Arabic and 25 000 words for French. If no continuous trigram full path is found, the POS tagger tries to use bigrams at the points where the trigrams were not found in the matrix. The accuracy of the part-of-speech tagger is around 91% for Arabic and 94% for French.
- A Syntactic analyzer which is used to split word graph into nominal and verbal chain and recognize dependency relations (especially those within compounds) by using a set of syntactic rules. We developed a set of dependency relations to link nouns to

other nouns, a noun with a proper noun, a proper noun with the post nominal adjective and a noun with a post nominal adjective. These relations are restricted to the same nominal chain and are used to compute compound words. For example, in the nominal chain "توزيع المياه" (water supply), the syntactic analyzer considers this nominal chain as a compound word (توزيع_مياه) composed of the words "توزيع" (supply) and "مياه" (water).

- A Named Entity recognizer which uses name triggers (e.g., President, lake, corporation, etc.) to identify named entities (Abuleil and Evens, 2004). For example, the expression "الأوّل مِن شَهْر مَارس" (The first of March) is recognized as a date and the expression "الشَّرْق الأوْسَط" (The Middle East) is recognized as a location.
- Eliminating Empty Words consists in identifying words that should not be used as search criteria and eliminating them. These empty words are identified using only their parts of speech (such as prepositions, articles, punctuations and some adverbs).
- Finally, words are normalized by their lemma. In the case the word has a set of synonymous lemmas, only one of these lemmas is taken as a normalization. Each normalized word is associated with its morpho-syntactic tag.

2.2 Statistical Analysis

The role of the statistical analysis is to attribute a weight to each word or a compound word according to the information the word or the compound word provides in choosing the document relevant to a query. This weight is computed by an idf formula (Salton and McGill, 1983). The weight is maximum for words appearing in one single document and minimum for words appearing in all the documents. This weight is used by the comparator to compute the semantic intersection between query and documents containing different words. A similarity value is associated with each semantic intersection. This value corresponds to the sum of the weights of words present in the documents. The search engine groups documents into classes (semantic intersections) characterized by the same set of words. These classes constitute a discrete partition of the indexed documents. For example, the search engine returns 12 classes for the query "إدارة موارد المياه" (water resources management) (Table 1).

Class	Query terms
1	إدارة_موارد_مياه
2	موارد_مياه, إدارة_موارد
3	مياه, إدارة_وارد
4	إدارة, موارد_مياه
5	إدارة_موارد
6	موارد_مياه
7	إدارة, موارد, مياه
8	إدارة, مياه
9	إدارة, موارد
10	موارد, مياه
11	مياه
12	موارد

Table 1. Relevant classes returned by the search engine for the query "إدارة موارد المياه"

The query term "إدارة_موارد_مياه" is a compound word composed of three words: "إدارة" (management), "موارد" (resources) and "مياه" (water). This compound word is computed by the syntactic analyzer.

2.3 Query Reformulation

The role of query reformulation is to infer new words from the original query words according to a lexical semantic knowledge. The reformulation can be used to increase the quality of the retrieval in a monolingual interrogation. It can also be used to infer words in other languages. The query terms are translated using bilingual dictionaries. Each term of the query is translated into several terms in target language. The translated words form the search terms of the reformulated query. The links between the search terms and the query concepts can also be weighted by a confidence value indicating the relevance of the translation. Reformulation rules can be applied to all instances of a word or to a word only when it is playing a specific part-of-speech. Semantic relations can also be selected: translations, synonyms, word derived from the same root, etc. The cross-language search engine has a monolingual reformulation for French and two bilingual reformulations for Arabic-French and French-Arabic language pairs.

2.4 Query and Documents Comparison

The search engine indexer builds the inverted files of the documents on the basis of their linguistic analysis: one index is built for each language of the document collection. This indexer builds separate indexes for each language. The search engine uses a comparison tool to evaluate all possible intersections between query words and documents, and computes a relevance weight for each intersection. This relevance weight corresponds to the sum of the weights of words present in the documents.

3 The Sentence Aligner

Parallel text alignment based on cross-language information retrieval consists in building a database of sentences of the target text and considering each sentence of the source text as a "query" to that database (Figure 2).

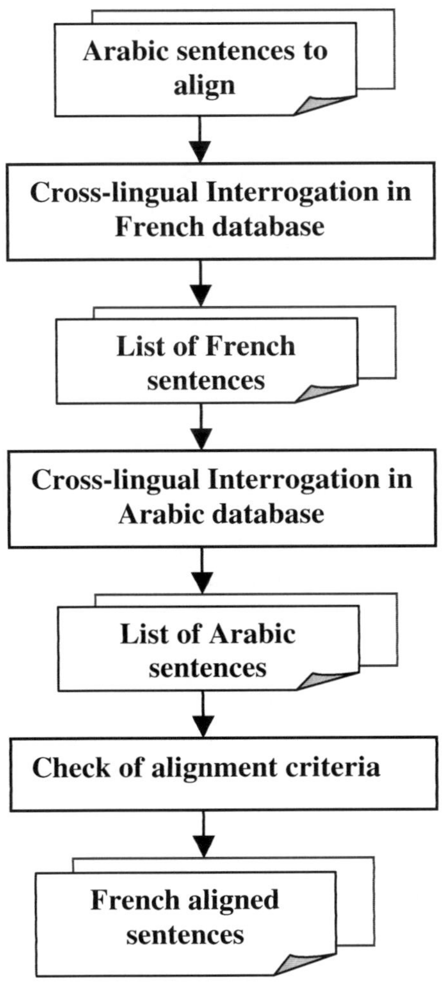

Figure 2. Sentence alignment steps

To evaluate whether the two sentences are translations of each other, we use three criteria:

- Number of common words between the source sentence and the target sentence (semantic intersection) must be higher than 50% of number of words of the target sentence.
- Position of the sentence to align must be in an interval of 10 compared to the position of the last aligned sentence.
- Ratio of lengths of the target sentence and the source sentence (in characters) must be higher or equal than 1.1 (A French character needs 1.1 Arabic characters): *Longer sentences in Arabic tend to be translated into longer sentences in French, and shorter sentences tend to be translated into shorter sentences.*

The alignment process has four steps:

1. Exact match 1-1 alignment: The goal of this step is to obtain an alignment with a maximum precision by using the three criteria: Number of common words between the source sentence and the target sentence; Position of the sentence to align; Ratio of lengths of the target sentence and the source sentence.
2. 1-2 alignment: This alignment consists in merging an unaligned sentence with one preceding or following already aligned sentence. We use to validate this alignment only the first two criteria.
3. 2-1 alignment: The goal of this alignment is to find for the two sentences following an aligned sentence a sentence in the target language taking into account the position of the last aligned sentence. This alignment is validated by using only the first two criteria.
4. Fuzzy match 1-1 alignment: This alignment proposes for the sentence to align the first sentence of the first class returned by the cross-language search engine. This type of alignment is added to take into account alignments which are partially correct (The source sentence is not completely aligned but some of its words are translated).

We describe below the algorithm of the Exact Match 1-1 alignment which is the base of the other aligners. This algorithm uses the functions of the cross-language search engine API.

- `PerformCrosslinguageSearch(Query, Corpus, Source language, Target language)`: returns the set of relevant classes corresponding to the question "Query" in the database "Corpus". Each class is composed of a set of sentences in the target language.
- `GetNumberOfCommonWords(Class)`: returns the number of common words between the source sentence and the target sentence (semantic intersection).
- `GetNumberOfWords(Sentence)`: returns the number of words of a sentence.
- `GetNumberOfCharacters(Sentence)`: returns the number of characters of a sentence.

```
function GetExactMatchOneToOneAlignments(Corpus_Ar, Corpus_Fr)
  for each Arabic sentence P_jAr ∈ Corpus_Ar do
    C_Fr←PerformCrosslinguageSearch(P_jAr, Corpus_Fr, Ar, Fr)
    R←0; Initialize the position of the last aligned sentence.
    for each class C_lFr ∈ C_Fr do
      for each French sentence P_mFr ∈ C_lFr do
        C_Ar←PerformCrosslinguageSearch(P_mFr, Corpus_Ar, Fr, Ar)
        for each class C_qAr ∈ C_Ar do
          for each Arabic sentence P_qAr ∈ C_qAr do
            if P_qAr=P_jAr then
              NM_Fr=GetNumberOfCommonWords(C_lFr);
              NM_Ar=GetNumberOfWords(P_jAr);
              NC_Ar=GetNumberOfCharacters(P_jAr);
              NC_Fr=GetNumberOfCharacters(P_mFr)
              if (NM_Fr ≥ NM_Ar/2) and (R-5 ≤ m ≤ R+5) and (NC_Fr=(1.1)*NC_Ar) then
                The sentence P_mFr is the alignment of the sentence P_jAr;
                R←m
              end if
            end if
          end for
        end for
      end for
    end for
  end for
end function
```

For example, to align the Arabic sentence [4/30] (sentence of position 4 in the Arabic corpus containing 30 sentences) " في ايطاليا ادت طبيعة الاشياء الى اقناع غالبية الناخبين في طريقة غير مرئية بأن زمن الاحزاب التقليدية قد بلغ نهايته " (In Italy, the order of things persuaded in an invisible way a majority of electors that time of traditional parties was finished), the exact match 1-1 aligner proceeds as follows:

- The Arabic sentence is considered to be a query to the French sentence database using the cross-language search engine. Retrieved sentences for the two first classes are illustrated in Table 2.

Class	Number of retrieved sentences	Retrieved sentences
1	1	[4/36] En Italie, l'ordre des choses a persuadé de manière invisible une majorité d'électeurs que le temps des partis traditionnels était terminé
2	3	[32/36] Au point que, dès avant ces élections, un hebdomadaire britannique, rappelant les accusations portées par la justice italienne contre M. Berlusconi, estimait qu'un tel dirigeant n'était pas digne de gouverner l'Italie, car il constituait un danger pour la démocratie et une menace pour l'Etat de droit [34/36] Après le pitoyable effondrement des partis traditionnels, la société italienne, si cultivée, assiste assez impassible (seul le monde du cinéma est entré en résistance) à l'actuelle dégradation d'un système politique de plus en plus confus, extravagant, ridicule et dangereux [36/36] Toute la question est de savoir dans quelle mesure ce modèle italien si préoccupant risque de s'étendre demain à d'autres pays d'Europe

Table 2. Retrieved sentences corresponding to the Arabic sentence [4/30]

- Results of cross-language querying show that the sentence [4/36] is a good candidate to alignment. To confirm this alignment, we use the French sentence as a query to the Arabic database. Relevant sentences corresponding to the French query "En Italie, l'ordre des choses a persuadé de manière invisible une majorité d'électeurs que le temps des partis traditionnels était terminé" are grouped into two classes in Table 3.

Class	Number of retrieved sentences	Retrieved sentences
1	1	[4/30] في ايطاليا ادت طبيعة الاشياء الى اقناع غالبية الناخبين في طريقة غير مرئية بأن زمن الاحزاب التقليدية قد بلغ نهايته □
2	3	[26/30] يشكل هؤلاء الرجال اكثر ثلاثية مثيرة للسخرية والتقزز في اوروبا، الى درجة ان احدى المجلات الاسبوعية البريطانية اعتبرت في معرض استعادتها للاتهامات القضائية الموجهة الى السيد برلوسكوني قبل هذه الانتخابات ان مسؤولا من هذا النوع ليس جديرا بحكم ايطاليا وانه يمثل خطرا على الديموقراطية وعلى دولة القانون □ [28/30] وقد تبينت صحة هذه التوقعات المتشائمة، فبعد الانهيار المثير للشفقة للاحزاب التقليدية، شهد المجتمع وف بثقافته ومن دون ان الايطالي المعر يبدي حراكا باستثناء قطاع السينما الذي لجأ الى المقاومة التدهور الراهن لنظام سياسي يعاني المزيد من الغموض والشطط والسخف والخطورة □ [30/30] وكل المسألة تكمن في معرفة الى اي مدى يمكن هذا النموذج الايطالي المثير ان اوروبية للقلق ان ينتشر غداً في بلد اخرى □

Table 3. The two classes corresponding to the French sentence [4/36]

The first proposed sentence is the original one and more of 50% of the words are common to the two sentences. Furthermore, the length ratio between the French sentence and the Arabic sentence is superior than 1.1 and positions of these two sentences in the databases are the same. Therefore, the exact match 1-1 aligner considers the French sentence [4/36] as a translation of the Arabic sentence [4/30].

4 Experimental Results

The sentence aligner has been tested on the MD corpus of the ARCADE II project which is composed of news articles from the French newspaper "Le Monde Diplomatique" (Chiao et al., 2006). This corpus contains 5 Arabic texts (244 sentences) aligned at the sentence level to 5 French texts (283 sentences). The test consisted to build two databases of sentences (Arabic and French) and to consider each Arabic sentence as a "query" to the French database.

To evaluate the sentence aligner, we used the following measures:

$$\text{Precision} = \frac{|A \cap A_r|}{|A|} \text{ and Recall} = \frac{|A \cap A_r|}{|A_r|}$$

A corresponds to the set of alignments provided by the sentence aligner and $\mathbf{A_r}$ corresponds to the set of the correct alignments.

The results we obtained at sentence level (Table 4) show an average precision around 97% and an average recall around 93%. These results do not take into account alignments which are partially correct (Fuzzy match 1-1 alignment).

Parallel Text	Precision	Recall
1	0.969	0,941
2	0,962	0,928
3	0,985	0,957
4	0,983	0,952
5	0,966	0,878

Table 4. Results of alignment at sentence level

Analysis of these results shows that our sentence aligner is not sensitive to missing sentences. This is because the first criterion used by our aligner is not related to surface information (sentence position or sentence length) but on the semantic intersection of these sentences.

Moreover, we have noted that precision depends on the discriminate terms which can occur in the source and target sentences.

5 Conclusion and Perspectives

We have proposed a new approach to sentence alignment based on a cross-language information retrieval model combining different information sources (bilingual lexicon, sentence length and sentence position). The results we obtained show correct precision and recall even when the parallel corpus includes changes in sentence order and missing sentences. This is due to the non-sequential strategy used by the sentence aligner. In future work, we plan to improve the alignment with syntactic structures of source and target sentences and to use the aligned bilingual parallel corpus as a translation memory in a computer-aided translation tool.

References

Abuleil S., and Evens M. 2004. Named Entity Recognition and Classification for Text in Arabic. In *Proceedings of IASSE-2004.*

Besançon R., de Chalendar G., Ferret O., Fluhr C., Mesnard O., and Naets H. 2003. Concept-Based Searching and Merging for Multilingual Information Retrieval: In *Proceedings of CLEF-2003.*

Brown P., Lai L., and Mercier L. 1991. Aligning Sentences in Parallel Corpora. In *Proceedings of ACL-1991.*

Chiao Y. C., Kraif O., Laurent D., Nguyen T., Semmar N., Stuck F., Véronis J., and Zaghouani W. 2006. Evaluation of multilingual text alignment systems: the ARCADE II project. In *Proceedings of LREC-2006.*

Darwish K. 2002. Building a Shallow Arabic Morphological Analyzer in One Day. In *Proceedings of ACL-2002.*

Debili F. and Zouari L. 1985. Analyse morphologique de l'arabe écrit voyellé ou non fondée sur la construction automatique d'un dictionnaire arabe, *Cognitiva*, Paris.

Debili F. and Sammouda E. 1992. Appariement des Phrases des Textes Bilingues. In *Proceedings of the 14th International Conference on Computational Linguistics.*

Fluhr C., Bisson F., and Elkateb F. 2000. *Parallel text alignment using cross-lingual information retrieval techniques.* Boston: Kluwer Academic Publishers.

Gale W.A. and Church K. W. 1991. A program for aligning sentences in bilingual corpora. In *Proceedings of the 29th Annual Meeting of Association for Computational Linguistics.*

Gaussier E. 1995. *Modèles statistiques et patrons morphosyntaxiques pour l'extraction de lexiques bilingues.* Ph.D. Thesis, Paris VII University.

Grefenstette G. 1997. *Cross-language information retrieval.* Boston: Kluwer Academic Publishers.

Grefenstette G., Semmar N., and Elkateb-Gara F. 2005. Modifying a Natural Language Processing System for European Languages to Treat Arabic in Information Processing and Information Retrieval Applications. In *Proceedings of ACL-2005 Workshop.*

Kay M. and Röscheisen M. 1993. *Text-translation alignment.* Computational Linguistics, Special issue on using large corpora, Volume 19, Issue 1.

Larkey L. S., Ballesteros L., and Connel M. E. 2002. Improving Stemming for Arabic Information Retrieval: Light Stemming and Co-occurrence Analysis. In *Proceedings of the 25th annual international ACM SIGIR conference on Research and development in information retrieval.*

Melamed I. D. 1996. A Geometric Approach to Mapping Bitext Correspondence. In *Proceedings of the Conference on Empirical Methods in Natural Language Processing.*

Papageorgious H., Cranias, L., and Piperidis, S. 1994. Automatic Alignment in Parallel Corpora. In *Proceedings of the 32nd Annual Meeting of the Association for Computational Linguistics.*

Salton G. and McGill M. 1983. *Introduction to Modern Information retrieval.* New York: McGraw Hill.

An Arabic Slot Grammar Parser

Michael C. McCord

IBM T. J. Watson Research Center
P.O.B. 704
Hawthorne, NY 10532
mcmccord@us.ibm.com

Violetta Cavalli-Sforza
Language Technologies Institute
Carnegie Mellon University
5000 Forbes Avenue
Pittsburgh, PA 15213
violetta@cs.cmu.edu

Abstract

We describe a Slot Grammar (SG) parser for Arabic, ASG, and new features of SG designed to accommodate Arabic as well as the European languages for which SGs have been built. We focus on the integration of BAMA with ASG, and on a new, expressive SG grammar formalism, SGF, and illustrate how SGF is used to advantage in ASG.

1 Introduction

In this paper we describe an initial version of a Slot Grammar parser, **ASG**, for Arabic. Slot Grammar (SG) (McCord, 1980. 1993) is dependency-oriented, and has the feature that deep structure (via logical predicate arguments) and surface structure are both shown in parse trees.

A new formalism **SGF** (**S**lot **G**rammar **F**ormalism) for SG syntax rules has been developed (McCord, 2006), and the ASG syntax rules are written in SGF. SGF is largely declarative, and can be called "object-oriented" in a sense we will explain. The rules in SGF all have to do with slot filling.

ASG uses BAMA (Buckwalter, 2002), in a version from Qamus, as its morphological analyzer. All the internal processing of ASG is done with the Buckwalter Arabic transliteration – though of course ASG can take real Arabic script (in UTF-8 form) as input. We use BAMA features in the processing (and parse trees), but augmented with other features more unique to ASG. The Penn Arabic Treebank (ATB), which also uses BAMA features, has served as a development guide in the work. But SG is a rule-based system, and there is no automatic training from the ATB.

Prior to this work, SGs had been written for English (McCord), German (Claudia Gdaniec), and for the Romance languages (Esméralda Manandise) Spanish, French, Italian and Portuguese. For handling Arabic, there have been two main new adaptations of SG.

One adaptation is in the treatment of features in the form that BAMA delivers. This treatment includes a *feature lexicon* in ASG, which can specify two kinds of relations among features, which we will describe below. We also take steps to handle the large number of analyses returned by BAMA. Special treatment of features appears as well in the SGF syntax rules. The other main adaptation is in the treatment of clitics, where special things happen in Arabic for proclitics.

Although the basic ideas of SG have not changed in treating Arabic, ASG has been serving as a test bed for the new syntax rule formalism SGF.

Overall, the design of the SG system has become neater by including Arabic as well as the European languages. For instance, the new treatment of features generalizes the existing treatment in the German SG. And the new treatment of clitics will make the treatment of clitics for the Romance languages neater.

In Section 2, we discuss the ASG feature system. Section 3 briefly describes the ASG slot frame lexicon. Sections 4 and 5 deal with syntactic analysis. In Section 6, we discuss current performance of ASG (coverage and speed), and in Section 7, related work.

Proceedings of the 5th Workshop on Important Unresolved Matters, pages 81–88,
Prague, Czech Republic, June 2007.

2 The Feature System

Features for an SG parser for language *X* are specified externally as character strings, listed by the grammar writer in the *feature lexicon* *X*feas.lx (Arfeas.lx for Arabic). Internally, features are represented in two ways, for efficient processing: (1) The features themselves are "atoms", represented by integers. (2) The set of features for a parse node is represented by a bit string, where each feature atom is assigned a bit position. For ASG, these bit strings are currently of length 512. But these internal representations are invisible to the grammar writer.

In the set of features for a node, some subsets can be viewed disjunctively. For instance if a noun is ambiguously singular or plural, it might have both features `sg` and `pl`. This situation occurs very much for Arabic text input because of the ambiguity due to unvocalized script. In order not to choke the parse space, the SG-BAMA interface combines some BAMA analyses, basically ones that have the same stem and POS, so that nodes have disjunctive BAMA features. But agreement rules or slot filler constraints often reduce the ambiguity. Such rules, specified in a perspicuous way in SGF, as we will see below, are implemented internally by intersecting the bit string representations of relevant feature sets.

For ASG, there are two categories of features. One category consists of BAMA compound features like

```
NOUN+NSUFF_FEM_PL+CASE_DEF_ACC
```

(indicating a feminine plural definite accusative noun). Although such features are compound in intent, they are treated as atomic symbols by ASG (as are all features specified in *X*feas.lx).

Features of the other category are more special to ASG. Some of them have to do with syntactic structure (like presence of an overt subject), and others are morphological. Typical morphological features are standard, simple ones that appear in sets of values for attributes like case, number, gender, and definiteness – for example:

```
nom, acc, gen
sg, dual, pl
m, f,
def, indef
```

Besides declaring features, *X*feas.lx can specify relations between features. One way is to specify simple hierarchical relations. An entry of the form

$x < y \ldots z \ldots$

specifies that feature *x* implies features *y* ... *z*. This means for instance that if the feature *x* is marked on a node, then a test in the grammar for feature *y* will succeed. Hierarchical information like this is stored internally in bit string arrays and allows efficient processing.

If an entry is of the form

$x < \ldots > u \ldots v$

then we say that *x* *extends* the feature set {*u* ... *v*}, and *x* is an *extending* feature. The basic idea is that *x* is a kind of abbreviation for the disjunction of the set {*u* ... *v*}, but *x* may appear on a node independently of that set. We will explain the exact meaning in the section below on the syntax rules. A typical example of an extending feature rule in Arfeas.lx is as follows:

```
gen < >
  NOUN+NSUFF_FEM_DU_GEN
  NOUN+NSUFF_FEM_PL+CASE_DEF_GEN
  NOUN+NSUFF_FEM_PL+CASE_INDEF_GEN
   . . .
```

where we list all BAMA compound features that include a genitive subfeature. Rules in the syntax component can test simply for extending features like `gen`, as we will see below. The syntax component does not even mention BAMA features. But this representational scheme allows us to keep BAMA compound features as units -- and this is important, because the morphological analysis (with ambiguities shown) requires such groupings. The internal representation of an extending feature relationship of *x* to {*u* ... *v*} associates with the atom for *x* the disjunction of the bit strings for *u* ... *v*, and the processing is quite efficient.

Although the features in *X*feas.lx are generally morphosyntactic, and have internal atom and bit string position representations in limited storage areas, SG also allows open-ended features, which may be used in the SG lexicon and tested for in the syntax component. These are typically semantic features.

3 The SG Lexicon

Although BAMA contains lexicons for doing Arabic morphological analysis, an SG needs its *SG lexicon* to drive syntactic analysis and help produce parse trees that show (deep) predicate argument structure. The main ingredients associated with index words in an SG lexicon are *sense frames.* A sense frame can specify a part of speech (POS), features (typically semantic features), a *slot frame*, and other ingredients. The most important ingredient is the slot frame, which consists of an ordered list of *(complement) slots.* Slots can be thought of as grammatical relations, but also as names for logical arguments for word sense predicates. An example from the ASG lexicon, called Ar.lx, is:

```
Eoniy < v (obj n fin)
```

This says that `Eoniy` (عْنِي) is a verb (stem) with a direct object slot (`obj`) which can be filled by either an NP (indicated by the `n`) or a finite VP (indicated by the `fin`). A slot can be either an atomic symbol or a list of the form

(*SlotName* $Option_1$ ... $Option_n$)

where the options are terms that specify conditions on the fillers of the slot. If no options are specified, then defaults are used. The `Eoniy` (عْنِي) example shows no subject slot, but the default is that every verb has a subject slot (even though it may not be overtly filled). One can specify a subject slot (`subj`) if it needs non-default options.

For the index words for ASG, we are currently using vocalized stems – stems as in the ATB, or as produced by BAMA. To produce a starter for Ar.lx, we extracted stems from the ATB, listed by frequency, and associated default sense frames based on the BAMA features in the ATB. Using vocalized stems entails some repetition of sense frames, since there can be more than one vocalized stem for a given word sense.

Index words in the SG lexicon can also be multiwords. Some multiword entries occur in Ar.lx.

Morpholexical analysis for ASG combines BAMA analysis with look-up in Ar.lx. BAMA provides morphological features (BAMA compound features) associated with vocalized stems. Also, an algorithm in ASG separates clitics out of the BAMA analyses and represents them in a form convenient for the parser. The vocalized stems are looked up in Ar.lx, and the sense frames found there (if look-up is successful) are merged with compatible analyses from BAMA. If look-up in Ar.lx fails, then the BAMA analyses can still be used, with default slot frames assigned. In the other direction, look-up in BAMA may fail, and special entries in Ar.lx can cover such words (specifying morphological features as well as slot frames).

4 The Parsing Algorithm

The SG parser is a bottom-up chart parser. Initial chart elements are one-word (or one-multiword) phrases that arise from morpholexical analysis. All further chart elements arise from binary combinations of a *modifier* phrase *M* with a *higher* phrase *H*, where *M* fills a slot *S* in *H*. The slot *S* could be a complement slot which is stored with *H*, having arisen from the lexical slot frame of the word sense head of *H*. Or *S* could be an adjunct slot associated with the POS of *M* in the syntax rule component *X*.gram. In both cases, the conditions for filling *S* are specified in *X*.gram. The parser attaches postmodifiers first, then premodifiers.

Normally, *M* and *H* will be existing adjacent phrases in the chart. But there is an interesting treatment of clitics that is especially relevant for Arabic. The SG data structure for a phrase *P* includes two fields for clitics associated with the head word of *P* – a list of proclitics, and a list of enclitics. Each clitic is itself a (one-word) phrase data structure, ready to be used for slot filling. So the parsing algorithm can combine not only adjacent phrases in the chart in the normal way, but can also combine a phrase with one of its clitics. For Arabic, all enclitics (typically pronouns) for a phrase *P* are attached to *P* (by postmodification) before *P* enters into any other slot filling. On the other side, proclitics (typically conjunctions and prepositions) of *P* are used only as higher phrases where *P* is the modifier. But a proclitic can get "passed upwards" before it is treated as a higher phrase. A non-deterministic option in the parser is that a phrase *M* becomes a premodifier of an adjacent phrase *H* in the chart, and the proclitic list of *M* is passed up to become the proclitic list of *H*. For instance a conjunction like "w"/"wa" [وَ , "and"] might be attached as a proclitic to the first word in a (premodifying) subject of a clause *C*, and the conjunction proclitic gets passed upwards until it finally takes C as a postconjunct modifier.

Although SG is a rule-based system, it does use a numerical scoring system for phrases during parsing. Real numbers are attached to phrases, indicating, roughly, how likely it is that the phrase is a good analysis of what it spans. Partial analyses (phrases) can be pruned out of the chart if their scores are too bad. Also, final parses get ranked by their scores. Scores can arise from rules in the syntax component, in the lexicon, or in the shell. A general rule in the shell is that complement slots are preferred over adjunct slots. The specific values of scores are normally determined by the grammar writer, with regression testing.

5 The ASG Syntax Rule Component

In an SG syntax rule component *X*.gram (Ar.gram for Arabic), the rules are written in the formalism SGF (McCord, 2006). Each rule deals with slot filling, and is either a complement slot rule or an adjunct slot rule. Each rule is of the form

S < *Body*

where *S* is the *index,* which is a complement slot for a complement slot rule, or a POS for an adjunct slot rule. The *Body* is basically a logical expression (in a form we will describe) which is true iff the corresponding slot filling can succeed. The rules can be viewed largely declaratively, even though there are some operators that look like commands.

The rule system is applied by the parsing algorithm when it is looking at specific phrases *M* and *H* that are adjacent or have a clitic relationship, and asking whether *M* can fill a slot in *H*. For a yet unfilled complement slot *S* of *H*, with a chosen slot option, the parser looks for the complement slot rule in *X*.gram indexed by *S,* and applies its body, requiring that to be true before doing the slot filling. And the parser also looks at the POS of *M*, finds the corresponding adjunct slot rule indexed by that POS, and applies its body. In this case, the body determines what the adjunct slot and option are; and it can do so non-deterministically: The body may be a disjunction, with operator ||, of several sub-bodies, which are all tried for insertion of the filled version of *H* into the chart. Complement slot rules can also use the infix operator || for disjunctions of the body on the top level, but in this case the || behaves deterministically – as in an if-then-else.

A simple example of a complement slot rule is the following, for the object of a preposition:

```
objprep <
   ri
   (opt n)
   (mpos noun)
   (extmf gen)
   (removemf nom acc)
   satisfied
```

The body is a sequence of tests which are viewed conjunctively. The first test, `ri`, means that the filler *M* is on the "right" of *H* (a postmodifier). The `opt` test checks that the slot option is `n`, requiring an NP. The next test requires that the filler *M* has POS `noun`. In SGF rules, the letter `m` in operators indicates the filler *M* as an implicit operand, and `h` indicates the higher phrase *H*.

The term `(extmf gen)` is an *ext*ending feature test on *M* for the feature `gen` (genitive). This will succeed iff either `gen` is marked explicitly on *M* or *M* has at least one of the BAMA features associated with `gen` in the extending feature rule for `gen` in Arfeas.lx (see Section 2). The test `(removemf nom acc)` always succeeds, and it will remove explicit occurrences of `nom` or `acc` on *M*, as well as any BAMA features associated with those features by extending feature rules.

Finally, the test `satisfied` succeeds iff *M* has no unfilled obligatory complement slots.

The syntax of the SGF formalism is Cambridge Polish (Lisplike), except for the uses of the binary operators < and ||. There are quite a number of "built-in" operators in SGF, and many of them can take any number of arguments.

Tests in SGF can be nested; some operators, including all the logical operators, can contain other tests as arguments. We mentioned that SGF is "object-oriented" in a certain sense. In any given test, however much embedded, there is always a *phrase in focus*, which is an implicit argument of the test. The phrase in focus can be considered like `this` in object-oriented languages. The default phrase in focus on top-level tests is *M* (the modifier). But some operators can shift the focus to another phrase, and this can happen an unlimited number of times in nested tests. For example, a test of the form

(rmod $Test_1$ ... $Test_n$)

searches the postmodifiers of the current phrase in focus and succeeds iff, for one of them as a new phrase in focus, all of the test arguments are satisfied. This scheme allows for quite compact expressions for searching and testing parse trees.

Now let us look at (a modified form of) an adjunct slot rule in Ar.gram, for adjectives that postmodify nouns:

```
adj <
   ri
   (hf noun)
   (agreef nom acc gen)
   (agreef def indef)
   (if (& (exthf pl) (nhf h))
       /* then */
       (extmf sg f)
       /* else */
       (& (agreef sg pl dual)
          (agreef m f) ) )
   satisfied
   (setslot nadj)
   (setopt aj)
```

So the filler *M* should be an adjective phrase. The first two tests check that *M* postmodifies *H*, and *H* is a noun phrase. The main operator here is **agreef**, which works with a list of extending features. The list of features should consist of the possible values of an attribute like case, number, gender, etc. The **agreef** test will succeed iff *M* and *H* agree along this dimension. For at least one of the argument features, both *M* and *H* should have this feature (as an extending feature). Furthermore, **agreef** takes care of reducing feature ambiguity in *M* and *H* (if it succeeds): If *x* is an argument feature such that one of *M* and *H* has *x* (as an extending feature) but the other does not, then *x* is removed from the other (as an extending feature).

For the **adj** rule at hand, the **if** statement can be interpreted as follows: If *H* (the noun) is plural and not human, then *M* (the adjective) must be singular and feminine; otherwise *M* and *H* must agree in number and gender. The actual current rule in Ar.gram skips the agreement test for plural non-human nouns, because we do not currently have enough marking of the human (**h**) features.

For subject-verb agreement, we have the situation that verbs do not use the same extending feature names as nouns do. (This has to do with corresponding BAMA features.) To handle this, **agreef** can take as arguments *pairs* of features, like **(sg vsg)**, where the first element is checked for *M* (the subj noun), and the second is checked for *H* (the verb). Here is a shortened form of the subject slot rule of ASG, which contains the current subject-verb agreement rule for ASG:

```
subj <
   (opt n)
   (mpos noun)
   (if (mf pron)
    /* then */
     (& (agreef (m vm) (f vf))
        (agreef (sg vsg)
                (pl vpl)
                (dual vdual))
        (agreef (pers1 vpers1)
                (pers2 vpers2)
                (pers3 vpers3)) )
    /* else */
     (& (exthf vpers3)
       (if (| (^ (extmf pl)) (mf h))
          (&
            (agreef (m vm) (f vf))
            (if le
               /* subj before verb */
               (agreef (sg vsg)
                       (pl vpl)
                       (dual vdual))
               /*subj after verb: */
               (exthf vsg) ) ) ) )
   )
```

The agreement part is the outer **if** test, and can be interpreted as follows:

1. If *M* is a pronoun, then *M* agrees with *H* in gender, number and person;
2. else *H* must be 3rd-person and if *M* is non-plural or human, then:
   a. *M* agrees with *H* in gender and
   b. if *M* premodifies *H* then it agrees with *H* in number,
   c. else *H* is singular.

This formulation shows the way we are currently ignoring agreement for plural non-human nouns, until we get human markings on nouns.

Now let us illustrate how an adjunct slot rule can overcome a seeming problem for dependency grammars when there is a "missing head word" for a phrase. Consider n the sentence shown in Figure 1, along with its ASG parse tree.

وهذه ظاهرة شائعة جداً قد يسببها الخوف او الاضطرابات المعوية.

wh*h ZAhrp $A}Ep jdAF qd ysbbhA Alxwf Aw AlADTrAbAt AlmEwyp.

[This is a very common phenomenon, which may be caused by fear or intestinal disorder.]

```
-----------------------------------------------------------------------
o----------- top     wa(111,u,1)        noun pron
`----------- rconj   h`*ihi(1)          noun pron
  `--------- npred   ZAhir(2)           noun sg cn def indef nom f
    `------- nadj    $A}iE(3)           adj sg def indef nom acc gen f
    | `----- adjpost jid~(4)            noun cn indef acc qualnoun
    | .----- vadv    qad(5)             adv
    `-+----- nrel    sab~ib(6,8,113)    verb pronobj
      `----- obj(n)  hA(113)            noun pron acc encliticf
      | .--- lconj   xawof(7)           noun cn def nom acc gen
      `-+--- subj(n) Oaw(8,7,9)         noun pl cn def nom acc f
        `--- rconj   {iDoTirAb(9)       noun pl cn def nom acc gen f
          `- nadj    miEawiy~(10)       adj sg def nom acc gen f
-----------------------------------------------------------------------
```

Figure 1. Handling a "missing head word"

Here Arabic does without a form of "be". In the ATB, the parse tree shows an S node with three daughters:

```
(S
  (CONJ wa)
  (NP-SBJ
    (DEM_PRON_F h`*ihi))
  (NP-PRD
    (NP (NOUN… ZAhir+ap+N))
      ... )
)
```

Since the ATB does not use a dependency tree scheme, there is no need for a word acting as a verb head of this S.

In ASG we solve the problem of the "missing head word" by letting the "clause" be a nominal phrase with head **h`*ihi** [هذه "this"] (this is the subj in the ATB tree), where the predicate NP fills an adjunct slot **npred** of the head NP. Logically, this is not unreasonable, because adjuncts often predicate logically on the phrase they modify. And a predicate NP for a "be" verb can do just that.

The **npred** rule in Ar.gram is as follows (in abbreviated form):

```
noun <
    ri
    (hf noun)
    (exthf nom)
    (extmf nom)
    (^ (mf propn) (hf propn))
    (nhf ri1 num)
    satisfied
    (^ (lmod lconj (rmod nrel)))
    (removehf acc gen)
    (removemf acc gen)
    (setslot npred)
    (setopt n)
```

The rule is indexed under the POS **noun**, since the **npred** filler *M* is an NP. (Actually the **noun** rule has several other disjunctive components, separated by the operator ||, for other ways NPs can modify other phrases as adjuncts.) So this rule requires that *M* postmodifies *H*, *H* is an NP, both *M* and *H* have extending features **nom**, neither *M* nor *H* is a proper noun, *H* has no postmodfiers, and is not a number, and *H* is satisfied. The test

```
(^ (lmod lconj (rmod nrel)))
```

illustrates two focus-shifting operations (see above). This says that it is not the case that *M* has a preconjunct which has a postmodifying relative clause. Finally, the rule removes the extending features **acc** and **gen** from both *H* and *M*, sets the adjunct slot to **npred**, and sets its option to **n**.

The parse in Figure 1 illustrates several other interesting features of Arabic syntax, for instance the resumptive pronoun in the relative clause (adjunct slot **nrel**). And this pronoun is an enclitic, treated by the ASG methods described in Section 4. (The conjunction "wa" in the tree is marked as a noun, because (coordinating) conjunctions in SG inherit features from their conjuncts. In SG, a phrase's features are carried on its head word.)

6 Performance of ASG

Since SG has its own linguistic choices (including being a dependency grammar), it is difficult to measure ASG automatically against the ATB without considerable conversion efforts. We plan to look into comparisons with the Prague Treebank (Hajič et al., 2006), but have not had time yet. The best approach, however, may be to create a treebank that simply uses the ASG design. The SG system has some tools for doing that – using SG parsing as a starter, and hand-correcting the trees.

For the immediate purposes of getting some idea of where ASG currently stands, we did a short measurement (hand-scored) on 20 untrained-on segments from the ATB chosen at random, scoring only the first (highest-ranked) parse for each segment. The scoring consisted of marking each parse tree node *N* for *correctness* of *N* in the sense that *N* has the correct mother node and the correct POS. (The parser does make an assignment of POS and mother for every word/node, even when there is no complete (segment-spanning) parse for the segment.) Note that correctness of all mother nodes implies correct tree shape. With this measurement, the percentage of correct nodes in the test set was 64%.

On 1,000 sentences from ATB3 of length 13 to 20 words, the percentage of complete parses (phrase analyses that span the whole segment) was 72% (with no guarantee of correctness of these parses).

Speed of ASG analysis seems good. On the 1,000 sentences mentioned above, parsing was at the rate of 2,500 words per second (on a laptop). This is with SGF being used in *interpreted* mode. There is a compiler for SGF (compiling *X*.gram to a C program) that provides about a twofold speed-up for syntactic analysis, although the compiler is not currently up-to-date with the latest set of operators for SGF.

For the morpholexical processing part of analysis, the rate was 10,000 words per second. This includes look-up and morphology in BAMA, and look-up in Ar.lx – the complete morpholexical process.

7 Related Work

Surprisingly little information is available regarding existing Arabic parsers and their performance, though some commercial parsers must exist. Until very recently, the focus of published research for Arabic NLP has been on low-level forms of processing, including morphological analysis, part-of-speech tagging, automatic diacriticization, and named entity transliteration; and frequently the term "parsing" in the context of Semitic languages refers to morphological and not syntactic parsing.

One symbolic approach to parsing Arabic (Othman et al., 2003, 2004) uses a unification-based grammar formalism and a chart parser implemented in Prolog. Information in the lexicon on "subject rationality" and "object rationality" is combined with "rationality" features on head nouns and noun phrases to eliminate some of the choices proposed by the morphological analyzer. No information is provided regarding the coverage of the grammar or the performance of the parser.

More performance data is available for two related statistical parsers trained on Arabic treebank data. Bikel's (2004) implementation of the Collins (2003) parser, trained on the Arabic TreeBank 1 (ATB1), reached recall/precision = 75.4/76.0 on sentences of 40 words or less and 72.5/73.4 on all sentences. Kulick et al. (2006) used the Bikel parser on a revised version of the ATB1 with results comparable to Bikel, and then on ATB3, where initial performance dropped slightly. A number of successive improvements allowed the parser to achieve recall/precision = 78.14/80.26 on sentences of 40 words or less and 73.61/75.64 on all sentences. The two most substantial improvements were obtained by changing the handling of punctuation and choosing a tagset that preserves a bit more information than the severely reduced one distributed with the ATB segments.

Other statistical parsers that have been used with Arabic include one trained on a segment of the Prague Arabic Dependency TreeBank (Hajič et al.,

2004) and then used to assist in the annotation of the remainder, but little seems to be published about its performance. The Stanford Parser has been used with Arabic (http://nlp.stanford.edu/downloads/ lex-parser.shtml), but no specific performance information could be found. It is based on the ideas that there are advantages in factoring out the phrase structure tree and the lexical dependency tree models and estimating them separately, and that significant improvements can be achieved without including any lexical dependency information by adding a few linguistically motivated annotations to phrase structure tree models (Klein and Manning, 2002, 2003).

Finally Chiang et al. (2006) used both Bikel's (2002) and Chiang's (2000) parsers to develop different approaches to parsing text in Levantine Arabic based on the Arabic Treebank data.

Even less information was found for parsing of other Semitic Languages (with the exception of http://www.cs.technion.ac.il/~winter/Corpus-Project/project-description.html) and Wintner's (1998) discussion of Hebrew syntax form a computational perspective. However, while the authors are not very familiar with this language, known similarities with Arabic give us reason to believe that some of our work on ASG could be readily reusable for Hebrew SG.

References

Daniel M. Bikel. 2002. Design of a multi-lingual, parallel processing statistical parsing engine. In *Proceedings of International Conference on Human Language Technology Research* (HLT).

Daniel M. Bikel. 2004. *On the Parameter Space of Lexicalized Statistical Parsing Models*. PhD thesis, Department of Computer and Information Sciences, University of Pennsylvania.

Tim Buckwalter. 2002. *Arabic Morphological Analyzer Version 1.0*. Linguistic Data Consortium catalog number LDC2002L49, ISBN 1-58563-257-0.

David Chiang. 2000. Statistical parsing with an automatically-extracted tree adjoining grammar. *In Proceedings of the 38th Meeting of the Association for Computational Linguistics (ACL'00)*, Hong Kong, China, 456–463.

David Chiang, Mona Diab, Nizar Habash, Owen Rambow, and Safiullah Sharif. 2006. Parsing Arabic Dialects. In *Proceedings of the 11th Conference of the European Chapter of the Association for Computational Linguistics*, Trento, Italy, 369–376.

Michael Collins. 2003. Head-driven statistical models for natural language parsing. *Computational Linguistics*, 29:589–637.

Jan Hajič, Otakar Smrž, Petr Zemánek, Jan Šnaidauf, and Emanuel Beška. 2004. Prague Arabic Dependency Treebank: Development in Data and Tools. *In Proceedings of NEMLAR 2004*.

Jan Hajič et al. 2006. *Prague Dependency Treebank Version 2.0*. Linguistic Data Consortium catalog number LDC2006T01, ISBN 1-58563-370-4.

Seth Kulick, Ryan Gabbard, and Mitchell Marcus. 2006. Parsing the Arabic Treebank: Analysis and Improvements. In Hajič J. and Nivre, J. (eds.): *Proceedings of the TLT 2006,* pp. 31-42. Institute of Formal and Applied Linguistics, Prague, Czech Republic.

Dan Klein and Christopher D. Manning. 2002. Fast Exact Inference with a Factored Model for Natural Language Parsing. In *Advances in Neural Information Processing Systems* 15 (NIPS 2002).

Dan Klein and Christopher D. Manning. 2003. Accurate Unlexicalized Parsing. In *Proceedings of the 41st Meeting of the Association for Computational Linguistics*.

Michael C. McCord. 1980. Slot Grammars. *Computational Linguistics*, 6:31-43.

Michael C. McCord. 1993. Heuristics for Broad-Coverage Natural Language Parsing. In *Proceedings of the ARPA Human Language Technology Workshop*. Morgan-Kaufmann, 127-132.

Michael C. McCord. 2006. *A Formal System for Slot Grammar*. Technical Report RC 23976, IBM T.J. Watson Research Center.

E Othman, K Shaalan, A Rafea. 2003. A Chart Parser for Analyzing Modern Standard Arabic Sentence. In *Proceedings of the MT Summit IX Workshop on Machine Translation*.

E Othman, K Shaalan, and A Rafea. 2004. Towards Resolving Ambiguity in Understanding Arabic Sentences. In *Proceedings of NEMLAR 2004*.

Shuly Wintner. 1998. Towards a linguistically motivated computational grammar for Hebrew. In *Proceedings of the ACL-98 Workshop on Computational Approaches to Semitic Languages*, 82-88.

Improved Arabic Base Phrase Chunking with a new enriched POS tag set

Mona T. Diab
Center for Computational Learning Systems
Columbia University
mdiab@cs.columbia.edu

Abstract

Base Phrase Chunking (BPC) or shallow syntactic parsing is proving to be a task of interest to many natural language processing applications. In this paper, A BPC system is introduced that improves over state of the art performance in BPC using a new part of speech tag (POS) set. The new POS tag set, ERTS, reflects some of the morphological features specific to Modern Standard Arabic. ERTS explicitly encodes definiteness, number and gender information increasing the number of tags from 25 in the standard LDC reduced tag set to 75 tags. For the BPC task, we introduce a more language specific set of definitions for the base phrase annotations. We employ a support vector machine approach for both the POS tagging and the BPC processes. The POS tagging performance using this enriched tag set, ERTS, is at 96.13% accuracy. In the BPC experiments, we vary the feature set along two factors: the POS tag set and a set of explicitly encoded morphological features. Using the ERTS POS tagset, BPC achieves the highest overall $F_{\beta=1}$ of 96.33% on 10 different chunk types outperforming the use of the standard POS tag set even when explicit morphological features are present.

1 Introduction

Base Phrase Chunking (BPC), also known as shallow syntactic parsing, is the process by which adjacent words are grouped together to form non-recursive chunks in a sentence. The base chunks form phrases such as verb phrases, noun phrases and adjective phrases, etc. An English example of base phrases is *[I]$_{NP}$ [would eat]$_{VP}$ [red luscious apples]$_{NP}$ [on Sundays]$_{PP}$*. The BPC task is proving to be an enabling step that is useful to many natural language processing (NLP) applications such as information extraction and semantic role labeling (Hacioglu & Ward, 2003). In English, these applications have shown robust relative performance when exploiting BPC when compared to using full syntactic parses. In general, BPC is appealing as an enabling technology since state of the art performance for BPC is higher ($F_{\beta=1}$ 95.48%) than that for full syntactic parsing ($F_{\beta=1}$ 90.02%) in English (Collins, 2000; Kudo & Matsumato, 2000). Moreover, since BPC had been cast as a classification problem by Ramshaw and Marcus (1995), the task is performed with greater efficiency and is easily portable to new languages in a supervised manner (Diab et al., 2004; Diab et al., 2007). For Arabic, BPC is especially interesting as it constitutes a viable alternative to full syntactic parsing due to the low performance in Arabic full syntactic parsing (labeled $F_{\beta=1}$ = ~80% compared to $F_{\beta=1}$=91.44% for BPC) (Bikel, 2004; Diab et al., 2007; Kulick et al., 2006).

In this paper, we present a support vector machine (SVM) based supervised method for Arabic BPC. The new BPC system achieves an $F_{\beta=1}$ of 96.33% across 10 base phrase chunk types. We vary the feature sets along two different factors: the usage of explicit morphological features, and the use of different part of speech (POS) tag sets. We introduce a new enriched POS set for Arabic which comprises 75 POS tags. The new POS tag set enriches the standard reduced POS tag set (RTS), distributed

Proceedings of the 5th Workshop on Important Unresolved Matters, pages 89–96,
Prague, Czech Republic, June 2007.

with the LDC Arabic Treebank (ATB) (Maamouri et al., 2004), by adding definiteness, gender and number information to the basic RTS. We devise an automatic POS tagger based on the enriched tag set, ERTS. We use the same unified discriminative model approach to both POS tagging and BPC. The POS tagging results using ERTS are comparable to state of the art POS tagging using RTS with an accuracy of 96.13% for ERTS and 96.15% for RTS. However, using the ERTS as a feature in the BPC task, we note an overall significant increase of 1% absolute $F_{\beta=1}$ improvement over the usage of RTS alone. Moreover, we experiment with different explicit morphological features together with the different POS tag sets with no significant improvement.

The paper is laid out as follows: Section 2 discusses state of the art related work in the field of BPC in both English and Arabic; Section 3 illustrates our approach for both POS and BPC in detail; Section 4 presents the experimental setup, results and discussions.

2 Related Work

English BPC has made a lot of head way in recent years. It was first cast as a classification problem by Ramshaw and Marcus (1995), as a problem of NP chunking. Then it was extended to include other types of base phrases by Sang and Buchholz (2000) in the CoNLL 2000 shared task. Most successful approaches are based on machine learning techniques and sequence modeling of the different labels associated with the chunks. Both generative algorithms such as HMMs and multilevel Markov models, as well as, discriminative methods such as Support Vector Machines (SVM) and conditional random fields have been used for the BPC task. The closest relevant approach to the current investigation is the work of Kudo and Matsumato (2000) (KM00) on using SVMs and a sequence model for chunking. A la Ramshaw and Marcus (1995), they represent the words as a sequence of labeled words with *IOB* annotations, where the *B* marks a word at the beginning of a chunk, *I* marks a word inside a chunk, and *O* marks those words (and punctuation) that are outside chunks. The *IOB* annotation scheme for the English example described earlier is illustrated in Table 1.

word	IOB label
I	*B-NP*
would	*B-VP*
eat	*I-VP*
red	*B-NP*
luscious	*I-NP*
apples	*I-NP*
on	*B-PP*
Sundays	*I-PP*
.	*O*

Table 1: *IOB* annotation example

KM00 develop a sequence model, YAMCHA, over the labeled sequences of words.[1] YAMCHA is based on the TinySVM algorithm (Joachims, 1998). They use a degree 2 polynomial kernel. In their work on the task of English BPC, YAMCHA achieves an overall $F_{\beta=1}$ of 93.48% on five chunk types. They report improved results of 93.91% using a combined voting scheme (Kudo & Matsumato, 2000).

As far as Arabic BPC, Diab et al. (2004 & 2007) adopt the KM00 model for Arabic using YAMCHA. They cast the Arabic data from the ATB in the *IOB* annotation scheme. They use the reduced standard LDC tag set, RTS, as their only feature. Their system achieves an overall $F_{\beta=1}$ of 91.44% on 9 chunk types.

3 Current Approach

This paper is a significant extension to the Diab et al. (2007) work. Similar to other researchers in the area of BPC, we adopt a discriminative approach. A la Ramshaw and Marcus (1995), and Kudo and Matsumato (2000), we use the IOB tagging style for modeling and classification.

Various machine learning approaches have been applied to POS and BPC tagging, by casting them as classification tasks. Given a set of features extracted from the linguistic context, a classifier predicts the POS or BPC class of a token. SVMs (Vapnik, 1995) are one such supervised machine learning algorithm, with the advantages of: discriminative training, robustness and a capability to handle a large number of (overlapping) features with good generalization per-

[1] http://www.chasen.org/ taku/software/yamcha/

formance. Consequently, SVMs have been applied in many NLP tasks with great success (Joachims, 1998; Hacioglu & Ward, 2003).

We adopt a unified tagging perspective for both the POS tagging and the BPC tasks. We address them using the same SVM experimental setup which comprises a standard SVM as a multi-class classifier (Allwein et al., 2000).

A la KM00, we use the `YAMCHA` sequence model on the SVMs to take advantage of the context of the items being compared in a vertical manner in addition to the encoded features in the horizontal input of the vectors. Accordingly, in our different tasks, we define the notion of context to be a window of fixed size around the segment in focus for learning and tagging.

3.1 POS Tagging

Modern Standard Arabic is a rich morphological language, where words are explicitly marked for case, gender, number, definiteness, mood, person, voice, tense and other features. These morphological features are explicitly encoded in the full tag set provided in the `ATB`. These full morphological tags amount to over 2000 tag types (FULL). As expected, such morphological tags are not very useful for automatic statistical syntactic parsing since they are extremely sparse.[2] Hence, the LDC introduced the reduced tag set (RTS) of 25 tags. RTS masks case, mood, gender, person, definiteness for all categories. It maintains voice and tense for verbs, and some number information for nouns, namely, marking plural vs. singular for nouns and proper nouns. Therefore, in the process it masks duality for nouns and number for all adjectives. It should be noted, however, that it is extremely useful to have these morphological tags in order to induce features. There exists a system that produces the full morphological POS tag set, MADA, with very high accuracy, 96% (Habash & Rambow, 2005).

In this work, we introduce a new tag set that explicitly marks gender, number, and definiteness for nominals (*namely*, nouns, proper nouns, adjectives and pronouns). Verbs, particles, as well as, the person feature on pronouns, are not affected by this enrichment process, since neither person nor mood are explicitly encoded. Morphological case is also not explicitly encoded in ERTS. The new tag set, ERTS, is derived from the FULL tag set where there is an explicit specification in the tag itself for the different features to be encoded. We restricted ERTS to this set of features as they tend to be explicitly marked in the surface form of unvowelized Arabic text. In ERTS, definiteness is encoded with a present (D) or an absent one. Gender is encoded with an F or an M, corresponding to Fem and Masc, respectively. Number is encoded with (Du) for dual or an (S) for plurals or the absence of any marking for singular. For example, Table 2 illustrates some words with the FULL morphological tag and their corresponding RTS and ERTS definitions.[3]

Our approach: ERTS comprises 75 tags. For the current system, only 57 tags are instantiated. We develop a POS tagger based on this new set. We adopt the `YAMCHA` sequence model based on the `TinySVM` classifier. The tagger trained for ERTS tag set uses lexical features of +/-4 character n-grams from the beginning and end of a word in focus. The context for `YAMCHA` is defined as +/-2 words around the focus word. The words before the focus word are considered with their ERTS tags. The kernel is a polynomial degree 2 kernel. We adopt the one-vs-all approach for classification, where the tagged examples for one class are considered positive training examples and instances for other classes are considered negative examples. We present results and a brief discussion of the POS tagging performance in Section 4.

3.2 Base Phrase Chunking

In this task, we use a setup similar to that of Kudo & Matsumato (2000) and Diab et al. (2004 & 2007), with the *IOB* annotation representation: Inside *I* a phrase, Outside *O* a phrase, and Beginning *B* of a phrase. However, we designate 10 types of chunked phrases. The chunk phrases identified for Arabic are *ADJP, ADVP, CONJP, INTJP, NP, PP, PREDP, PRTP, SBARP, VP*. Thus the task is a one of 21 classification task (since there are *I* and *B* tags for each chunk phrase type, and a single *O* tag). The 21 *IOB* tags are listed: {*O, I-ADJP, B-ADJP, I-ADVP,*

[2]Dan Bikel, personal communication.

[3]All the romanized Arabic is presented in the Buckwalter transliteration scheme (Buckwalter, 2002).

		Gloss	*FULL*	*RTS*	*ERTS*
حصيلة	*HSylp*	'outcome'	NOUN+NSUFF_FEM_SG+CASE_IND_NOM	NN	NNF
نهائية	*nhA}yp*	'final'	ADJ+NSUFF_FEM_SG+CASE_IND_NOM	JJ	JJF
حادث	*HAdv*	'accident'	NOUN+CASE_DEF_ACC	NN	NNM
النار	*AlnAr*	'the-fire'	DET+NOUN+CASE_DEF_GEN	NN	DNNM
الجماعي	*AljmAEy*	'group'	DET+ADJ+CASE_DEF_GEN	JJ	DJJM
شخصين	*$xSyn*	'two persons'	NOUN+NSUFF_MASC_DU_GEN	NN	NNMDu

Table 2: Examples of POS tag sets RTS, ERTS and FULL

B-ADVP, I-CONJP, B-CONJP, I-INTJP, B-INTJP, I-NP, B-NP, I-PP, B-PP, I-PREDP, B-PREDP, I-PRTP, B-PRTP, I-SBARP, B-SBARP, I-VP, B-VP}.

The training data is derived from the ATB using the ChunkLink software.[4] ChunkLink flattens the tree to a sequence of base (non-recursive) phrase chunks with their *IOB* labels. For example, a token occurring at the beginning of a noun phrase is labeled as *B-NP*. The following Table 3 Arabic example illustrates the *IOB* annotation scheme:

Tags	*B-VP*	*B-NP*	*I-NP*	*O*
Arabic	وقع	مساء	الجمعة	.
Translit	wqE	msA'	AljmEp	.
Gloss	happened	night	the-Friday	.

Table 3: An Arabic *IOB* annotation example

Chunklink, however, is tailored for English syntactic structures. Hence, in order to train on reasonable Arabic chunks, we modify Chunklink's output using linguistic knowledge of Arabic syntactic structures. Some of the rules used are described below (we illustrate using ERTS for ease of exposition).

• **IDAFA**: This syntactic structure marks possession in Arabic. It is syntactically the case where an indefinite noun is followed by a definite one. The Chunklink output is modified to ensure that they form a single NP. Example: مساء الجمعة *msA' AljmEp* 'night of Friday' is *IOB* annotated as [*msA'* DNN B-NP, *AljmEp* DNNM I-NP].

• **NOUN-ADJ**: Nouns followed by adjectives and they agree in their morphological features of gender, number and definiteness form a single NP chunk. Example: حصيلة نهائية رسمية *HSylp nhA}yp rsmyp* 'final official outcome' is *IOB* annotated as [*HSylp* NNF B-NP, *nhA}yp* JJF I-NP, *rsmyp* JJF I-NP]

• **Pronouns**: This is an artifact of the ATB style of clitic tokenization. All pronouns, except in nominative position in the sentence such as *hw* and *hy*, are chunk internal.

• **Interjections**: If an interjection is followed by a noun, the noun is marked as internal to the interjective phrase.

• **Prepositional Phrases**: Nouns following prepositions are considered internal to the prepositional phrase and are *IOB* annotated, I-PP.

Phrase Types: The different phrase types are described as follows.

• **ADJP**: This is an adjectival phrase. The adjectival phrase could comprise a single adjective if mentioned in isolation such as جيدا *jydA* 'well', or multiple words such as قريبا جدا *qrybA jdA* 'very soon'. The latter is *IOB* annotated [*qrybA* B-ADJP] and [*jdA* I-ADJP], respectively.

• **ADVP**: This is an adverbial phrase. It may comprise a single adverb following a verb, such as سريعا *sryEA* 'quickly', or multiple words such as لكن ها *lkn hA* 'but she'.[5] The latter is *IOB* annotated [*lkn* B-ADVP] and [*hA* I-ADVP], respectively.

• **CONJP**: This chunk marks conjunctive phrases. We see single word CONJP when the conjunction appears before a verb phrase or a prepositional phrase such the conjunction و *w* 'and'. But we also have multiword conjunctive phrases when the conjunction is followed by a noun. For instance, و الفلسطينيون *w AlflsTynywn* 'and the Palestinians'

[4]http://ilk.uvt.nl/ sabine/chunklink

[5]This is a result of the ATB clitic tokenization style.

is *IOB* annotated [*w* B-CONJP] and [*AlflsTynywn* I-CONJP].

• **INTJP**: This is an interjective phrase. The interjective phrase could comprise a single interjection if mentioned in isolation such as نعم *nEm* 'yes'. Or with multiple words such as يا اخت *yA Axt* 'Oh sister', where it is *IOB* annotated [*yA* B-INTJP] and [*Axt* I-INTJP].

• **NP**: This is a noun phrase. It may comprise a single noun or multiple nouns or a noun and one or more adjectives. In this phrase type, we see typical noun adjective constructions as in الزفاف الجماعي *AlzfAf AljmAEy* 'the group wedding', where the initial noun is marked as [*AlzfAf* B-NP], and the folowing adjective is *IOB* annotated [*AljmAEy* I-NP]. We also encounter *idafa* constructions. For example, ملك الاردن *mlk AlArdn* 'king of Jordan', where *mlk* 'king' is an indefinite noun, and *AlArdn* 'Jordan' is a definite one. This phrase is *IOB* annotated [*mlk* B-NP] and [*AlArdn* I-NP].

• **PP**: This is a prepositional phrase. The phrase starts with a preposition followed by a pronoun, noun or proper noun. If the noun or proper noun is itself the beginning of an NP, the whole NP is internal to the PP. For example, خلال حفل الزفاف الجماعي *xlAl Hfl AlzfAf AljmAEy* 'during the group wedding party', *xlAl* is the preposition and is *IOB* annotated [*xlAl* B-PP], [*Hfl* I-PP] (if *Hfl* were not preceded by a preposition it would have been annotated [*Hfl* B-NP]), then for the noun [*AlzfAf* I-PP], and finally the adjective [*AljmAEy* I-PP].

• **PREDP**: This is a predicative phrase. It typically begins with a particle إن *An* '[is]', followed by a noun phrase. For example, إن الاصلاح الديني مهمة المجددين *An AlASlAH Aldyny mhmp Almjddyn* 'religious improvement is the reformers' task'. In our data, since we do not mark recursive structures in this BPC level, only the predicative particle is *IOB* annotated with B-PREDP. If it were followed by a possessive pronoun, the pronoun is annotated I-PREDP.

• **PRTP**: This phrase type marks particles such as negative particles that precede both nouns and verbs. A particle could be single word or a complex particle phrase. An example of a simple word particle is لم *lm* 'not', and a complex one is لا سيّما *lA sy∼mA* 'not as long'. In the latter case, it is *IOB* annotated [*lA* B-PRTP] and [*sy∼mA* I-PRTP].

• **SBARP**: This phrase structure marks the subjunctive constructions. SBARP phrases typically begin with a particle meaning 'that' such as أن *An* or مما *mmA* or الذي *Al*y* followed by a verb phrase.

• **VP**: This is a verb phrase. VP phrases are typically headed by a verb. All object pronouns proceeding a verb are *IOB* annotated I-VP. Moreover, we observe cases where a VP is headed by nominals (nouns and adjectives, in particular). The majority of these nominals are the active participle. The active participle in the ATB is tagged as an adjective. Active participles in Arabic are equivalent to predicative nominals in English (gerunds). Hence, some VPs are headed by JJs. An example active participle heading a verb phrase in our data is متهما *mthmA* 'accusing'.

Our Approach: We vary two factors in our feature sets: the POS tag set, and the presence or absence of explicit morphological features. We have three possible tag sets: RTS, ERTS and the full morphological tag set (FULL). We define a set of 6 morphological features (and their possible values): CASE (*ACC, GEN, NOM, NULL*), MOOD (*Indicative, Jussive, Subjunctive, NULL*), DEF (*DEF, INDEF, NULL*), NUM (*Sing, Dual, Plural, NULL*), GEN (*Fem, Masc, NULL*), PER (*1, 2, 3, NULL*).

From the intersection of the two factors, we devise 10 different experimental conditions. The conditions always have one of the POS tag sets and either no explicit features (noFeat), all explicit features (allFeat), or some selective features of: case mood and person (CASE_MOOD_PER), or definiteness gender and number (DEF_GEN_NUM). Therefore, the experimental conditions are as follows: RTS-noFeat, RTS-allFeat, RTS-CASE_MOOD_PER, RTS-DEF_GEN_NUM, ERTS-noFeat, ERTS-allFeat, ERTS-CASE_MOOD_PER, ERTS-DEF_GEN_NUM, FULL-noFeat, FULL-allFeat.

The BPC context is defined as a window of $+/-2$ tokens centered around the focus word where all the features for the specific condition are used and the tags for the previous two tokens before the focus token are also considered.

4 Experiments and Results

4.1 Data

The dev, test and training data are obtained from ATB1v3, ATB2v2 and ATB3v2 (Maamouri et al., 2004). We adopt the same data splits introduced by Chiang et. al (2006). The corpora are all news genre. The total development data comprises 2304 sentences and 70188 tokens, the total training data comprises 18970 sentences and 594683 tokens, and the total test data comprises 2337 sentences and 69665 tokens.

We use the unvocalized Buckwalter transliterated version of the ATB. For both POS tagging and BPC, we use the gold annotations of the training and test data for preprocessing. Hence, for POS tagging, the training and test data are both gold tokenized in the ATB clitic tokenization style. And for BPC, the POS tags, the morphological features, and, the tokenization is all gold. We derive the gold ERTS deterministically from the FULL set for the BPC results reported here.

The IOB annotations on the training and gold evaluation data are derived using Chunklink followed by our linguistic fixes described in Section 3.

4.2 SVM Setup

We use the default values for YAMCHA with the C parameter set to 0.5. It has a degree 2 polynomial kernel. YAMCHA adopts a one-vs-all binarization method.

4.3 Evaluation Metric

Standard metrics of Accuracy (Acc.), Precision, Recall, and F-measure $F_{\beta=1}$, on the test data are utilized. For both POS tagging and BPC, we use the CoNLL shared task evaluation tools.[6]

4.4 Results

4.4.1 ERTS POS Tagging Results

Table 4 shows the results obtained with the YAMCHA based POS tagger, *POS-TAG*, and the results obtained with a simple baseline, *BASELINE*. *BASELINE* is a supervised baseline, where the most frequent POS tag associated with a token from the training data is assigned to it in the test set, regardless of context. If the token does not occur in the training data, the token is assigned the *NN* tag as a default tag.

POS tagset	Acc.%
RTS	96.15
ERTS	96.13
BASELINE	86.5

Table 4: Results of POS-TAG on two different tag sets RTS and ERTS

POS-TAG clearly outperforms the most frequent baseline. Looking closely at the data, the worst obtained results are for the NO_FUNC category, as it is randomly confusable with almost all POS tags. Then, the imperative verbs are mostly confused with passive verbs 50% of the time, however the test data only comprises 8 imperative verbs. VBN, passive verbs, yields an accuracy of 68% only. It is worth noting that the most frequent baseline for VBN is 21%. VBN is a most difficult category to discern in the absence of the passivization diacritic which is naturally absent in unvowelized text (our experimental setup). The overall performance on the nouns and adjectives is relatively high. However, confusing these two categories is almost always present due to the inherent ambiguity. In fact, almost all Arabic adjectives could be used as nouns in Arabic.[7]

4.4.2 Base Phrase Chunking (BPC)

Table 5 illustrates the overall obtained results by our BPC system over the different experimental conditions.

The overall results for all the conditions significantly outperform state of the art published results on Arabic BPC of $F_{\beta=1}$=91.44% in Diab et al. (2004 & 2007). This is mainly attributed to the better quality annotations associated with tailoring of the Chunklink *IOB* annotations to the Arabic language characteristics.

All the $F_{\beta=1}$ results yielded by ERTS POS tag set outperform their counterparts using the RTS POS tagset. In fact, ERTS-noFeat condition outperforms all other conditions in our experiments.

We note that adding morphological features to the RTS POS tag set helps the performance slightly

[6]http://cnts.uia.ac.be/conll2003/ner/bin/conlleval

[7]This inherent ambiguity leads to inconsistency in the ATB gold annotations.

Condition	$F_{\beta=1}$	Condition	$F_{\beta=1}$
RTS-noFeat	95.41	ERTS-noFeat	**96.33**
RTS-CASE_MOOD_PER	95.73	ERTS-CASE_MOOD_PER	**96.32**
RTS-DEF_GEN_NUM	95.8	ERTS-DEF_GEN_NUM	**96.33**
RTS-allFeat	95.97	ERTS-allFeat	**96.25**
FULL-noFeat	96.29	FULL-allFeat	96.22

Table 5: Overall $F_{\beta=1}$ % results yielded for the different BPC experimental conditions

as we see a sequence of small jumps in performance from RTS-noFeat (95.41%) to RTS-allFeat (95.97%). However adding these features to the ERTS and FULL conditions does not help. In fact, in both the allFeat conditionsfor both ERTS and FULL, we note a slight decrease. The ERTS condition performance goes down from 96.33% (ERTS-noFeat) to 96.25% (ERTS-allFeat), and the FULL condition performance goes down from 96.29% (FULL-noFeat) to 96.22% (FULL-allFeat). This suggests that the features are not adding much information over and above what is already encoded in the POS tag set, and, in fact adding the explicit morphological features might be adding noise.

There is no significant difference between using ERTS and FULL in the overall results. However, we note that ERTS conditions slightly outperform the FULL conditions. This may be attributed the consistency introduced by ERTS over FULL, i.e., if FULL is not consistent in assigning CASE or MOOD or PER, for instance, ERTS, being insensitive to these features masks these inconsistencies present in the FULL tag set.

RTS-DEF_GEN_NUM may be viewed as an explicit encoding of the features in ERTS-noFeat, however, ERTS-noFeat outperforms it. Explicitly encoding the CASE MOOD and PER features does not help ERTS, in fact we see a slight drop in overall performance. However, upon closer inspection of the results per phrase type, we note slight relative improvement on PRTP and VP chunk types performance when the CASE, MOOD and PER are explicitly encoded. In ERTS-CASE_MOOD_PER, VP yields an $F_{\beta=1}$ of 99.3% and PRTP yields 97.2%, corresponding to ERTS-noFeat where VP yields an $F_{\beta=1}$ of 99.2% and PRTP an $F_{\beta=1}$ of 96.8%.

To better assess the quality of the performance and impact of the new POS tag set, we examine closely in Table 6 the phrase types directly affected by the added information whether encoded in the POS tag set or explicitly used as independent features. These phrase types are the ADJP, INTJP, NP and PP. The PP scored highly across the board with $F_{\beta=1}$ over 99% for all conditions, hence, it is not included in Table 6.

Condition	ADJP	INTJP	NP
RTS-noFeat	68.42	55.17	92.98
RTS-CASE_MOOD_PER	69.47	59.26	93.72
RTS-DEF_GEN_NUM	71.57	**64.29**	93.71
RTS-allFeat	72.22	57.14	94.15
ERTS-noFeat	72.35	57.14	**94.92**
ERTS-CASE_MOOD_PER	**73.16**	61.54	94.86
ERTS-DEF_GEN_NUM	72.6	**64.29**	**94.92**
ERTS-allFeat	72.91	59.26	94.78
FULL-noFeat	71.84	51.85	94.81
FULL-allFeat	72.52	57.14	94.67

Table 6: $F_{\beta=1}$ Results for ADJP, INTJP, and NP, across the different experimental conditions

As illustrated in Table 6, ERTS outperforms RTS and FULL in all corresponding conditions where they have similar corresponding morphological feature settings. ERTS-noFeat yields better results than RTS-noFeat and FULL-noFeat for the three different phrase types. The INTJP phrase is the worst performing of the three phrase types, however it marks the most significant change in performance depending on the experimental condition. We note that adding explicit morphological features to the base condition RTS yields consistently better results for the three phrase types. The highest performance for NP is yielded by ERTS-noFeat and ERTS-DEF_GEN_NUM with an $F_{\beta=1}$ of 94.92%.

The highest scores yielded for ADJP (73.16) and INTJP (64.29) are in an ERTS experimental condition. We also observe a slight drop in performance in NP for the ERTS conditions when the CASE MOOD and PER features are added. This might be due to the inconsistent or confusable assignment of these different features in the ATB.

5 Conclusions and Future Work

In this paper, we address the problem of Arabic base phrase chunking, BPC. In the process, we introduce a new enriched POS tag set, ERTS, that adds definiteness, gender and number information to nominals. We present an SVM approach to both the POS tagging with ERTS and the BPC tasks. The POS tagger yields 96.13% accuracy which is comparable to the results obtained on the standard reduced tag set RTS. On the BPC front, the results obtained for all conditions are significantly better than state of the art published results. This indicates that better linguistic tailoring of the *IOB* chunks creates more consistent data. Overall, we show that using the enriched POS tag set, ERTS, yields the best BPC performance. Even using ERTS with no explicit morphological features yields better results than using RTS in all conditions with or without explicit morphological features. These results are confirmed by closely observing specific phrases that are directly affected by the change in POS tag set namely, ADJP, INTJP and NP. Our results strongly suggests that choosing the POS tag set carefully has a significant impact on higher level syntactic processing.

6 Acknowledgements

This work was funded by DARPA Contract No. HR0011-06-C-0023. Any opinions, fi ndings and conclusions or recommendations expressed in this material are those of the author and do not necessarily reflect the views of DARPA.

References

Erin L. Allwein, Robert E. Schapire, and Yoram Singer. 2000. *Reducing multiclass to binary: A unifying approach for margin classifiers*. Journal of Machine Learning Research, 1:113-141.

Daniel Bikel. 2004. *Intricacies of Collins Parser*. Computational Linguistics.

Tim Buckwalter. 2002. *Buckwalter Arabic Morphological Analyzer Version 1.0*. Linguistic Data Consortium, University of Pennsylvania, 2002. LDC Catalog No.: LDC2002L49

David Chiang, Mona Diab, Nizar Habash, Owen Rambow, and Safi ullah Shareef. 2006. *Parsing Arabic Dialects*. Proceedings of the European Chapter of ACL (EACL).

Michael Collins. 2000. *Discriminative Reranking for Natural Language Parsing*. Proceedings of the 17th International Conference on Machine Learning.

Mona Diab, Kadri Hacioglu and Daniel Jurafsky. 2004. *Automatic Tagging of Arabic Text: From Raw Text to Base Phrase Chunks*. Proceedings of North American Association for Computational Linguistics.

Mona Diab, Kadri Hacioglu and Daniel Jurafsky. 2007. *Automated Methods for Processing Arabic Text: From Tokenization to Base Phrase Chunking*. Book Chapter. In Arabic Computational Morphology: Knowledge-based and Empirical Methods. Editors Antal van den Bosch and Abdelhadi Soudi. Kluwer/Springer Publications.

Nizar Habash and Owen Rambow. 2005. *Arabic Tokenization, Morphological Analysis, and Part-of-Speech Tagging in One Fell Swoop*. Proceedings of the Conference of American Association for Computational Linguistics (ACL).

Kadri Hacioglu and Wayne Ward. 2003. *Target word Detection and semantic role chunking using support vector machines*. HLT-NAACL.

Thorsten Joachims. 1998. *Text Categorization with Support Vector Machines: Learning with Many Relevant Features*. Proc. of ECML-98, 10th European Conf. on Machine Learning.

Seth Kulick, Ryan Gabbard, and Mitch Marcus. 2006. *Parsing the Arabic Treebank: Analysis and Improvements. in* Treebanks and Linguistic Theories.

Taku Kudo and Yuji Matsumato. 2000. *Use of support vector learning for chunk identification*. Proc. of the 4th Conf. on Very Large Corpora, pages 142-144.

Mohamed Maamouri, Ann Bies, Tim Buckwalter, and Wigdan Mekki. 2004. *The Penn Arabic Treebank : Building a Large-Scale Annota ted Arabic Corpus*. NEMLAR Conference on Arabic Language Resources and Tools. pp. 102-109.

Lance A. Ramshaw and Mitchell P. Marcus. 1995. *Text Chunking using transformational based learning*. Proc. of the 3rd ACL workshop on Very Large Corpora

Erik Tjong, Kim Sang, and Sabine Buchholz. 2000. *Introduction to the CoNLL-2000 shared task: Chunking*. Proc. of the 4th Conf. on Computational Natural Language Learning (CoNLL), Lisbon, Portugal, 2000, pp. 127-132.

Vladamir Vapnik. 1995. *The Nature of Statistical Learning Theory*. Springer Verlag, New York, USA.

Smoothing a Lexicon-based POS Tagger for Arabic and Hebrew

Saib Mansour
Computer Science, Technion
Haifa, 32000, Israel
saib@cs.technion.ac.il

Khalil Sima'an
ILLC
Universiteit van Amsterdam
Amsterdam, The Netherlands
simaan@science.uva.nl

Yoad Winter
Computer Science, Technion
Haifa, 32000, Israel
and Netherlands Institute for Advanced Study
Wassenaar, The Netherlands
winter@cs.technion.ac.il

Abstract

We propose an enhanced Part-of-Speech (POS) tagger of Semitic languages that treats Modern Standard Arabic (henceforth *Arabic*) and Modern Hebrew (henceforth *Hebrew*) using the same probabilistic model and architectural setting. We start out by porting an existing Hidden Markov Model POS tagger for Hebrew to Arabic by exchanging a morphological analyzer for Hebrew with Buckwalter's (2002) morphological analyzer for Arabic. This gives state-of-the-art accuracy (96.12%), comparable to Habash and Rambow's (2005) analyzer-based POS tagger on the same Arabic datasets. However, further improvement of such analyzer-based tagging methods is hindered by the incomplete coverage of standard morphological analyzer (Bar Haim et al., 2005). To overcome this coverage problem we supplement the output of Buckwalter's analyzer with synthetically constructed analyses that are proposed by a model which uses character information (Diab et al., 2004) in a way that is similar to Nakagawa's (2004) system for Chinese and Japanese. A version of this extended model that (unlike Nakagawa) incorporates synthetically constructed analyses also for known words achieves 96.28% accuracy on the standard Arabic test set.

1 Introduction

Part-of-Speech tagging for Semitic languages has been an active topic of research in recent years. (Diab et al., 2004; Habash and Rambow, 2005; Bar-Haim et al., 2005) are some examples for this line of work on Modern Standard Arabic and Modern Hebrew. POS tagging systems aim at classifying input sequences of lexemes by assigning each such sequence a corresponding sequence of most probable POS tags. It is often assumed that for each input lexeme there is a set of *a priori* possible POS tag categories, or a probability function over them, and the tagger has to choose from this limited set of candidate categories. We henceforth use the term *lexicon* to refer to the set of lexemes in a language and the mapping that assigns each of them candidate POS tags, possibly with additional probabilities.

Two ways to obtain a lexicon can be distinguished in recent works on POS tagging in Semitic languages. *Data-driven* approaches like (Diab et al. 2004) employ the lexicon only implicitly when extracting features on possible POS tags from annotated corpora that are used for training the POS tagger. *Lexicon-based* approaches (Habash and Rambow, 2005; Bar-Haim et al., 2005) use a lexicon that is extracted from a manually constructed morphological analyzer (Buckwalter 2002 and Segal 2001 respectively).

In this paper we show that although lexicon-based taggers for Arabic and Hebrew may initially outperform data-driven taggers, they do not exhaust the advantages of data-driven approaches.

Proceedings of the 5th Workshop on Important Unresolved Matters, pages 97–103,

Consequently, we propose a hybrid model of data-driven methods and lexicon-based methods, and show its advantages over both models, in a way that is reminiscent of Nakagawa's (2004) results for Chinese and Japanese.

As a first step, we develop a Part-of-Speech tagger that treats Arabic and Hebrew using the same probabilistic model and architectural setting. We start out from MorphTagger, a lexicon-based tagger for Hebrew developed by Bar-Haim et al. (2005), which uses standard Hidden Markov Model techniques. We port the existing MorphTagger implementation to Arabic by exchanging Segal's (2001) morphological analyzer with Buckwalter's (2002) morphological analyzer, and then training the tagger on the Arabic Treebank (Maamouri et al., 2001). Remarkably, this gives state-of-the-art accuracy (96.12%) on the same Arabic datasets as Habash and Rambow (2005). To the best of our knowledge, this is the first time the same POS tagging architecture is used both for Arabic and Hebrew texts with comparable accuracy.

Despite the initial advantages of this setting, our empirical study shows that in both languages, further improvement in accuracy is hindered by the incompleteness of the morphological analyzer. By "incompleteness" we refer not only to the well-studied problem of unknown words (out-of-vocabulary). Our results show that for both Arabic and Hebrew, a more serious problem involves words for which the analyzer provides a set of analyses that does not contain the correct one. We find out that this is the case for 3% of the words in the development set. This obviously sets an upper bound on tagger accuracy using methods that are purely based on a manually constructed lexicon. We refer to this problem as the "incomplete lexicon" problem.

We focus on devising a solution to the incomplete lexicon problem by smoothing. We supplement the output of Buckwalter's analyzer with synthetically constructed analyses that are proposed by a model which uses character information (Diab et al., 2004) in a way that is similar to Nakagawa's (2004) system for Japanese. Unlike Nakagawa's method, however, our smoothing method incorporates synthetically constructed analyses also for known words, though only when all available taggings of the sentence have low probabilities according to our model. A version of this extended model achieves a modest improvement (96.28%) in accuracy over the baseline on the standard Arabic test set.

This paper is structured as follows. In section 2 we start with a brief discussion of previous work. Section 3 describes our adaptation of Bar Haim et al.'s POS tagging system to Arabic. In section 4 we show that an architecture like Bar Haim et al.'s, which relies on a morphological analyzer, is likely to suffer from coverage problems under any configuration where it is used as a stand-alone. In section 5 we present our new architecture and the method of combining the models. Section 6 concludes.

2 Relation to Previous Works

Quite a few works have dealt with extending a given POS tagger, mainly by smoothing it using extra-information about untreated words. For example, (Church, 1988) uses the simple heuristic of predicting proper nouns from capitalization. This method is not applicable to Arabic and Hebrew, which lack typographical marking of proper nouns. More advanced methods like those described by Weischedel et al. (1993) incorporate the treatment of unknown words within the probability model. Weischedel et al. use derivational and inflectional endings to infer POS tags of unknown words. Nakagawa (2004) addresses the problem of unknown words for Japanese and Chinese, and uses a hybrid method of word-level and character-level information. In his model, Nakagawa uses character information (only) when handling unknown words, claiming that in word-level methods information about known words helps to achieve higher accuracy compared to character-level models. On the other hand, when it comes to unknown words, Nakagawa uses a character-level method, which is hypothesized to be more robust in such cases than word-level methods.

Virtually all works that dealt with coverage problems of POS taggers have concentrated on the problem of "unknown" words – words that have no analysis in the initial tagging system. However, in the context of analyzer-based tagging systems, we also have to deal with the problem of "known" words that miss the correct analysis in the morphological analyzer. In the Arabic and Hebrew datasets we have examined, this problem is more severe than the unknown words problem. Unlike previous works, we propose to smooth the word-segment driven model also for "known" words. To avoid overgeneration, this is done only when all taggings of the sentence have low probability.

3 Adapting a Hebrew POS-tagger to Arabic

Bar Haim et al.'s (2005) POS tagging system, MorphTagger, was developed initially for Hebrew. Our work is mainly developed for Arabic and tested over Arabic data. Due to the similarity in the morphological processes in Hebrew and Arabic and the generality of Bar Haim et al.'s architecture, the adaptation process was fairly simple. However, as far as we know this is the first implementation of a unified model for Arabic and Hebrew that achieves state-of-the-art accuracy. MorphTagger requires two components: a morphological analyzer to produce a set of analyses for every lexeme, and a POS tagged corpus for acquiring an HMM disambiguator. The HMM disambiguator assigns a probability to every pair $\langle w_1^n, t_1^n \rangle$, where $w_1^n = w_1 ... w_n$ is a sentence and $t_1^n = t_1 .. t_n$ a corresponding sequence of POS tags hypothesized by the analyzer. This probability is approximated in a standard HMM fashion:

$$P(w_1^n, t_1^n) = P(t_1^n) P(w_1^n \mid t_1^n) = \prod_{i=1}^{n} P(t_i \mid t_{i-1}, t_{i-2}) P(w_i \mid t_i)$$

For an input sentence w_1^n, the pair $\langle w_1^n, t_1^n \rangle$ with the highest probability is selected. The language ($P(t_i \mid t_{i-1}, t_{i-2})$) and lexical ($P(w_i \mid t_i)$) models' parameters are estimated from the tagged corpus by Maximum-Likelihood Estimator (MLE) followed by Katz backoff smoothing for the language model and Add-λ smoothing for the lexical model, where a small λ=1 count is given to analyzes provided by the analyzer but not found in the training corpus. Furthermore, MorphTagger employs an array of other smoothing techniques explained in Bar Haim et al. (2005).

Our implementation of MorphTagger for Arabic was developed using Buckwalter's (2002) Morphological Analyzer v1.0 (BMA1.0), and the Arabic Treebank part 1 v2.0 (ATB1), Part 2 v2.0 (ATB2) and Part 3 v1.0 (ATB3). The ATB was chosen not only because of its size and comprehensiveness, but also because Buckwalter's analyzer was developed in accordance with the ATB, which makes the task of combining information from both sources easier. In all our experiments we use a tag-set of 24 tags which was mapped from the original tag-set (191 tags in ATB1) using the mapping script of the ATB distribution.

To check the ambiguity level and the difficulty of the task at hand, we ran BMA1.0 over a testing set extracted from ATB1. The average number of analyses per word is 1.83, and the average number of segmentations per word is 1.2, however, the task of disambiguating Arabic is still not easy, as 46% of the data is ambiguous. Those results are comparable to the results of Bar Haim et al. for Hebrew, according to which the average number of analyses per word is 2.17 with 1.25 segmentations on average per word, and 54% of the words are ambiguous.

The performance of MorphTagger over Arabic was measured using the same test settings of Diab et al. (2004). Habash and Rambow (2005) use a different test setting drawn from ATB1. Although we could not reproduce the exact setting of Habash and Rambow, comparison to their reported accuracy is still quite telling due to the similarity of the data. The comparison between the accuracy of the three systems is summarized in Table 1. The results in this table were obtained using the correct ("gold") segmentation and applying the standard F-measure for POS tagging accuracy. The result of Diab et al. was reproduced on their setting, and the result of Habash and Rambow is as reported in their paper.

System	Tagging accuracy
MorphTagger	96.12
Diab et al.	95.81
Habash and Rambow	97.5

Table 1 - Comparison between systems over ATB1

The result achieved by MorphTagger slightly exceeds Diab et al.'s result (on the same test setting) and is slightly inferior to Habash and Rambow's reported result. Overall, it is an encouraging result that the MorphTagger system that was developed for Hebrew could be easily ported to Arabic and yield state-of-the-art results.

In Table 2, we present the accuracies achieved for MorphTagger on a cross validated, 10-fold test, including the standard deviation results in parentheses. The results are reported both for gold-segmentation (GS) and without GS.

Test setting	Accuracy per word (%)		$F_{\beta=1}$ per Word-segment (%)	
	Segmentation	Tagging	Segmentation	Tagging
GS	100	94.89 (0.62)	100	95.436 (0.53)
without GS	99.015 (0.24)	94.374 (0.64)	98.854 (0.28)	94.727 (0.56)

Table 2 - MorphTagger performance cross validated

Note that by tagging accuracy per word we mean the percentage of words correctly segmented and tagged. The tagging F-measure is calculated in the standard way, counting the correctly tagged word-segments and dividing it by the number of "gold" word-segments for recall, and further by the number of outputted word-segments for precision.

Analyzing the POS tagging errors of MorphTagger, we found that about 2.8% of the words in ATB1 were not correctly analyzed by the morphological analyzer. Such "incomplete lexicon" problems inevitably lead to tagging errors in MorphTagger's architecture. This problem is more serious still on data taken from ATB2 and ATB3, where respectively 4.5% and 5.3% of the data led to "incomplete lexicon" problems. We conclude that a morphological analyzer can be used to improve upon Diab et al.'s results, as done in Habash and Rambow and in our straightforward application of MorphTagger to Arabic. However, this method still suffers from considerable coverage problems, which are discussed in the following section.

4 Coverage of Morphological Analysis for Arabic

In order to analyze the coverage problem, we tested the coverage of BMA1.0 over parts of the ATB which were composed from articles taken on different periods of times. The results are summarized in Table 3. The schema of the table includes, for each part of the ATB: (i) the number of tokens that include at least one Arabic character (henceforth "*Arabic words*"[1]); (ii) Out-of-Vocabulary (OOV) words, unanalyzed by BMA1.0; (iii) the percentage of proper nouns (NNP) out of the OOV words; (iv) the number of "no correct" words – words for which BMA1.0 found at least one solution but the correct analysis according to the ATB was not among them; and (v,vi,vii) the number of proper nouns (NNP), nouns (NN) and adjectives (JJ) from "no correct". A problem that is unique to the ATB is that some words in the corpus were not manually annotated and were given the NO_FUNC tag. Those words are counted as Arabic words, but are ignored in the rest of the statistics of Table 3.

The noticeable difference in OOV words between ATB1 and ATB2/ATB3 is expected, because the lexicon of BMA1.0 was developed using information extracted from ATB1. ATB2 and ATB3, which were developed after BMA1.0 was released (using a more advanced version of Buckwalter's analyzer), show a different picture. In those two parts the OOV problem is not too hard: a heuristic that would assign NNP to each OOV word would be sufficient in most of the cases. However, the "No Correct" problem is more difficult: NNPs account for 5% in ATB2 and 18% in ATB3 of these words, which are mostly dominated by missing adjectives and missing nouns (54% jointly in ATB2 and 37% jointly in ATB3).

Taken together, the OOV problem and the "No Correct" problem mean that more than 5% of the words in ATB2 and ATB3 cannot be tagged correctly using BMA1.0 unless further data are added to those provided by the morphological analyzer. A similar coverage result was reached for Hebrew by Bar Haim et al., using a morphological analyzer for Hebrew (Segal, 2001). Bar Haim et al. report that for about 4% of the Hebrew words in their corpus, the correct analysis was missing. From these data we conclude that on top of systems like the ones proposed by Bar Haim et al. and Habash and Rambow, we need to enhance the morphological analyzer using additional analyses.

[1] This definition of Arabic words is taken from Buckwalter's analyzer.

ATB part	Arabic words	OOV	NNP of OOV	No Correct	NNP of No Correct	NN of No Correct	JJ of No Correct
1	123798	126 (0.11%)	21 (16.67%)	3369 (2.82%)	0	517 (15.35%)	980 (29.09%)
2	125729	958 (0.77%)	497 (51.88%)	5663 (4.53%)	282 (4.98%)	1254 (22.14%)	1818 (32.1%)
3	293026	6405 (2.2%)	5241 (81.83%)	15484 (5.32%)	2864 (18.5%)	2238 (14.45%)	3494 (22.57%)

Table 3 - Coverage of Buckwalter's Analyzer

5 Smoothing Using a Data-driven Character-based Model

So far we have shown that POS tagging models that use a morphological analyzer achieve high accuracy but suffer from coverage problems that can not be solved by a simple heuristic. On the other hand, models that use character-based information are likely to make relatively good predictions for words that are out of the vocabulary of the morphological analyzer. We hypothesize that this may be especially true for Semitic languages, due to their rich and systematic pattern (template) paradigms. Such patterns add constant characters to root characters, and features of substrings of words may therefore help in predicting POS tags from those patterns.

Our baseline models for the experiments are MorphTagger with a NNP heuristic (MorphTagger+NNP) and ArabicSVM (Diab et al.'s system). As we have already reported in section 3, MorphTagger+NNP achieved 96.12% tagging accuracy and ArabicSVM achieved 95.87% over the same testing data used by Diab et al. One simple hybrid model would be adding the analyses produced by the SVM to the morphological analyzer analyses and disambiguate these analyses using MorphTagger's HMM. This system has improved accuracy – it achieved accuracy of 96.18%, higher than both of the base models.

The problem with such model is over-generation of the SVM: when checked over ATB1 and ATB2, 40% of the new analyses introduced by the SVM are correct analyses, and 60% are wrong. To avoid this problem, we suggest conditioning the addition of SVM analyses on the sentence's tagging probability calculated by the HMM model. This is justified due to the fact that there is correlation between the probability of the tagging of a sentence given by a language model and the accuracy of the tagging. The relation is shown in Figure 1.

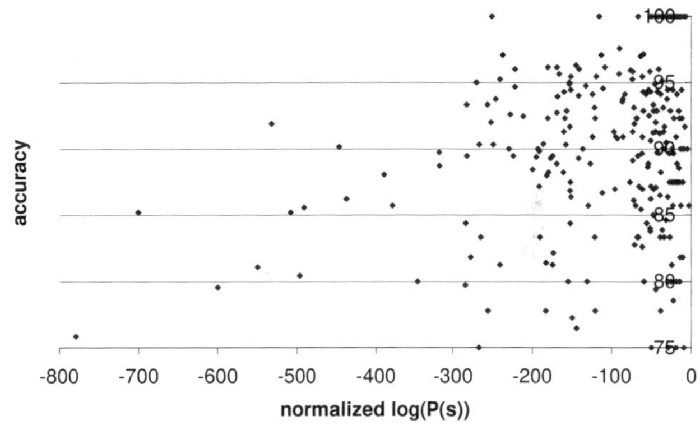

Figure 1 Probability VS Accuracy

Figure 1 shows the relation between the accuracy of the tagging and the normalized logarithmic probability of the tagging. We normalize the probability of the tagging by the sentence length as longer sentences usually have lower probabilities.

Following the previous conclusions, we propose a hybrid model which adds the analyses of the SVM only in cases where the tagging probability by the basic MorphTagger system is lower than an empirically calculated threshold. If the HMM is confident about the tagging it produces, the probability of the tagging will be high enough to pass the threshold, and then the tagging will be outputted without adding the SVM analyses which might add noise to the morphological analyzer output. A general algorithm is shown in Figure 2.

Given a sentence *s*, perform the following steps:

1. Produce analyses for each word in *s* using the morphological analyzer combined with the corpus analyses.
2. Calculate lexical and contextual probabilities using available annotated corpora (using Maximum Likelihood Estimation).
3. Run Viterbi's Algorithm for HMM disambiguation, and calculate a rank of the tagging which is composed from the probability given by the model and the length of the sentence.
4. If [rank>threshold] output tagging.

4'. [Otherwise] run the character based model over the sentence and add the new analyses generated.

5'. Combine the analyses generated by the morphological analyzer and the character-based model, update the lexical probabilities and rerun the model.

Figure 2 - Enhanced Tagging Algorithm

Note that in the algorithm, a new (word, tag) pair introduced by the morphological analyzer or by the character model does not appear in the tagged corpus, therefore a small count $\lambda=1$ is given in such cases. This method can be improved further, especially for the analyses produced by the data-driven character-based method.

The accuracy we obtained using this system was 96.28% which shows slight improvement over the previous simple hybrid system. Examining the errors in the simple hybrid method and the conditioned method, we see that the improvement is not smooth: the conditioned model includes errors which did not exist in the simple model. These errors occur when correct analyses of the character-based model were discarded. In general, however, the conditioned method chooses more correct analyses. It should be noted that adding the character-based model analyses boosted the coverage from 97% to 98%, but the accuracy did not improve to the same level. The main cause for this is the weak relation between the probability of a sentence and the accuracy. As it is difficult to model this relation, we believe that more time should be invested to improve the HMM probabilities especially for the character model analyses, which can boost the chances of choosing good analyses.

6 Conclusions and Future Work

This paper demonstrates that it is possible to successfully port a POS tagger originally built for Hebrew to Arabic using a morphological analyzer and a tagged corpus. The POS tagger (called MorphTagger) achieves state-of-the-art results both on Hebrew and Arabic. Despite this positive result we find that further improvement of accuracy is hindered by the coverage of the morphological analyzer. Contrary to earlier work on POS tagging, the problem turns out not so much in unknown (OOV) lexemes as much as in known lexemes for which the correct tag is missing. We showed empirical evidence that this problem arises for the available treebanks and morphological analyzers for both Arabic and Hebrew. We propose an approach that smoothes a given lexical model (obtained from a morphological analyzer and an annotated corpus) by adding synthetically constructed analyses, obtained from a POS tagger that combines character-level information. Unlike earlier work, we apply this smoothing only when the probabilistic model assigns probabilities lower than a threshold to all possible POS taggings of the input sentence. This way we obtain moderate improvement in Arabic POS tagging.

The problem of missing lexeme-POS pairs in POS taggers for Semitic languages is more severe than in languages like English. We conjecture that this is because of the more complex morphology of Semitic languages.

In future work it might be worthwhile to consider morphological processes that are more complex than the standard affixation (suffixing/prefixing) processes in order to generalize better over cases in the training data. Such a generalization may provide better coverage of lexeme-POS pairs and would increase the upper bound on accuracy.

References

Roy Bar Haim, Khalil Sima'an and Yoad Winter. 2005. *Choosing an Optimal Architecture for Segmentation and POS-Tagging of Modern Hebrew.* ACL Workshop on Computational Approaches to Semitic Languages. A revised and extended version to appear in Journal of *Natural Language Engineering.*

Eric Brill. 1995. *Transformation-based error-driven learning and natural language processing: a case study in part of speech tagging.* In Computational Linguistics 21, pages 543-565.

Tim Buckwalter. 2002. *Arabic Morphological Analyzer Version 1.0.* Linguistic Data Consortium, University of Pennsylvania.

Kenneth W. Church. 1988. *A stochastic parts program and noun phrase parser for unrestricted text.* Proceedings of the second conference on Applied natural language processing, Pages 136-143.

Mona Diab, Kadri Hacioglu, and Daniel Jurafsky. 2004. *Automatic Tagging of Arabic Text: From Raw Text to Base Phras e Chunks.* In HLT-NAACL: Short Papers, pages 149-152.

Nizar Habash and Owen Rambow. 2005. *Arabic Tokenization, Part-of-Speech Tagging and Morphological Disambiguation in One Fell Swoop.* In Proceedings of the 43rd Annual Meeting of the Association for Computational Linguistics, pages 573-580, Ann Arbor.

Young-Suk Lee, Kishore Papineni, Salim Roukos, Ossama Emam, and Hany Hassan. 2003. *Language model based Arabic word segmentation.* In ACL, pages 399-406.

Mohamed Maamouri and Ann Bies. 2004. *Developing an Arabic treebank: Methods, guidelines, procedures, and tools.* In Proceedings of the Workshop on Computational Approaches to Arabic Script-based Languages (COLING), Geneva.

Christopher D. Manning and Hinrich Schütze. 1999. *Foundations of Statistical Natural Language Processing.* The MIT press, Cambridge, Massachusetts.

Tetsuji Nakagawa. 2004. *Chinese and Japanese word segmentation using word-level and character-level information.* In Proceedings of the 20th International Conference on Computational Linguistics, pages 466-472, Geneva.

Erel Segal. 2001. *Hebrew morphological analyzer for Hebrew undotted texts.* Master's thesis, Computer Science Department, Technion, Haifa, Israel.

Ralph Weischedel, Marie Meteer, Richard Schwartz, Lance Ramshaw and Jeff Palmucci. 1993. *Coping with Ambiguity and Unknown Words through Probabilistic Models.* Computational Linguistics (Special issue on using large corpora: II) volume 19, pages 361-382.

An Amharic Stemmer : Reducing Words to their Citation Forms

Atelach Alemu Argaw
Department of Computer and Systems Sciences
Stockholm University/KTH, Sweden
atelach@dsv.su.se

Lars Asker
Department of Computer and Systems Sciences
Stockholm University/KTH, Sweden
asker@dsv.su.se

Abstract

Stemming is an important analysis step in a number of areas such as natural language processing (NLP), information retrieval (IR), machine translation(MT) and text classification. In this paper we present the development of a stemmer for Amharic that reduces words to their citation forms. Amharic is a Semitic language with rich and complex morphology. The application of such a stemmer is in dictionary based cross language IR, where there is a need in the translation step, to look up terms in a machine readable dictionary (MRD). We apply a rule based approach supplemented by occurrence statistics of words in a MRD and in a 3.1M words news corpus. The main purpose of the statistical supplements is to resolve ambiguity between alternative segmentations. The stemmer is evaluated on Amharic text from two domains, news articles and a classic fiction text. It is shown to have an accuracy of 60% for the old fashioned fiction text and 75% for the news articles.

1 Introduction

Stemming is the process of reducing morphological variants of a word into a common form. For morphologically less complex languages like English or Swedish, this usually involves removal of suffixes. For languages like Amharic or Arabic, that have a much richer morphology, this process also involves dealing with prefixes, infixes and derivatives in addition to the suffixes. Stemming is widely used in IR, with the assumption that morphological variants represent similar meaning. It is applied during indexing and is used to reduce the vocabulary size, and it is used during query processing in order to ensure similar representation as that of the document collection. In cross language information retrieval (CLIR) where a query is typically posed in one language, and the document collection from where the documents are retrieved is in another language, some form of translation is required. For low resource languages such as Amharic, machine readable dictionaries (MRDs) play a crucial role by enabling look up of translations of query terms. In most cases such MRDs have all entries represented only by their citation form. Thus in CLIR applications, it is of outmost importance that query terms in the source language are reduced to the exact corresponding citation form as presented in the MRD. In this paper we address this particular problem of stemming Amharic words and reducing them to their citation forms for CLIR applications.

The remainder of the paper is organized as follows. Section 2 provides a background information about the Amharic language, followed by related work in Section 3 and a brief description of Amharic morphology in Section 4. Section 5 presents the resources utilized, while Section 6 deals with a detailed description of the stemmer. In section 7 we describe experiments conducted to evaluate the performance of the stemmer and discuss the obtained results. We give concluding remarks in Section 8.

Proceedings of the 5th Workshop on Important Unresolved Matters, pages 104–110,
Prague, Czech Republic, June 2007.

2 The Amharic Language

Amharic is the official working language of the federal government of the Federal Democratic Republic of Ethiopia and is estimated to be spoken by well over 20 million people as a first or second language. Amharic is the second most spoken Semitic language in the world (after Arabic). It is today probably the second largest language in Ethiopia (after Oromo, a Cushitic language) and possibly one of the five largest languages on the African continent. Following the Constitution drafted in 1993, Ethiopia is divided into nine fairly independent regions, each with it's own nationality language. However, Amharic is the language for country-wide communication and was also for a long period the principal literal language and medium of instruction in primary and secondary schools of the country, while higher education is carried out in English. Despite it's wide speaker population, computational linguistic resources for Amharic, as most 'low resource' languages, are very limitted and almost non existent.

Written Amharic uses a unique script which has originated from the Ge'ez alphabet (the liturgical language of the Ethiopian Orthodox Church). Written Ge'ez can be traced back to at least the 4th century A.D. The first versions of the language included consonants only, while the characters in later versions represent consonant-vowel (CV) phoneme pairs. In the modern Ethiopic script each syllable pattern comes in seven different forms (called orders), reflecting the seven vowel sounds. The first order is the basic form; the other orders are derived from it by more or less regular modifications indicating the different vowels. There are 33 basic forms, giving 7*33 syllable patterns (syllographs), or fidels. Two of the base forms represent vowels in isolation, but the rest are for consonants (or semi-vowels classed as consonants) and thus correspond to CV pairs, with the first order being the base symbol with no explicit vowel indicator. The writing system also includes four (incomplete, five-character) orders of labialised velars and 24 additional labialised consonants. In total, there are 275 fidels, but not all the letters of the Amharic script are strictly necessary for the pronunciation patterns of the spoken language; some were simply inherited from Ge'ez without having any semantic or phonetic distinction in modern Amharic. There are many cases where numerous symbols are used to denote a single phoneme, as well as words that have extremely different orthographic form and slightly distinct phonetics, but with the same meaning. So are, for example, most labialised consonants basically redundant, and there are actually only 39 context-independent phonemes (monophones): of the 275 symbols of the script, only about 233 remain if the redundant ones are removed. The script also has a unique set of punctuation marks and digits. Unlike Arabic or Hebrew, the language is written from left to right.

The Amharic writing system uses multitudes of ways to denote compound words and there is no agreed upon spelling standard for compounds. As a result of this - and of the size of the country leading to vast dialectal dispersion - lexical variation and homophony is very common.

3 Related work

Pioneering the work on morphological analysis of Amharic verbs, Abiyot (Bayou, 2000) designed and implemented a prototype word parser for Amharic verbs and their derivation. He designed a knowledge-based system that parses verbs, and nouns derived from verbs. He used root pattern and affixes to determine the lexical and inflectional category of the words. He tested his system on a limited number of words (200 verbs and 200 nouns) and the result showed that 86% of the verbs and 84% of the nouns were recognized correctly. Another prototype morphological analyzer for Amharic was developed by Tesfaye Bayu (Bayu, 2002) where he used an unsupervised learning approach based on probabilistic models to extract morphemic components (prefix, stem and suffix) to construct a morphological dictionary. He also investigated an approach whereby he applied the principle of Auto segmental Phonology to identify morphemic component of a stem such as consonantal root, vocalic melodies and CV-templates. The first system was able to parse successfully 87% of words of the test data (433 of 500 words). This result corresponds to a precision of 95% and a recall of 90%. Tested with 255 stems, the second system identified the morphemic componentes of 241 (or 94% of the) stems correctly.

Fissaha and Haller (Fissaha and Haller, 2003) discuss the morphology of Amharic verbs in the context of Machine Translation and present an implemetation of a morphological analyser for Amharic using Xerox Finite State Tools (XFST). The different classification shemes for Amharic verbs that have been forwarded are discussed followed by the implication such classifications have on the implementation strategy. They claim that morphological analysis for Amharic with XFST can handle most of the morphologcal phenomena except some derivation processes which involve simultaneous application of both stem interdigitation and reduplication. Saba and Gibbon (Amsalu and Gibbon, 2005) extend the XFST implementation of Amharic morpholgy to include all word categories. Testing with 1620 words text from an Amharic bible, they report recall levels of 94% for verbs, 85% for nouns, and 88% for adjectives while they report precisions of 94% for nouns, 81% for adjectives, 91% for adverbs, and 54% for verbs, at the above specified recall levels.

A more recent work that applies Conditional Random Fields to segment and part of speech tag Amharic words is done by Fissaha (Adafre, 2005). He reports an accuracy of 84% for the word segmentation. The work deals with bound morphemes of prepositions, conjunctions, relative markers, auxiliary verbs, nagation marker and coordinate conjunction, but leaves out other bound morphemes such as definite article, agreement features such as gender and number, case markers, etc, and considers them to be part of the word. The best result (84%) is obtained by using character, morphological and lexical features.

There has been a work done by Alemayehu and Willet (Alemayehu and Willett, 2002) which investigates the effectiveness of stemming in information retrieval for Amharic. They compare performance of word-based, stem-based, and root-based retrieval of 40 Amharic queries against 548 Amharic documents, and show better recall levels for stem and root based retrieval over word based, but they don't provide information on the precision of these experiments.

All the above mentioned works attempt to address the need to develop a morphological analyser for Amharic, and show that there has been a great deal of effort put in the design and implementation of each system. Although that is the case, none of them are publicly available, and/or are limitted in some way. For our current task of stemming for the purpose of CLIR dictionary lookup, full fledged morphological analysis is most likely an overkill since we only need citation forms of words, and precision plays a very important role.

4 Amharic Morphology

Amharic has a rich verb morphology which is based on triconsonantal roots with vowel variants describing modifications to, or supplementary detail and variants of the root form. A significantly large part of the vocabulary consists of verbs, which exhibit different morphosyntactic properties based on the arrangment of the consonant-vowel patterns. For example, the root *sbr*, meaning 'to break' can have the perfect form *säbbär* with the pattern CVC-CVC[1], imperfect form *säbr* with the pattern CVCC, gerund form *säbr* with the pattern CVCC, imperative form *sbär* with the pattern CCVC, causative form *assäbbär* with the pattern *as*-CVCCVC, passive form *täsäbbär* with the pattern *tä*-CVCCVC, etc. Subject, gender, number, etc are also indicated as bound morphemes on the verb, as well as objects and possesion markers, mood and tense, beneficative, malfactive, transitive, dative, negative, etc, producing a complex verb morphology.

Amharic nouns can be inflected for gender, number, definiteness, and case, although gender is usually neutral. Adjectives behave in the same way as nouns, taking similar inflections, while prepositions are mostly bound morphemes prefixed to nouns. The definte article in Amharic is also a bound morpheme, and attaches to the end of a noun. We have given a very brief description of some aspects of Amharic morphology, detailed information can be found in (Bender, 1968), (Bender and Fulas, 1978), (Yimam, 1995).

We have constructed 65 rules based on the entire Amharic morphology for the purpose of this study. The rules vary from simple affixation rules to each word category to allowed combinations of prefixes and suffixes for each word category and set of affixes.

[1]C stands for consonants and V for vowels

5 Resources

5.1 The Corpora

We have utilized three different sources of text for the development of the stemmer and the experiments. The first is a collection of news articles from an online news repository, Ethiopian News Headlines (ENH), which is available at http://www.ethiozena.net. This corpus consists of 3.1 million words of Amharic news text in a little more than 10,000 articles. This corpus was used to collect word frequency and prefix and suffix statistics i.e. the number of times an affix occurs attached to a known stem, and the occurence statistics was used to disambiguate between alternative segmantations of a given word. The second text source is another Ethiopian news agency, Walta Information Center (WIC) which can be found at http://www.waltainfo.com. We used news items downloaded from WIC to evaluate the stemmer on independent news texts from another source. The third text, which was also used for evaluation, is from the Amharic novel "Fikir Iske Meqabir" (FIM) by the renowned Ethiopian author Dr. Hadis Alemayehu. This text (FIM) was selected for the evaluation in order to see how well the stemmer would perform on a text that differed substantially in style from the news collection.

5.2 The Dictionaries

The simplest and most straight forward way for the stemmer to verify that a suggested segmentation is correct is to try to look up the stem in a dictionary. For this purpose we used three different dictionaries, an Amharic - English, an Amharic - French, and an Amharic - Amharic dictionary. The Amharic - English dictionary, by Dr. Amsalu Aklilu, contains 15 000 Amharic words with their English translations (Aklilu, 1981). The Amharic - French dictionary (Abebe, 2004) has 12 000 Amharic entries while the Amharic - Amharic dictionary by Kesatie Birhan has 56 000 entries (Tesema,). All three dictionaries were made available to us in electronic form, transliterated to SERA and then merged and represented in a form suitable for the stemmer.

5.3 Transliteration

The dictionaries and all Amharic news texts mentioned above are published using Ethiopic script and using a variety of fonts, some of which are not Unicode compliant. In order to simplify the analysis and to have a unified representation of the texts, we transliterated all Amharic texts into SERA which is a system for ASCII representation of Ethiopic characters (Firdyiwek and Yacob, 1997).

The transliteration was done using a file conversion utility called `g2` which was made available to us by Daniel Yacob of the Ge'ez Frontier Foundation (http://www.ethiopic.org/).

6 The Stemmer

The stemmer first creates a list consisting of all possible segmentations of the word that is to be stemmed. In a second step, each such segmentation is then verified by matching each candidate stem against the machine readable dictionary. If no stem matches the dictionary, the stemmer will modfy the stem and redo the matching. If more than one stem matches, the most likely stem will be selected after disambiguating between the candidate stems based on statistical and other properties of the stems. In the cases when exactly one stem matches the dictionary then that segmentation will be presented as the output from the stemmer.

6.1 Segmentation

For each new word the stemmer first creates a list of possible segmentations by applying a list of morphological rules for allowed prefixes and suffixes. In this way, the word `Indeminorewna` would for example be segmented into the following 9 different ways:

```
(1)   Indeminorewna
(2)   Indeminorew -na
(3)   Indeminore -w -na
(4)   Inde- minorewna
(5)   Inde- minorew -na
(6)   Inde- minore -w -na
(7)   Inde- mi- norewna
(8)   Inde- mi- norew -na
(9)   Inde- mi- nore -w -na
```

For each of the 9 possible segmentations, the remaining stem is then matched against the (merged) three dictionaries. In this case, the only one that is found as entry in the dictionary is `nore`, so alternative 9 is selected as the most likely segmentation of the word.

6.2 Disambiguation

If more than one of the candidate stems are matched in the dictionary, those segmentations that have a stem that matches an entry in the dictionary are ranked according to length and frequency of the stem. The longest stem that have a match in the dictionary is selected and if more than one stem of equal length matches the dictionary then the stem that is more frequent is preferred before the less frequent. The frequency score is based on how often the stem occurs in the ENH corpus described above. The word `beteyazew` would for example be segmented in the following ways:

```
(1)  beteyazew
(2)  beteyaze -w
(3)  beteyaz -e -w
(4)  be- teyazew
(5)  be- teyaze -w
(6)  be- teyaz -e -w
(7)  be- te- yazew
(8)  be- te- yaze -w
(9)  be- te- yaz -e -w
```

In this case the three stems `teyaze` (5), `yaze` (8) and `yaz` (9) all have matching entries in the dictionary but `teyaze` is selected as the most likely stem since it is the longest.

6.3 Modification

For approximately 30% of the words, the stem does not match the dictionary. In these cases, the stem will be slightly modifed and a second attempt to match the entries in the dictionary will be done. For example the word `IndegeleSut` should correctly be segmented into `Inde- geleSe -u -t`. With the approach described so far, the segmentation based on prefixes and suffixes would yield the stem `geleS` which will not have a match in the dictionary. Instead, for the dictionary lookup to succeed, we first need to add the vowel `e` at the end of the stem. For the word `astawqWal` which should correctly segment into `astaweqe -W -al` we will first have to insert `e` both between `w` and `q` and again after `q` to reach the correct form of the stem. This process of modifying the stem by adding vowels, is applied to the candidate stems if no matches by the unmodifed stems are made in the dictionary. For the current implementation of the stemmer, this is done by inserting one of the vowels 'e' or 'a' between the consonants if the unmatched stem contains two consecutive consonants, or after the last consonant if the stem ends in a consonant. If exactly one of the modifed stems will match the dictionary, then that segmentation will be ranked as the most likely. If more than one modifed stem matches, then the longest will be selected. For the words where this modification of the stem is done, approximately 30% will successfully match their correct entry in the dicionary while 20% make an incorrect match and the remaining 50% will not match the dictionary at all.

6.4 Out-of-dictionary terms

Finally, the approximately 15% of the words that do not have any stem that matches entries in the dictionary (even after the modifiaction) will be ranked according to the length of the stem and the number of times that the stem occurs in the ENH corpus. In this case, it is the shorter stems that are preferred. For example the word `bekomixnu` will have four possible segmentations, none of which occurs in the dictionary.

```
(1) bekomixnu
(2) bekomixn -u
(3) be- komixnu
(4) be- komixn -u
```

In this case, alternative 4, `komixn` is the shortest stem that occurs as a unique word in the reference corpus and is therefor selected as the most likely segmentation before either one of the alternative stems `bekomixnu`, `bekomixn` or `komixnu`.

7 Experimental Evaluation

In order to evaluate the performance of the stemmer, we selected the first 1503 words (= 1000 unique words) from the WIC corpus described above. We also selected a 470 words long text from the book "Fikir Iske Meqabir" to get a text with 300 unique words.

On the WIC data the stemmer had an overall accuray of 76.9 %. For 48 % of the words, the stemmer found exactly one segmentation with a stem that was matching the dictionary, and for these words it had an accuracy of 83.75 %. For 36.3 % of the words, the stemmer found more than one segmentation that matched the dictionary and therefor needed to do additional disambiguation between alternative segmentations. For these words, the stemmer had an accuracy of 69.1 %. For the remaining 15.7 % of the words, the stemmer found no match in the dictionary for any of the possible segmentations. For these words the stemmer had an accuracy of 73.9 %. In the cases when there is only one match in the dictionary, the extra sources for error that are introduced by having to disambiguate between alternative segmentations are avoided and hence the stemmer has best accuracy for those words that have exactly one segmentation with a stem that will match the dictionary.

For the 300 unique words from Fikir Iske Meqabir, the stemmer had an overall accuracy of 60.0 % In a similar fashion as for the WIC data, the stemmer performed best on the subset of words for which there was exacly one match in the dictionary. For this group the performance was 68.8 % correct but the overall accuracy was lowered by the fact that the stemmer performed worse on the words that had either more than one match, or no match at all in the dictionary. These numbers were 54.8 % and 42.1 % respectively.

8 Conclusion

We have presented the design and development of an Amharic stemmer which reduces words to their citation forms for the purpose of dictionary lookup in CLIR. Given the resource constraints we have, and the specificity of the stemmer, the overall performance could be acceptable, but needs further improvment. The stemming depends highly on word entries in the three MRDs for verification purposes. These MRDs altogether consist of a limitted amount of entries, overall 83000, with a very high level of overlap, leaving 47176 unique entries. Although it is not the largest source of error, it accounts for around 15% of the words segmentation decided on corpus statististics only since they are not found in the dictionaries. We intend to use more dictionaries with the assumption that there will be a performance increase with the increasing number of citation forms to refer to. On the other hand, increasing the amount of citation forms also will increase the percentage of words that will have more than one match in the dictionaries. That would lead us to focus on the disambiguation strategy in the future. So long as the morphological rule exists, we are able to get the correct segmentation for a word in a possible segmentations list. And when we have two or more likely segmentations that are picked out since they have matching stems in dictionaries, we need to design a smarter way of disambiguation that would take into account contextual information and part of speech tags, etc, in addition to the currently used occurence frequency approach.

Although conducting a full fledged morphological analyser for Amharic is beyond the scope of this paper, we would like to note that there is a need to create a forum for collaboration and exchange among researchers involved in developing NLP resources for Amharic and other Semitic languages and organize the considerable effort that is being made individually. We also hope that some of the ideas and procedures that are described in this paper could be more generally applicable to other Semitic languages as well.

Acknowledgements

The copyright to the two volumes of the French-Amharic and Amharic-French dictionary ("Dictionnaire Francais-Amharique" and "Dictionnaire Amharique-Francais") by Dr Berhanou Abebe and Eloi Fiquet is owned by the French Ministry of Foreign Affairs. We would like to thank the authors and the French embassy in Addis Ababa for allowing us to use the dictionary in this research.

The content of the "English - Amharic Dictionary" is the intellectual property of Dr Amsalu

Aklilu. We would like to thank Dr Amsalu as well as Daniel Yacob of the Geez frontier foundation for making it possible for us to use the dictionary and other resources in this work.

We would also like to thank Ato Negash of Walta Information Center for allowing us to use part of their news texts in this research.

References

Berhanou Abebe. 2004. *Dictionnaire Amharique-Francais*. Shama Books, Addis Ababa, Ethiopia.

Sisay Fissaha Adafre. 2005. Part of speech tagging for amharic using conditional random fields. In *Proceedings of ACL-2005 Workshop on Computational Approaches to Semitic Languages*.

Amsalu Aklilu. 1981. *Amharic - English Dictionary*. Mega Publishing Enterprise, Ethiopia.

Nega Alemayehu and Peter Willett. 2002. The effectiveness of stemming for information retrieval in amharic. In *Short Communication*.

Saba Amsalu and Dafydd Gibbon. 2005. Finite state morphology of amharic. In *Proceedings of RANLP*.

Abiyot Bayou. 2000. Design and development of word parser for amharic language. Masterthesis, Addis Abeba Univeristy.

Tesfaye Bayu. 2002. Automatic morphological analyser: An experiment using unsupervised and autosegmental approach. Masterthesis, Addis Ababa University.

M. Lionel Bender and Hailu Fulas. 1978. Amharic verb morphology. In *East Lansing: Michigan State University, African Studies Center*.

M. Lionel Bender. 1968. *Amharic Verb Morphology: A Generative Approach*. Ph.D. thesis, Graduate School of Texas.

Yitna Firdyiwek and Daniel Yacob. 1997. System for ethiopic representation in ascii.

Sisay Fissaha and Johann Haller. 2003. Amharic verb lexicon in the context of machine translation. In *Actes de la 10e conference TALN, Batz-sur-Mer*.

Kesatie Birhan Tesema. *YeAmarinja Mezgebe Qalat*. Adis Abeba.

Baye Yimam. 1995. *ye amargna sewasew (Amharic Grammar)*. EMPDA.

Author Index

Association for Computational Linguistics
209 N. Eighth Street
Stroudsburg, Pennsylvania 18360